In this carefully researched, winsc
Michael Morgan invites his readers to join John Newton and some of his friends around the family table for conversation and mutual encouragement. Having experienced God's amazing grace in their own lives, this remarkable circle of friends challenged each other to spread the Gospel and to apply its teaching in such important tasks as building the church, feeding the hungry, reforming the prisons and helping to end the practice of slavery. In each of these endeavors, they drew strength from both the teaching of the Bible and from the friendships they shared. In an era of fragmentation, individualism and division, they have much to teach each one of us.

Garth M. Rosell, *M.Div., Th.M., Ph.D., Senior Research Professor of Church History, Gordon-Conwell Theological Seminary*

Michael gives us an insight here into the lasting impact of Newton's ministry of authentic friendship – a talent which this godly man 'cherished, nurtured, and sustained' as 'a careful steward'. He shows Newton as 'a lightening rod for social reform' and 'compassionate ministries' in areas as diverse as politics, literature, education and the church (established and dissenting), both at home and abroad in world missions. This is an outstanding encapsulation of Newton's ministry, gleaning practical hints from the past to apply today. I hope that this makes it into wide circulation, especially Bible Colleges and areas of training. It will be an eye-opener to the general public (and doubtless also to many to pastors).

Marylynn Rouse, *Director, The John Newton Project*

This is an awesome and important work, brimming with riches that illustrate the beautiful truth that evangelical safety is found neither in scepticism, aloofness nor caution, but in the rock of ages. In the one who says *abide in me*. Crammed with extraordinary stories of the flowerings of grace in Newton. In a fragmented, disintegrated age in which we are *alone together*, Newton shows us with welcoming arms the example of someone who knows where Home is, and the one who has opened the door. A privilege to recommend.

Ben Virgo, *Director, Christian Heritage London*

'Change the world' is such an overused, over-promising slogan today that we hardly notice it anymore. So it is astonishing to read how John Newton really did change the world while rarely leaving his modest parish, all through the power of friendship. Michael Morgan charts a way that all faithful pastors can be world-changers with the insight of both a historian and a pastor who follows in his subject's footsteps.

Cory Hartman, *Founder and Principal writer, Fulcrum Content*

In this excellent book, Michael Morgan shows us just how powerful friendship is in the life of a pastor. In analyzing the amazing life of John Newton, Morgan encourages all of us in pastoral ministry to see that faithfully shepherding our congregations, while at the same time caring for the poor and the oppressed in our communities is possible, namely, as we lean on and link arms with our brothers and sisters in Christ.

Mark Hallock, Lead Pastor of Calvary Church in Englewood, Colorado; Author of *The Shepherd Preacher*

JOHN NEWTON

Catalyst for Compassion

John Newton: Catalyst for Compassion

Published 2018 by Acoma Press
40 W. Littleton Blvd. Suite 210, PMB 215
Littleton, CO 80120
www.acomapress.org

Requests for information should be addressed to:

The Calvary Family of Churches
40 W. Littleton Blvd. Suite 210, PMB 215
Littleton, CO 80120
www.thecalvary.org
office@thecalvary.org

Cover Design: Evan Skelton

Interior Layout: Evan Skelton

First Printing, 2019

Printed in the United States of America

Paperback ISBN: 978-1-7341644-0-4
PDF ISBN: 978-1-7341644-1-1

JOHN NEWTON

catalyst for COMPASSION

MICHAEL MORGAN

Contents

Table of Figures

For Kate.

Acknowledgments

A number of people have been an enormous help to me in putting this project together. First of all, a special thanks to the individuals who allowed me to interview them about their own life and calling, and the way Newton's ministry from the eighteenth century can continue to shape our ministries today. Lisa Shapiro's creativity in the original design was wonderful, as well as Evan Skelton's new cover and artwork; I am truly grateful to you both. Many thanks to Cory Hartman for both dialoguing over and editing the content herein. I also would like to extend my deep appreciation to Marylynn Rouse of the John Newton Project (www.johnnewton.org) for her invaluable help in the initial stages of this work, her generosity in allowing me to utilize her draft copy of the Newton and Wilberforce correspondence, and her keen eye in the editing process. To Dr. Garth Rosell and Dr. Robert Mayer I owe profound gratitude for their support, insight, and encouragement along the way; it has been invaluable. Joshua, Abigail, and Patrick—you are the good stuff in life. And finally, to my "virtuous and amiable comfort," my truest companion, and dearest friend, Kate. Thank you.

Introduction

I have called you friends.

—Jesus (John 15:5)

Many pastors today concede helplessness against overwhelming social injustice in light of never-ending ministry responsibilities. More often than not, the problem is not a lack of concern or compassion; most pastors lack time. But even when time is carved out of a pastor's busy schedule, where is he supposed to start when the problematic issues are widespread and the general consensus is apathy or acceptance? What is a pastor to do? As Timothy Keller has noted, "Churches and Christians who seek to do justice have poor families and neighborhoods nearby. The problems seem vast and intractable. How do we even begin to think about how we can help?"[1]

It is obvious that we cannot do it alone.

That is where friends come in to play. Friendship, one of the most basic relationships in life, also happens to be one to which most of us give little reflection. We rightly emphasize marriage and parenting; the importance of healthy relationships in the home cannot be overstated. Many of us also proclaim, week after week, the need for people in our churches to build relationships with neighbors and coworkers as we seek to reach a lost world with the gospel. And to be fair, we do encourage people to engage in discipleship, as well as to practice accountability with our peers. That said, little effort is given to understand the power of friendship itself.

Yet, "Friendship still is, and will always continue to be, a central figure of human existence. Our hearts yearn for friends. Our minds dream about the possibilities, promises, and pitfalls of friendship. Our souls are willing to take extraordinary risks to experience true and authentic friendship."[2]

There is untapped power here that many of us have failed to appreciate. This is particularly the case in a "mentor-friendship." Mentor-friends move beyond weekly appointments over coffee. They go beyond the objective of grounding another person in the basics of Christian theology. They are friends first, and mentors second, even if the mentor-friend is a bit further along in his Christian journey.

The truth is, most pastors have ample opportunity to be just this kind of friend to someone. We long to change the world, to make some kind of difference, when right under our noses is opportunity beyond our wildest dreams, not to mention the deep joy that real and lasting friendship can provide. Often, instead of engaging in the simplicity of friendship, those of us who attempt to tackle poverty, oppression, or systemic sin live life at a crazy pace, running from one initiative to the next, in hopes that somehow we can move the titan boulders of injustice just a smidgeon before we collapse in exhaustion. Who has time for friends?

However, there is another way. Perhaps we can learn from a spiritual giant that many pastors and historians overlook. Though some research has been done on his life, John Newton has not been given the academic attention that he warrants.[3] He is known as a homespun sage, a friendly chap who wrote great songs, and a former slave ship captain who never ceased to be amazed by the scandal of grace, but not as one whose prophetic voice echoed through those he mentored until the conscience of a nation was pierced. While this is a book for pastors, not scholars, his life deserves more reflection, not only as a central figure of the Evangelical Awakening in eighteenth-century England, but also as a key player, albeit primarily behind the scenes, in a remarkable number of justice and compassion efforts.[4] Perhaps more so than any other leader in the revival and reform movements of the eighteenth century, no one person's life was more dramatically shaped by friendships than John

Newton. In fact, Newton's entire life can be viewed through the prism of his friendships.

As his legacy attests, John Newton was a man forever amazed by grace. Arguably, his greatest impact was achieved through the cast of friendships that he developed and sustained. These friendships were honest, abiding, Christ-centered, and grew out of Newton's willingness to go to bat on another's behalf. His joy in Christ overflowed and enriched his friendships with luminaries such as Charles Simeon, William Carey, William Cowper, William Wilberforce, and many others. In turn, this network of friends would lead the charge in an amazing array of social reforms. The historical record is staggering. Through these friendships, most of the great social issues of the day were confronted and challenged, including slavery, poverty, illiteracy, prostitution, the caste system, widow burning, prison conditions, and even orphan care. "Social ministries . . . were developed to a degree which has never been equaled by later Evangelicals."[5]

How did Newton do it?

Answering that question is the task of the present volume. In Part One, we will reexamine Newton's life through the lens of his friendships, introduce his amazing circle of Christian friends, and chronicle Newton's powerful influence in each of their lives. Twelve notable Christian leaders such as Claudius Buchanan, Hannah More, Thomas Charles, and Richard Johnson will be introduced.

Part Two follows the most compelling reform movements and compassionate ministries that took place as a result of these friendships, tracing them from Newton to his disciples. Each of these efforts have John Newton's fingerprints all over them. This section demonstrates the powerful diversity of Newton's influential reach in society through politics, literature, and education, as well as his guidance to the Established and Dissenting church, both at home and abroad in world missions.[6]

Finally, Part Three builds on Newton's story and legacy by teasing out lessons that we can learn from him. There is much to glean: Newton was a pastor first, one who preached, and one who prayed. He befriended all who came his way, genuinely, and for the long haul, bolstering them at just the right moment. Time and again, Newton rehearsed his story of God's deliverance, encouraged others to stick it out in the sphere to which God had called them, and multiplied his life into others. He introduced these friends to one another, stood behind each one when they needed his support, and finally, got out of the way so that they could shine.

Make no mistake: we can become, as John Newton was, a great catalyst for compassion by loving, teaching, and empowering the friends whom God has placed in our lives.

If you are burdened by the plight of the poor, heartbroken over the reality of human trafficking in our own day, stirred by the cries of the oppressed, yet also overwhelmed with work, pulled in numerous directions, and confused about where to begin, take heart. There is a way to write sermons, perform weddings, attend meetings, follow up visitors, care for the sick and dying, reach out to the lost, and still seek justice and mercy. We know, because it has been done before, by countless pastors before us. One of the most exemplary cases is that of John Newton.

But how? How did Newton do it?

Well, in short, he called them friends.

PART ONE

the power of friendship:
THE LIFE OF JOHN NEWTON

CHAPTER ONE

Needing a Friend

JULY 1725—MARCH 1748: BAD FRIENDS

A hellion was born on July 24, 1725.[1] Though his mother was a faithful Dissenter who taught her child to memorize Scripture, her death in 1732, only weeks before John Newton's seventh birthday, had a disastrous effect on her only child.[2] His father, being an irreligious sailor who spent most of his time away at sea, left John to figure out life for himself. John was sent off to boarding school in Essex for two years, and his father promptly remarried a woman who never displayed any real attachment to her new stepson.[3]

At ten years old, Newton's formal education came to a close, and by the time he was eleven John sailed the seas with his father.4 The next seven years Newton was raised in large part on deck. The term "cuss like a sailor" exists for a reason, and John swiftly learned how to compete with the best of them. Even so, his mother's influence was not completely lost upon her son, and the young man vacillated numerous times between piety and total abandonment of God. Alarming circumstances, such as the death of a friend, or a close call, would grab John's attention for a season, only to eventually wear off.[5]

At around fifteen years of age, Newton decided to muster up his convictions, and began a two year journey of moral living.[6] At seventeen, John was exposed to Lord Shaftesbury's *Rhapsody*, and immediately taken in. Shaftesbury proposed a philosophy of natural religion, which Newton enthusiastically embraced and promoted, leading him further away from biblical Christianity.[7]

Though Newton's father was a man who inspired fear in his son, he did care about John, and tried repeatedly to set John up with steady employment through his seafaring connections. On one such occasion, in December of 1742, Newton was to set sail to Jamaica. He had a week before the ship would push off. In the meantime, he took a trip to visit the family of his late mother, whom he had not seen in a long time. That trip would change Newton's life forever, for unbeknownst to him, he was about to meet his future wife.[8]

Once John laid eyes on thirteen-year-old Mary Catlett, he threw all caution to the wind, and decided to turn a three-day visit into a three-week stay.[9] He had no desire to be in Jamaica, forced to be away from his new-found love for four to five years. Though he missed the ship, Newton's father forgave him rather quickly, and arranged for him to work on a ship sailing to Venice instead. Unfortunately, it was more opportunity for Newton to carouse with profane company.

By the end of 1743, Newton was back in England, visiting Mary again, extending his stay again, and missing his next voyage, again![10] Newton seemed to display almost no responsibility or concern for the consequences of his actions at this time. Because Newton missed his ship, he was available to be pressed into naval service upon the *Harwich*, a man of war. In his autobiography, Newton writes, "I here met with companions who completed the ruin of my principles."[11] Despite his father's connections, there was nothing that he could do to avoid it. Newton was stuck, whether he liked it or not.[12]

At least for a little while. In December 1744, Newton went absent without leave so that he could say goodbye to his beloved Mary.[13] After returning (and no longer in the good graces of his captain), John went

AWOL again, this time while he was on duty to ensure that no sailors would go AWOL! Upon being caught, Newton was put in chains, stripped, whipped, and demoted.[14] His superiors were happy to be rid of him when the *Harwich* came upon another ship needing men, and Newton volunteered to go. This vessel was on the way to Africa.[15] Once again, John had just made a little decision that would radically alter the rest of his life.

His naval days would not last long. Even though the new commander knew his father, and may have been inclined to show John favor, Newton promptly displayed his remarkable song-writing skill by composing a ditty that ridiculed the captain. His extraordinary powers of influence also showed as the whole crew directly learned to sing the song as well.[16]

Newton's sinful flamboyance reached new heights. He wrote in his *Authentic Narrative*,

> while I was passing from the one ship to the other, this was one reason why I rejoiced in the exchange, and one reflection I made upon the occasion, viz. that I now might be as abandoned as I pleased, without any controul: and, from this time, I was exceedingly vile indeed.[17]

Reflecting back on these early years, Newton wrote in 1778,

> How industriously is Satan served! I was formerly one of his most active under-tempters. Not content with running the broad way myself, I was indefatigable in enticing others; and had my influence been equal to my wishes, I would have carried all the human race with me. And doubtless some have perished, to whose destruction I was greatly instrumental, by tempting them to sin, and by poisoning and hardening them with principles of infidelity; and yet I was spared! When I think of the most with whom I spent my unhappy days of ignorance, I am ready to say, I only am escaped alive to tell thee.[18]

Having ruined his reputation and burned more bridges, Newton sought out a discharge, and received it, with the understanding that he would work with a slave trader on the coast of Africa. These were the circumstances that led Newton to end up on "the island of Benanoes, with little more than the clothes upon my back."[19] At the time, he had no idea about the kind of person with whom he had just thrown in his lot. Newton, without even realizing it, had just become a slave. Decades later, when campaigning against the trade, he reveals a little of his own story:

> My headstrong passions and follies plunged me, in early life, into a succession of difficulties and hardships, which, at length, reduced me to seek a refuge among the natives of Africa. There, for about the space of eighteen months, I was in effect, though without the name, a captive, and a slave myself; and was depressed to the lowest degree of human wretchedness.[20]

His new master's mistress hated him from the instant they met. She saw to it that John was insulted, mocked, only given leftover scraps of food to eat, and even chained to the deck of a ship while his master went ashore to do business, sometimes upwards of forty hours at a time.[21] His wretchedness stuck with him long, and in 1803, he could still say, "For forty years past, I have thought, every waking hour, on my former misery."[22] On his forty-eighth birthday, Newton wrote to a friend, "How unlike am I now to that poor slave of the slaves who wandered almost naked, and like a hungry dog was glad to receive a morsel of food from any hand that offered it!"[23]

Had his father not been so connected in the seafaring world, Newton may well have died on the coast of Africa as a young man. However, he was able to get a message sent to his father about his condition, who immediately contacted a friend to fetch his son.[24] But even after his rescue (which Newton almost botched with remarkable indifference) his heart had not changed in the least. His *Authentic Narrative* records his brazened conscience, ungrateful attitude, and reckless profligacy.[25]

Through this whole early period of Newton's life, he had ruined most of his friends, or they had helped ruin him. After a few years had passed, and Newton could see these ill effects, he wrote to his new bride, "the less we are connected with worldly people the better."[26] But for now,

Newton was the worldly person, and his influence on everyone around him was like a rotten apple.

Even his rescuer began to question what he had done, feeling that maybe he had taken a Jonah on board.[27] Perhaps he was right, because on March 10, 1748, a storm of biblical proportion overcame the ship, upon which a man, running from God, was hiding.

MARCH 1748—NOVEMBER 1754: NO FRIENDS

Just like Jonah, Newton was below deck, asleep, when the storm began to rage. As he was running up to help, he bumped into the captain, who sent him back below deck to fetch a knife. Before he could make it on deck again, the man in his place had been swept overboard.[28]

The *Greyhound*, violently beaten by the waves and leaking badly, was most of the way into the seven-thousand-mile journey back home.[29] Bedding was used to plug holes, while buckets frantically scooped out water, and for the next nine hours Newton pumped water out of the ship. He had been tied on deck with a rope, as "almost every passing wave [broke] over my head."[30] Faced with death, Newton finally realized his desperate need for mercy.

The storm raged on, and after an hour break, Newton was back on deck for eleven more hours. As time passed, he reflected upon his life, and conviction pierced him, but the gospel still had not gripped his heart.[31] The storm eventually waned, but the crew was not out of danger just yet, as most of the provisions had been washed overboard, and the sails were ripped and torn. It was April 8th before the ship finally found harbor in Ireland.[32]

But the hellion had been shaken. And during those four weeks, Newton had cracked open the Bible, and had begun to study and pray.[33] In Newton's own words,

> I no more questioned the truth of scripture, or lost a sense of the rebukes of conscience. Therefore I consider this as the beginning of my return to God, or rather of his return to me; but I cannot consider myself to have

> been a believer (in the full sense of the word) till a considerable time afterwards.[34]

During this period, however, Newton laments, "I had no christian friend or faithful minister to advise me . . . for six years after this period."[35]

Not surprisingly, one of his first stops once back on land was to go visit Mary, this time proposing marriage.[36] Yet to get married, Newton needed to get a job. Though his father died about this time, one of his father's friends offered John a much-needed position, and lovestruck, Newton blundered into his active participation in the slave trade. He was appointed first mate upon the *Brownlow*.[37] As Jonathan Aitken vividly describes,

> Tearing husbands away from their wives and children, shackling these screaming men in heavy fetters, and chaining them in horrific, overcrowded squalor that would have disgraced the animal pens of an abattoir were routine tasks for the ship's mate of a slave-trading ship. It is likely that Newton carried out all of them.[38]

Mary consented to the marriage plans, and the two would be happily joined on February 1, 1750,[39] possessing "only their clothes and seventy pounds in debt."[40] Although she did not show signs of God's saving work in her life for several more years,[41] Mary would have been heartbroken if she had known about the behavior of her fiancé. While away at sea, Newton experienced significant backsliding.[42] He was losing the battle to control his sinful urges.

It was not until a violent fever got his attention that Newton finally cast himself at the mercy of Jesus and came to trust in the grace of the gospel.[43] Newton was born again. His sins of leading others astray, drunkenness, and sexual immorality and abuse were truly, and finally, forgiven.[44]

Though fruit came quickly, friends were hard to come by. Newton's diary entry from December 22, 1751 reveals Newton's new faith, as he resolves first, to use his time for God, and second, "to choose for my companions only good people, from whom I may derive some improvement, or, if otherwise, such as I may hope to benefit by my influence."[45] That is easier said than done, and in truth, it was a lonely time for John Newton. In his autobiography, he speaks of having sweet communion with God, and then proceeding to spend "the evenings in vain and worthless company" as a spectator.[46]

In 1750, John became captain of the *Duke of Argyle*, and began holding worship upon his ship while at sea, even officiating the service himself.[47] Curiously, Newton spoke of his tenure aboard a slave ship as one of the sweetest times of communion he ever had with God.[48] It seems that Newton, almost embarrassed by these earlier statements, wanted to set the record straight in his 1788 publication, *Thoughts Upon the African Slave Trade*:

> Disagreeable I had long found it; but I think I should have quitted it sooner, had I considered it, as I now do, to be unlawful and wrong. But I never had a scruple upon this head at the time; nor was such a thought once suggested to me by any friend.[49]

Friendships were crucial to John Newton, but at this period of his life, apart from Mary, he did not have any. As an old man, Newton wrote,

> I had so many kind friends calling upon me from morning till night. But I remember when it was otherwise. When I had not one friend in the world to interrupt me, or to look upon me. Who hath given me all these?[50]

Newton took two more voyages as a slaver, now as captain of the *African*. On his last voyage, in remarkable testimony to his humane treatment, Newton did not lose a single person at sea, while others regularly lost a third or more of the slaves on board.[51] One other remarkable thing happened on that third journey as a slave-ship captain. John Newton made a friend.

Captain Alexander Clunie was John Newton's first Christian friend. The two met at St. Christopher's, an island in the West Indies. Clunie was a member of Samuel Brewer's Independent church on the east side of London. For six years, Newton had been isolated in his spiritual growth and development, not even receiving the benefit of evangelical preaching. But now, because of Clunie, Newton knew where to find solid teaching in London; moreover, "he taught me the advantage of christian converse."[52]

It was 1754, and Newton was scheduled to make his next voyage as a slave ship captain at the end of the year. Ten years later, while writing his *Authentic Narrative*, Newton admitted: "I was sometimes shocked with an employment that was perpetually conversant with chains, bolts, and shackles. In this view I had often petitioned, in my prayers, that the Lord, in his own time, would be pleased to fix me in a more humane calling."[53] God answered those prayers by "a severe mercy." Two days before setting sail on his fourth journey, John Newton had a seizure that lasted one hour.[54] His days as a slave ship captain were over. And so were his days without friends.

NOVEMBER 1754—MARCH 1764: FINDING FRIENDS

In August of 1755, Newton landed an enviable position as Tide Surveyor in Liverpool. It was a rather easy appointment, freeing him to pursue some new connections that he had learned of from Captain Clunie.[55] Clunie had impressed upon Newton the importance of these new friendships. His diary entry from February 15, 1755 records Newton's reflection upon a sermon about the importance of fellowship, as well as Clunie's influence:

> He [Rev. James Webb] treated of the benefit of Christian conference, and communicating of experiences, which so far as I have been enabled to attempt, I can thankfully witness to, with him. . . . My acquaintance with Clunie was greatly blessed to me in this point and since by his means I have been brought to converse with many more excellent Christians, who have been I hope of great use to me, and from a knowledge of my circumstances have been led to glorify God on my behalf. It is my judgement that societies formed on this view, will by divine blessing be abundantly useful, in promoting a spiritual and vital Godliness. I pray that I may always see it my duty to attempt the forming of such, or frequenting them when I have opportunity to do so.[56]

Frequent them, he did. To put it mildly, Newton was a sponge. He began traveling to London with great regularity, taking in four sermons every Sunday! If that were not enough, Newton tried to attend worship on Tuesdays, Wednesdays, and Fridays as well.[57] He was thirty years old, starting fresh, seeing for the first time that friendship can be "abundantly useful" in expanding the kingdom of God, and he determined to purposely pursue these kinds of relationships for the rest of his life.

His connections and correspondence began expanding rapidly in this period, and Nonconformist pastors such as Samuel Brewer and Samuel Hayward took immediate interest in Newton, mentoring this bright young man with such a checkered past.[58] These new friendships were exhilarating, and Newton could not help but record his feelings in his diary on May 28, 1755: "Every fresh acquaintance I make of this kind, is a new confirmation of my faith and hope, and I bless God for the many witnesses I have been of late brought to the knowledge of."[59]In his diary on January 1, 1756, Newton listed five reasons why 1755 had been the best year of his life. Reason number four:

> For an acquaintance with many valuable Christian friends both in the ministry and out of it, by whom my heart has been often warmed, my faith strengthened, and in whose prayers I hope I have a daily share and benefit.[60]

Several of these acquaintances were quite noteworthy. Brewer and Hayward introduced Newton to George Whitefield in the summer of 1755, and the two became close friends and correspondents.[61] In 1756, we find Newton writing Whitefield, and asking him to come and preach in Liverpool again. He then updates Whitefield on his own well-being: "The time you was down was a harvest season with me, the Lord enlarged my heart to hear his word from your mouth & I continued for about a week after in a frame beyond my common attainment; but for the most part sinse I have been in the Valley."[62] In fact, Newton followed Whitefield around so much during this period, that he earned himself the nickname "young Whitefield."[63]

After taking in so much Calvinistic preaching, Newton was a bit cautious of John Wesley at first,[64] but by 1760 he had come to appreciate him as well, spending as much time with him as he could afford.[65] His own experience and depravity kept him from ever embracing the perfectionism of the Wesleys, yet he partnered with them in ministry for a period of four years.[66] In fact, Newton became so close to John Wesley's brother, Charles, that he served as a pall bearer in Charles' funeral.[67]

Figure 1. John Newton.

This season in Newton's life also provided him much time for study and reflection. He began to write, which would become a lifelong passion. His first published work was, not surprisingly, *Thoughts on Religious Associations*.[68] Friendships were important; he sent a copy to every minister in Liverpool.[69]

Though his formal schooling had come to a close at the age of ten, Newton had been self-taught in mathematics and the classics, and began the same undertaking in theological education,[70] becoming proficient in both Greek and Hebrew.[71] By 1757, he was already entertaining the idea of entering the pastorate.[72] On his birthday in 1758, Newton officially committed himself to the work of ministry, spending eleven hours in prayer and fasting.[73]

Yet, even though Newton had been suddenly surrounded by such a wonderful group of friends, becoming a pastor turned out to be much more difficult than he would have originally imagined. His first few sermons were train wrecks. The first time, likely trying to imitate Whitefield, Newton used no notes. He forgot his sermon halfway through, and the resident pastor had to finish up for him![74] Like a new driver, the next time around, Newton overcorrected. This time he brought too many notes into the pulpit, and ended up reading his sermon to the congregation.[75] Even so, Newton would find that preaching came easy compared to finding a church that he could pastor.

He had friends among the Calvinistic and Wesleyan Methodists, the Moravians, the Baptists, Independents, and Anglicans. The question of where he should serve was a difficult one for Newton to discern. Five attempts at becoming a Church of England curate were derailed because Newton was suspected to be a Methodist, and had no formal degree in divinity.[76] There even seems to be a short period in Newton's life where he avoided Whitefield and Wesley in hopes that his association with either of them would not block his prospects at becoming an Anglican clergyman.[77] At one point, he almost took an Independent church,[78] and at another, he almost became a Presbyterian.[79] It even appears that Newton almost planted a new Independent congregation in Liverpool, but in April 1761 he seems to have finally given up and begun preaching a Sunday evening service at his house.[80]

His life story was prominent in these early sermons; Newton viewed his life as a monument to God's mercy.[81] His testimony was wild, and fantastic, and people loved hearing it.[82] It should come as no surprise that one of Newton's friends asked him to write it down. Later, another friend asked for him to expand it even further.[83] That was how John Newton came to pen his autobiography when he was only thirty-nine years old. Little did he know at the time that his *Authentic Narrative* would also serve as the instrument that God would use to get him his first pastorate.

CHAPTER TWO

Being a Friend

MARCH 1764—DECEMBER 1807

March 4, 1764 must have been an exciting day. After seven years of waiting, it was this day that Newton's diary reveals that Lord Dartmouth, having read Newton's *Authentic Narrative*, offered him the curacy at the Anglican church in Olney.[1] So began the second half of Newton's amazing story.[2]

In the past, Newton had experienced life surrounded by bad friends, or isolated without any friends, and during his tenure in Liverpool, he had met many people who became wonderful friends. But as of yet, Newton was still relatively new to being a friend to others.

His time in Olney would change all of that. As a pastor, being a friend was part of the job, a part that was rooted in his own relationship with Christ. As the twelfth-century monk Aelred of Rievaulx stated, "God is friendship!" and, "For what more sublime than can be said of friendship, what more true, what more profitable, than that it ought to, and is proved to, begin in Christ, continue in Christ, and be perfected in Christ?"[3] Six hundred years later, Newton was affirming the same truth:

> I have a Friend, a rich, compassionate, powerful, unchangeable Friend; and the thought of him, who he is, where he is, what he has done, and what

> he is doing, somehow composes my mind and maintains my peace. Could he be taken from me, or my expectations founded upon him fail, I should instantly sink to the bottom of the bottomless pit of despair.[4]

Friendship was an integral part of Newton's spirituality. As a pastor, he was extending not only his own hand but the friendship of Christ to those around him; it was a means of grace.[5] He was also uniquely suited for it. As Josiah Bull noted,

> There must have been something marvelously winning about Mr. Newton to attract a circle of friends alike numerous and excellent. . . . Dartmouth and Wilberforce and the Thorntons, Charles Grant and Ambrose Serle and Mrs. Hannah More, with the elite of the clergy of all denominations. And these were not casual, but life-long friendships.[6]

These friendships were characterized by uncommon length, depth, and Christ-centeredness. Most of them flourished because Newton had assisted, encouraged, or promoted another at a pivotal moment in his or her journey. What is striking is that Newton seemed to be a friend to all, regardless of their circumstances.

TO CHILDREN

Newton let the little children come to him. In fact, one of the striking features of his early ministry in Olney was his effort to reach the children of the parish with the gospel. Every Thursday, Newton spent time catechizing children, teaching them the truths of Scripture.[7] Newton knew that money talks, and he began bribing children who could memorize the catechism with prizes of cash. Not surprisingly, that was a hit! While he could afford it, he had over two hundred children meeting with him weekly.[8] But even when the money ran out, interest among the children did not. He always had over forty, even in a little rural parish, but typically had fifty to seventy kids who could not wait to spend time with him.[9]

And for good reason: Newton was terribly fond of children. Although Mary and he never had children of their own, in 1774 the

Newtons adopted five-year-old Betsy Catlett, their niece, who had been orphaned.[10] Nine years later they did it again, bringing in another niece, Eliza Cunningham, after her mother died.[11] He loved these children as his own. Years later, when Betsy was in a psychiatric ward, Newton would take a daily walk to the hospital to wave at her through the window. Though he was almost blind and unable to see her, he would wave until the person walking with him could see Betsy waving her handkerchief back.[12] Then he would return home.

Yet this love for children did not stop with his own family. One of his earliest biographers, Josiah Bull, shares a memory from his own childhood. His father, Thomas Bull, found Josiah making a boat one day and remarked, "Ah, Mr. Newton used to make just such boats as these to please me when I was a child."[13] Newton clearly went out of his way to delight and entertain children.

One such child was a little boy around eleven years of age with a slight build, a precious voice, a quick wit, and a gleam in his eye. His name was William Wilberforce, and he had just been sent off to live with his aunt and uncle (Figure 2). His father had recently died, and his mother was dealing with serious depression, so his Uncle William and Aunt Hannah took him in and loved him as their own.[14] The couple had become good friends with Newton. "We are glad to have your promise of a visit this summer," Newton wrote to Hannah on June 9, 1770.[15] Perhaps this would be the occasion of his first encounter with little

Figure 2. Young William Wilberforce.

William. The exact date of their meeting is unknown, as the Wilberforce family often attended Newton's preaching, and he regularly visited to teach in their parlor.[16] It is also likely that the family made two more visits to stay at Olney the following summer.[17]

Newton took an immediate shine to Wilberforce, specifically noting "Master" William in his letters.[18] Despite the fact that the two were thirty-four years and twenty days apart,[19] they had an uncommon affection for one another from the start. Speaking of Newton, Wilberforce, who had recently lost his own father, is quoted as saying he revered Newton "as a parent when I was a child."[20] Over the next two years, Newton spent much time with William, sharing "about faith and about his journey from slave trader to servant of the Lord."[21]

It was a blow to them both when William's mother, Elizabeth Wilberforce, recovered her health, caught wind of the Methodist influence that was corrupting her child, and sent for him immediately.

Newton shared his concern for William with Hannah:

> I hope your nephew engages good bodily health, and his soul nourished and refreshed; and though he lives in a barren land, I trust he finds that the Lord can open springs and fountains in the wilderness. The word of grace and the throne of grace afford wells of salvation, from which he cannot be debarred; from thence, I hope, he will daily draw with joy the water of life, and, like a tree of the Lord's planting, strike root downwards, and bear fruit upwards, and experience that the Lord is able to keep, establish, and comfort him, though for a season he is deprived of the public ordinances of the Gospel.[22]

William's mother was determined to distract her son from spiritual pursuits with worldly pleasures. As his faith withered, from a distance Newton mourned. To a friend, he wrote,

> The strongest and most promising [religious convictions] I ever met with were in the case of Mr Wilberforce when he was a boy. But they now seem entirely worn off, not a trace left behind, except a deportment comparatively decent and moral in a young man of large fortune.[23]

Two years after their last encounter, Newton was still writing to William's uncle, "I beg to be remembered likewise to Master Wilberforce when you see him."[24] Though the two would have no contact for the next fifteen years, Newton never stopped praying for his young friend.[25]

It was a friendship that perhaps Newton thought was over, an insignificant friendship with a young boy. A friendship that, in time, would take on a significance of epic proportion.

TO SEEKERS

Six months after Newton's letter to William's uncle, he received one from an unlikely correspondent. Thomas Scott, the local heretic, who just so happened to be the curate of the neighboring parish at Weston, wrote him a letter (Figure 3). It was May of 1775, and Newton's ministry at Olney was flourishing. Two waves of revival had swept through the parish under Newton's leadership, and over one hundred people had experienced awakening.[26] The Tuesday evening prayer meeting grew so much that it was relocated to a room that could hold 130 people,[27] and every Sunday morning forty to fifty parishioners were praying for Newton before he preached.[28] He preached twice on Sundays[29] and led a group for singing and prayer every Sunday night.[30] He visited three to four families every afternoon[31] and opened his home to visitors every Wednesday

Figure 3. Thomas Scott.

and Friday.[32] On top of all of this, he had also gone to visit the sick in Scott's parish because Thomas Scott was too lazy to do it himself. Scott recalled:

> In January 1774, two of my parishioners, a man and his wife, lay at the point of death. I had heard of it, but according to my general custom, not being sent for, I took no notice of it: but one evening, the woman being already dead, and the man dying, I heard that my neighbor Mr. [Newton] had been several times to visit them. Immediately my conscience reproached me with being shamefully negligent, in sitting at home within a few doors of dying persons, my general hearers, and never going to visit them.[33]

Even after that, Scott "felt an eager desire of entering into a religious controversy, especially with a Calvinist."[34] Yet, Scott knew his opponent: "Concealing, therefore, the true motives of my conduct under the offer of friendship . . . I wrote him a long letter . . . as would introduce a controversial discussion of our religious differences."[35]

Newton did not have time for this. But the possibility of friendship was too enticing to pass up. Newton responded, "I set a great value upon your offer of friendship, which I trust will not be interrupted on either side by the freedom with which we mutually express our difference of sentiments when we are constrained to differ."[36] The two struck up a lively correspondence, with Newton writing eight substantial letters to Scott over the next six months.

Thomas Scott was a Socinian[37] and a Pelagian.[38] Though he had been ordained into the priesthood in 1772, he did not adhere to the *Thirty-Nine Articles*.[39] He had entered the ministry because it appeared easy, and it would afford him time to pursue other recreational activities.[40] In truth, he disdained Newton and those of his same evangelical ilk, even preaching against Methodism from the pulpit.[41]

Yet Newton could see through all of that to a man who was truly searching, a man who needed a friend on his way. Upon receiving Scott's first letter, Newton noted in his diary, "Received an unexpected letter from Mr. Scott. . . . It seems dictated by a spirit in search of the truth."[42]

It was in that compassionate tone that Newton, over the next six months, patiently began to answer Scott's questions, objections, and barbs. He pointed Scott to search the Scriptures with prayer,[43] sent him a book of evangelical doctrine,[44] and even affirmed that it was okay for Scott to wrestle through his questions and objections.[45] Newton did not yet view Scott as truly saved but as a seeker. Referring to his own journey, Newton wrote on October 21, 1775, "Then I was seeking, and now, through mercy, I have found, the Pearl of great price. It is both the prayer and the hope of my heart, that a day is coming when you shall make the same acknowledgement."[46]

Scott was less than convinced. In fact, he felt that Newton had disappointed him,[47] and Scott eventually broke off the correspondence.

> I made use of every endeavour to draw him into controversy, and filled my letters with definitions, inquiries, arguments, objections, and consequences, and required explicit answers: he, on the other hand, shunned everything controversial, as much as possible, and filled his letters with the most useful, and least offensive instructions.[48]

Newton pursued him anyway, writing three times without receiving any response.[49] It was certainly discouraging. "Much of my leisure. . . has been employed in writing to Mr. Scott. This correspondence takes up much time, and hitherto I seem to get but little ground."[50] Scott did not even like Newton: "To speak plainly, I did not care for his company, I did not mean to make any use of him as an instructor, and was unwilling the world should think us any ways connected."[51]

For the next year and a half, the two had almost no contact. However, when Scott was going through a difficult time, who else would he turn to but Newton? Newton, of course, continued to encourage him to search the Scriptures. Scott did, and even acquiesced to hear Newton preach. It made absolutely no sense to him, but because of their friendship, Scott kept coming back for more.[52] Over the next six months, Scott's thinking began to change. He began to listen to Newton regularly. Newton's diary is hopeful: "I think he gets forward into the light."[53] He must have made great strides, because Newton invited Scott to preach for him twice in October of 1777.[54]

In fact, by January 1778, Newton could say, "O my Lord, what a teacher art Thou! How soon, clearly, and solidly is he established in the knowledge and experience of Thy gospel, who but lately was a disputer against every point! I praise Thee for him."[55] By the following year, Scott had penned his own autobiography, *Force of Truth: An Authentic Narrative*. Even the title harkens back to the autobiography of the mentor who is featured so prominently in its pages. Not surprisingly, Newton helped with the revisions.[56] Scott was only thirty-one years old at the time.

The man who had been so antagonistic to orthodox Christianity was quickly becoming one of its prime defenders. In time, Scott would write a commentary on the Bible, which "was to be second only to [Matthew] Henry's in popularity."[57] This man, who at first was a terrible communicator, became, according to Newton, one of the best extempore preachers around.[58] In fact, when the living at St. Mary Woolnoth in London was offered to Newton in 1779,[59] Newton could not think of a better person to take his place at Olney. In his diary, Newton prayed for the congregation who had become so dear to his family:

> May Thy gracious hand, my Lord, wipe away their tears, and turn their mourning into joy. I trust it shall be so if Thou art pleased to favour my wishes and endeavours for Mr. Scott to supply my place, which he is willing to do.[60]

In the end, that is exactly what happened. John Newton moved to London in January of 1780,[61] and Thomas Scott became the curate at Olney.

London brought its own challenges, but it also brought amazing opportunity. Newton was fifty-four years old, and his circle of influence was clearly growing.[62] The only way to keep up with everyone was letter writing. Even that was an uphill battle. To a friend, he wrote, "I have about sixty unanswered letters, and while I am writing one I usually receive two; so that I am likely to die much in debt."[63] Yet Newton saw letter writing as a calling on his life,[64] believing that the Lord would use him "most by [his] letters."[65]

And for good reason. Newton wore his heart on his sleeve; his authenticity and wisdom shone brightly every time he set his pen to paper. "I number my Christian correspondents among my principle blessings, a few judicious, pious friends, to whom, when I can get leisure to write, I send my heart by turns."[66] His letters were so helpful, in fact, that Newton began to collect and publish them in volumes. One such was aptly titled, *Cardiphonia*—that is, "utterances of the heart"—published in 1781.

The next year, when Hannah More cracked open the volume, she was searching (Figure 4). A close friend had died.[67] More was a thirty-seven-year-old woman, who, a decade earlier, watched as her engagement failed. Now, though she was an accomplished poet and playwright who ran in London's elite literary circles, she wanted more. And she found it.

That same year we find her writing to a family member,

> Ask Dr. Stonehouse if he has read '*Cardiphonia*,' by Mr. Newton of Olney. There is in it much vital religion, and much of the experience of a good Christian, who feels and laments his own imperfections and weaknesses.[68]

So far, More had never known this "vital religion" and reading *Cardiphonia* opened her eyes to "a spiritual experience beyond anything she had known."[69]

Five years later, in 1787, More decided to seek out the author.[70] It was at this time that her life would take a dramatic turn.[71] She marked the day: "To-day (Tuesday) I have been into the city to hear good Mr. Newton preach; and afterwards went and sat an hour with him, and came home with pockets full of sermons." [72] The two developed a correspondence which lasted over fifteen years, during which Newton continued to fill both her pockets and her heart.[73]

We find her gushing about Newton's character and influence in a letter to him dated May 18, 1787, "I at once feel that degree of friendship for [you] which in other cases one does not arrive at but after much time and by slow gradations." And,

Figure 4. Hannah More.

> Your little book to your dissenting friend I opened the moment I came home, intending (for I was very busy) only to read a page or two; but I was so pleased with the candour, good sense, and Christian spirit of it, that I never laid it out of my hands while there was a page unread.[74]

More was "truly attached"[75] to old Newton, but to be fair, the feelings were reciprocal.

In a letter to Wilberforce (a mutual friend), Newton writes,

> If you see the Miss Mores, may I beg you to present my love to them, and to tell them, especially Miss Hannah and Miss Patty, that my heart is often hovering about Mendip,[76] particularly on a Sunday morning. I am thankful that I have seen Cowslip Green, I should be glad to see it again."[77]

Over the years, Newton prayed for Hannah to never get caught up in the "applause of the world,"[78] recommended books to her,[79] shared his own journey in approaching death,[80] encouraged her in her publishing efforts,[81] and checked up on her when she was sick.[82]

It was quite an investment, but not one that would return void. After meeting John Newton, Hannah More found a new circle of friends in the Clapham Sect (Wilberforce's tight-knit community) and decided to employ her literary talent, considerable drive, and eminent competence to scrub several of the darkest stains on England's skirt.

But not all seekers whom Newton befriended were so accomplished. Some were little more than traveling vagabonds. In 1791, the same year Newton went to visit Hannah More to see her latest undertaking, Newton himself had a visitor. Claudius Buchanan, a twenty-five-year-old, had run away from home in Scotland some time before with a desire to see the world (Figure 5). He wound up penniless, a drifter, living on whatever he could scrounge together by playing the violin to passersby. The prodigal wrote his mother, who sent word back that he needed to go hear Newton preach.

St. Mary Woolnoth was packed, as usual. What made this Sunday different is that Newton had a note in his hand from an anonymous visitor: "On the receipt of my mother's letter, I went the next Sunday evening to your church; and when you spoke I thought I heard the words of eternal life. I listened with avidity, and wished you had preached till midnight. . . . what shall I do to inherit eternal life?" The note ended by asking Newton to preach something suitable for someone who was seeking. Instead, Newton made an announcement to the congregation that if the anonymous person was present, he would love to meet with that person![83]

Figure 5. Claudius Buchanan.

At sixty-six years of age, befriending seekers was par for the course for John Newton. Buchanan reported what happened next in a letter to his mother,

> I called on him on the Tuesday following, and experienced such a happy hour as I ought not to forget. If he had been my father he could not have expressed more solicitude for my welfare. Mr. Newton encouraged me much. He put into my hands the *Narrative* . . . and gave me a general invitation to breakfast with him as often as I could.[84]

Under Newton, Buchanan came to saving faith, and through his connections, received financial aid to attend Cambridge. [85] Their correspondence during Buchanan's college years is incredibly insightful into Buchanan's estimation of his mentor. "Your letter, long looked for, amply repaid my patience. I should not like to part with it for its weight in gold. It is not only useful to me now, but will probably be often consulted by me in years to come."[86] At another point, Buchanan wrote, "Oh sir, what a seasonable gift were your books to a person in my situation! Next to the Oracles of Truth I consult *them*."[87] It is no surprise that Buchanan hoped, early on, to follow in Newton's footsteps. In considering vocational ministry, Buchanan asked Newton's advice on associating with other guys at college, what books to read, and if he "ever shall be able to preach extempore from the pulpit."[88]

It is clear that Buchanan hung on to almost every word that Newton said: "I hope to derive advantage from your advice."[89] Another time Buchanan made the (scary) assertion that he considered depending on the Lord, and depending on "the direction of his experienced Servant, by whom he frequently speaks, as nearly the same thing."[90] Though Buchanan's loyalty may have been misguided at times, his affection for Newton was abundantly clear. Imagine a twenty-seven-year-old man signing off, "Your little child in the gospel."[91] Buchanan loved Newton as a father. And Newton came to love this violin-playing vagabond as a son. In fact, after waiting four years for his ordination, [92] Claudius Buchanan became John Newton's curate at St. Mary Woolnoth in 1795.[93]

But it would not last long. Because, just as it happened in the case of Thomas Scott and Hannah More, after becoming friends with John Newton, Claudius Buchanan realized that God had greater things in store. He realized, all the while, it was not so much that he had been seeking God; rather, God had sought out him.

TO THE DEPRESSED

For a man who had experienced the depths of despair, stranded and alone on the coast of Africa, Newton seemed to possess a wonderful sense of joy. It was rooted in his relationship with Christ, and it overflowed in his friendships with others, especially with those who frequented the slough of despond. His sense of humor seemed to shine brightest in those relationships; moreover, Newton welcomed them. In a letter to his dear friend, William Bull, a pastor from a neighboring town, who freely admitted his "excessive propensity to dejection,"[94] Newton playfully writes,

> I shall hope to share—
> A Theosophic pipe with brother B.,
> Beneath the shadow of his favorite tree,
> And then how happy I! how cheerful he![95]

But he was not simply a buffoon with depressed people. He was also able to draw from his own experience and empathize with others by sharing his story and history of feeling abandoned and literally enslaved. We see him do this very thing in another letter to Bull.[96] Newton was no stranger to darkness. And it is a good thing, because three years into his first pastorate, we find him dealing with one of the darkest struggles with depression recorded in modern church history.

William Cowper was Newton's junior by six years (Figure 6).[97] His mother died when he was only six, and his father, a rector, sent him off to boarding school, where he was exposed to endless torment from one of the older boys.[98] Between losing his mother as a young child, his father sending him away, and the abuse that he endured at boarding school, William Cowper suffered from serious emotional trauma.

In 1752, when he was only twenty-one, Cowper experienced his first major bout of depression. Though he had won his cousin Theodora's

Figure 6. William Cowper.

heart, he had not won his uncle's. [99] He was heartbroken when told that marriage would be improper, and he sunk into deep despair. The poems of George Herbert proved to be a lifeline.[100] But, that was only the beginning.

A second major depression swept over Cowper in 1763 and lasted for a year and a half. His attempts to poison himself, drown himself, and hang himself all failed. [101] Two months later, he was sent to St. Albans Insane Asylum. It was there that Cowper experienced conversion, and there he stayed for over a year. Upon his release in 1765, he went to live with a retired pastor, Mr. Unwin, and his wife. Two years later, Mr. Unwin passed away.[102]

It seems unlikely that John Newton could have imagined that his going to visit this grieving family in a neighboring town would change their lives forever, but sometimes the truth is stranger than fiction. Newton proved to be such a joy, and support, that Mrs. Unwin decided it was time to relocate. She was moving to Olney. And Cowper was coming with her.[103]

William Cowper and John Newton got along smashingly. Reflecting back on their friendship, Newton told Wilberforce that for the seven years prior to Cowper's third bout of depression, "we were seldom separated seven waking hours."[104] All told, for twelve years, the two friends walked through life together: "The first six I passed in daily admiring and trying to imitate him; during the second six I walked pensively with him in the valley of the shadow of death."[105] Given that Cowper had recently been released from an insane asylum when they met, it appears that Newton is being humble concerning the part that he played in their friendship. As early as July 30, 1767, before Cowper had even moved to Olney, we find Newton writing Cowper a letter to help him through his depression.[106] When Cowper and Mrs. Unwin made the move in the fall of that year,[107] Newton pulled out all the stops to assist Cowper in every possible way.

He prayed for Cowper. His journal reveals the deep concern: "My dear friend still walks in darkness."[108] He gave up vacation time to stay with Cowper when he was struggling,[109] he "perform[ed] family worship morning and evening in two houses,"[110] (his own, and Cowper's), and the Newtons even took Cowper in to live with them on two occasions, once for about five months, and once for over a year.[111]

Whereas most would grow weary with such stubborn depression, Newton empathized deeply: "when you pipe, I am ready to dance; and when you mourn, a cloud comes over my brow, and a tear stands a-tiptoe in my eye."[112] In the same letter, Newton continued to point out the evidence of God's saving grace in Cowper's life, the very thing that Cowper failed to see himself, and the root of his deepest fears.

Such love and friendship did not go unnoticed. In one of his many poems, Cowper wrote, "True bliss, if man may reach it, is compos'd / Of hearts in union mutually disclos'd."[113] The editor of Cowper's *Works* assumes these words were written of Newton; perhaps the most joyful facet of Cowper's life was knowing the curate of Olney. Cowper once claimed that a "sincerer or more affectionate friend no man ever had."[114]

Hoping to turn his attention outward, Newton invited Cowper into the ministry of visiting the poor. Cowper became very involved; at his memorial, Newton said, "He was a great blessing to the Lord's poor. . . . he loved the poor, often visit[ing] them."[115] Once, Cowper signed a petition designed to help the poor in Olney. When another person refused to sign the document, thinking it was was composed poorly, Cowper remarked to Newton, "I dare say if his lordship does not comply with the prayer of it, it will not be because he thinks it of more consequence to write grammatically than that the poor should eat, but for some better reason."[116] Surely this writer was revealing his hand; some things were clearly more important that literary skill. Compassion was one of them.

Even so, both men had a lyrical bent, and such friendship, founded on Christ, naturally worked its way out in song. This was the genesis of the *Olney Hymns*. Newton and Cowper collaborated on a hymnbook to celebrate their friendship. Newton describes the intent in the preface:

> A desire of promoting the faith and comfort of sincere Christians, though the principal, was not the only motive to this undertaking. It was likewise intended as a monument, to perpetuate the remembrance of an intimate and endeared friendship.[117]

Unfortunately, two years into the project, Cowper was hit with another round of despondency,[118] and only completed sixty-seven hymns, leaving Newton to carry the bulk of the project. When the *Olney Hymns* went to press in 1779, Newton was the author of the other 281.[119]

Later that year, when John Newton moved away from Olney to take a pastorate in London, it is not surprising that Cowper's well-being was foremost in his thoughts.[120] It only makes sense that, before leaving, Newton would introduce Cowper to another close friend who understood depression. "Mr. Newton was very anxious, before he left Olney, that Mr. Bull should be acquainted with the poet Cowper."[121] That friendship blossomed as well,[122] and before long, Newton moved away.

Even though Newton was now gone, the testament to their friendship stood. The *Olney Hymns* went through five editions in the first year, and over the next hundred years, over 500,000 copies were circulating.[123] In 1779, no one could have imagined the future impact of such a work. How many times have God's people sung the refrains, "God moves in a mysterious way,"[124] "There is a fountain fill'd with blood,"[125] or "Amazing grace! (how sweet the sound) That sav'd a wretch like me!"?[126]

To think that the friendship of a country minister and a depressed parishioner could produce such fruit is incredible. To think that it also awakened Cowper's genius literary gifts (gifts that would be employed to eradicate deeply rooted systemic injustice) is almost unbelievable.

TO OTHER PASTORS

Denominational affiliation was never a hindrance to Newton's friendships. To him, the differences were much less important than unity in the gospel and love from the heart.

> I am somehow disqualified for claiming a full brotherhood with any party; but there are a few among all parties who bear with me, and love me, and with this I must be content at present. But so far as they love the Lord Jesus Christ, I desire, and by his grace, I determine (with or without their leave), to love them all.[127]

His affection for others despite ecclesiological differences, is illustrated, perhaps most vividly, in his relationship with the friend whom he entrusted with Cowper's care upon his move to London: the Reverend William Bull of Newport Pagnell (Figure 7).

Figure 7. William Bull.

It was 1766, and Newton was only two years into his ministry when the two met, beginning a friendship that lasted throughout the rest of Newton's life. Although they were not terribly fond of one another at first, once the two got to know each other, they became the best of friends.[128] William Bull was about thirteen years younger than Newton, but given Newton's late start in ministry, they both were ordained in 1764.[129] Bull was the pastor of the Independent congregation of the neighboring town. The warmth of their friendship becomes clear when one peruses the familiarity that fills their copious correspondence.[130]

As previously noted, Newton regularly attempted to encourage Bull in his depression, but the scope of their conversation was much broader. Anticipating a get-together, Newton seemed giddy with excitement: "I shall think of you hourly till I see you, as children count the hours for days before the fair."[131] The two joked often:

> A pig came to our house on Monday; and, though he neither brought an introductory letter, nor could tell us who sent him, we, being something in the habit of receiving strangers, bid him welcome. In return, he entertained us, Mr. Bacon, and Mrs. Gardiner, very agreeably at dinner, yesterday (Tuesday), but he was gone before yours came. I can only thank you now for both pig and letter.[132]

Besides laughing and eating,[133] the two smoked pipes together,[134] shared sermon ideas,[135] and talked theology.[136]

Newton greatly expanded Bull's circle of acquaintances by introducing him to John Thornton, patriarch of the Clapham Sect, and a generous, godly, and rich benefactor of Newton's. Bull's life would never be the same. Newton was asked to draw up a plan for a school that would train young men for ministry.[137] He did and suggested that Bull should be the first superintendent.[138] Thornton agreed to fund it, Bull agreed to lead it, and the Newport Pagnell Evangelical Institution for the Education of Young Men for the Christian Ministry was founded.[139]

It was also through this connection that Bull became more involved in compassionate ministry. Thornton told Bull that he would be his banker: "When you want assistance, you know where to come for it."[140] Once Thornton sent Bull twenty blankets in addition to his annual gift of twenty guineas to distribute to the poor.[141] Newton, of course, encouraged Bull in this as well. When Thomas Scott came down with a fever, Newton bragged:

> He caught it by attendance on the sick poor. A noble wound! Shall soldiers risk their lives, and stand as a mark for great guns, for sixpence a day, or for the word honour? and is it not worth venturing something in imitation of Him who went about doing good, and when the good we aim at is for his sake?[142]

With Bull, Newton shared his concern about the oppression in the East Indies,[143] as well as his broken heart over the trans-Atlantic slave trade.

> I preached (as I did last year) about the slave trade. I considered it not in a political but in a moral view, from Jer. ii. 34. I think myself bound in conscience to bear my testimony at least, and to wash my hands from the guilt, which, if persisted in, now things have been so thoroughly investigated and brought to light, will, I think, constitute a national sin of a scarlet and crimson dye.[144]

Three days later, Newton reiterated that he had "charged all who do not express their detestation of this traffic, now things are so thoroughly investigated, and notorious, with bloodguiltiness. Lord, lay not the sin to our charge."[145] Newton made it clear to Bull that unless people "express their detestation" of the slave trade, they themselves were guilty partners in it.

But Newton's line in the sand in no way tempered Bull's affection for his friend. In fact, of all the men that William Bull knew, he wanted his son to become a man like John Newton. He asked Newton to perform his son's wedding ceremony.

> It was, and still is, a matter of peculiar feeling and comfort to me, that you, the dearest and oldest friend I have left, should perform the sacred ceremony on this occasion. Oh, may your mantle, may a double portion of your spirit, fall upon this dear youth![146]

It is no surprise that Bull's grandson made the statement that John Newton moving away from Olney was one of the "greatest trials" that

William Bull ever faced.[147] Even so, years later, we find Newton's love for his old friend unabated:

> My dear old friend. . . . Though the flame of our affection is not much supported by the fruit of frequent letters and converse, I trust it still burns brightly, for it is fed from a secret, invisible, and inexhaustible source.[148]

It was indeed. But William Bull was not the only one who missed such a rich friendship with another pastor. Newton did as well.

It seems only natural, then, that after Newton moved to London, he pulled together three other close friends, and in 1783, the Eclectic Society was born.[149] It was meant to be a time for pastors (and a few laymen) to get together and discuss a predetermined topic.[150] What Newton enjoyed with William Bull was expanded and extended to others. There were rules governing attendance, and the men would typically meet for three hours at a time.[151] Newton was the clear leader of the group. He started it, took minutes for the first ten years,[152] and was twenty years older than most of the other members.[153] In time, the size of the club grew to about a dozen, and many fruitful discussions took place as they gathered (even after Newton's death) for over thirty years.[154]

Figure 8. Charles Simeon.

One of the country members of this society (who thereby received some leniency with the attendance requirements!) was a younger pastor at Cambridge named Charles Simeon (Figure 8). He was thirty-four years younger than Newton, and though he seemed to have never ending conflict from within his own parish, Simeon was an up-and-coming leader in the Established Church.[155] For almost six years, Newton and Simeon attended the Eclectic Society together.[156]

At the beginning of 1796, Simeon raised the idea of starting a new Anglican mission society. By this time, the Baptist and London Missionary Societies had formed, and although two Anglican societies were in existence, Simeon and later John Venn pushed for another Anglican missionary society that would reach the nations. Newton, of course, was on the original committee of twenty-four.[157] In 1799, under John Venn's leadership, the Church Missionary Society was born. Its effectiveness in the early years was extremely limited, but it did function to further expand Newton and Simeon's working relationship.

Earlier, Newton had invited Simeon to come preach at an event,[158] and Newton had done the same at least twice in Simeon's church.[159] They had also joined efforts in the past to find candidates for the India Mission,[160] and likely tried to find Richard Johnson a helper in Botany Bay.[161] Now they were working together once again, each hoping to find suitable missionaries that the new Society could send overseas.

Though Henry Venn (John Venn's father) can be credited as Simeon's mentor, Newton still seemed to exercise quite an influence in Simeon's life through their limited interactions. In fact, it is interesting to find Simeon writing to Newton after Henry Venn's death: "O that I may fight my fight as he has, & may be a partaker of the Glory that awaits him."[162] Yet, in the end, it seems that Simeon wished to end his life as Newton did, and not as his long-time mentor had:

> I had often thought with a kind of complacency, that as I had for many years accumulated, and was continuing daily to amass a great stock of Sermons upon the finest portions of Scripture, I should, if my life should be spared to attain the age of sixty, have a fund to go to, and be able to prosecute my work with more ease, at a time when I might expect my strength, according to the course of nature, to be diminished. My dear friend, old Mr. Venn, had suspended his labours entirely at that period of life: and I thought that I also, if spared till then, might be miles emeritus. This now appeared to me extremely wrong; and it seemed as if God in this

> dispensation said to me, 'Well, if you look forward with complacency to a relaxation from labour in my service at that period, you shall have it now, and be altogether disabled from serving me at all.' I now saw that I had sinned in entertaining such a thought, and I determined, through grace, that whatever measure of strength God should see fit to allot to me in future life, I would spend it for Him; and that whether my days should be more or less protracted, I would, like Mr. Newton, Mr. Romaine, and Mr. Wesley, die in harness.[163]

When it came to emulating someone who finished strong, John Newton was the first man on Simeon's list, not Henry Venn. In fact, exactly two months after Newton's death, Simeon wrote to Newton's executor:

> You are commissioned to publish his papers, *and those in particular which he has pointed out;* and you submit them to the judgment of myself and two other Ministers, who, in point of Christian experience, are mere babes to him. In consequence of this, because we cannot descend into his depths, we must bring him into our shallows, and reduce this and that expression to our standard. This is an injustice to him, and to the world. We have not ability to sit in judgment upon such a man, any more than babes just beginning to see the truth are to sit in judgment upon us.[164]

Despite denominational differences (as in the case of Bull), and geographical hurdles (as with Simeon), Newton seemed to go out of his way to foster friendships with other pastors. Unlike many in the pastorate, he was not territorial, did not get caught up with labels, and seemed to be free of ladder-climbing. He thought that relationships could be mutually beneficial, advancing the cause of the gospel. But perhaps even more fundamental to his motivations was the simple fact that John Newton loved befriending people—and none more than energetic, promising young people with a heart for ministry.

TO PROMISING YOUNG LEADERS

On his seventy-ninth birthday, August 4, 1804, Newton wrote his penultimate diary entry, "Let me retire as a thankful guest from a full table, and rejoice that others are coming forth to serve thee (I hope better) when I can do no more."[165] He never saw up-and-coming leaders as a threat, but instead as a joy, investing much time into their growth and development.

John Ryland Jr. is a prime example (Figure 9). His father was a well-known and influential Baptist pastor, and raised his son to be ambitious as well. Before Ryland reached his ninth birthday, he had already translated the Greek New Testament, and by the time he was twelve, he had gone through Genesis in the original Hebrew five times! [166] His first full-length book was published by his eighteenth birthday; by all appearances, John Ryland Jr. was meant for great things.[167]

Figure 9. John Ryland, Jr.

Born on January 29, 1753, Ryland was twenty-eight years younger than Newton. [168] The two first met around 1765, and three years later, when Ryland visited Olney, he stayed a week in the curate's house.[169] Ryland was only fifteen years old at the time. Egged on by his father, though Ryland was quite sharp, he was also quite proud in those early years. After Newton saw the preface of one of his publications, where Ryland stated that not a single person had assisted him in one line,[170] he responded with a letter to his recent visitor, telling him that "there is too much confidence in your manner."[171]

Surprisingly, Ryland listened, and so began three decades of correspondence between the two, with over eighty of Newton's letters still surviving today.[172] In 1824, the year before Ryland died, he wrote,

"Mr. Newton invited me to visit him at Olney in 1768; and from thence to his death, I always esteemed him, and Mr. Hall of Arnsby . . . as my wisest and most faithful counsellors, in all difficulties."[173]

Ryland began to seek out Newton's advice about a number of topics. After he preached 138 times as an eighteen-year-old, Newton advised him to slow down.[174] He did. When the American Revolution was taking place, Ryland wanted to know Newton's opinion on the war. Newton obliged.[175] Soon Ryland was having girl problems, and Newton reminded him, "You were sent into the world for a nobler end than to be pinned to a girl's apron string; and yet if the Lord sees it not good for you to be alone, he will provide you a help-mate."[176] There's almost no topic that the two overlooked.[177]

Not surprisingly, Newton also counseled Ryland to remember the least of these. Ryland wanted to get married, and Newton pointed out that to get married, one needed money. "Besides, you would be grieved not to find an occasional shilling in your pocket to bestow upon one or other of the Lord's poor."[178] Ministry priorities were also influenced by this concern. Once, when Ryland asked for Newton's financial help to repair a decrepit church building, Newton declined, stating that he would not be involved in building campaigns when there were so many poor that needed help.[179] Even Ryland's estimation of brilliant American theologians, with whom he was enamored, was tempered by Newton's assessment of their concern for the poor:

> I think, in some things they run too much into refinements, and I bless God for a plain Gospel, designed to be preached to the poor, which can be received by faith into the heart, by those who have little taste or capacity for nice distinctions.[180]

Not only did Ryland listen to Newton's advice, but early on he began the practice of transcribing all of Newton's letters in his notebook.[181] Obviously, he found Newton's perspective both valuable and fresh. Although Ryland came from a hyper-Calvinistic background, Newton's tender way and evangelistic zeal resonated with the young man. "I pray the Lord to give you a gentle and loving spirit towards all men, and a practical conviction that grace alone has made you to differ."[182] Newton's prayers were answered, and over time, John Ryland Jr. parted with his father's High Calvinism, and moved to a warmer evangelical Calvinism.[183]

Though Ryland's father was a godly man and a prominent leader, Newton seemed to wield almost as much influence over the young man. In fact, when Ryland had difficulty with his father in later years, not surprisingly, he turned to Newton for help.[184] At twenty-eight years old, he had become his father's assistant pastor at the church. A few years later his father moved away, allowing him to assume the helm.[185] Now he was being attacked for his new views.[186] It seems likely that at one point, even John Ryland Sr. published a pamphlet against his son.[187] What should he do? Encouraging as always, Newton wrote,

> The Lord has given you a heart to serve him, and he will stand by you. The sailors have a saying, that if it was always fine weather the old women would go to sea; but the skill of the mariner is seen in the storm. Trust in your pilot, and manage your sails, and all will be well.188

Ryland resisted the urge to respond, as Newton had counseled, and in time, all was well.[189]

So well, in fact, that in 1792, John Ryland Jr. was asked to become the president of Bristol Baptist College, and the pastor of Broadmead Church. [190] That same year he served as the moderator of the Northamptonshire Baptist Association meetings.[191] He was now in a position where his new views, gleaned from Newton, would help change the trajectory of Baptist life for the next two hundred years.

It was at those same Baptist associational meetings that another promising, young leader broke into the spotlight. He was a close friend to Ryland, having been baptized by Ryland nine years before.[192] His name was William Carey (Figure 10), and at one of those meetings, he preached a "deathless" sermon from Isaiah 54:2-3:

> Enlarge the place of your tent,
> and let the curtains of your habitations be stretched out;
> do not hold back; lengthen your cords
> and strengthen your stakes.
> For you will spread abroad to the right and to the left,
> and your offspring will possess the nations
> and will people the desolate cities.

The text echoes one of Newton's letters to Ryland from almost twenty years prior: "It rejoices me to hear that . . . the Lord is lengthening your cords, and I hope strengthening your stakes."[193] Whether Ryland passed that idea on to Carey is impossible to determine. What is clear is that this young man, born in 1761, rocketed into Christian history almost out of nowhere.

Figure 10. William Carey.

Just a few years before, Carey was working in a cobbler shop, fixing shoes.[194] After coming to faith, and desiring to enter into the ministry, he united with John Sutcliff's independent church in Olney.[195] By that time, Newton was no longer curate at Olney, but Newton's disciple, Thomas Scott, filled the pulpit of the Anglican church there. In a letter to Ryland, Carey wrote, "If there be anything of the work of God in my soul, I owe much of it to [Scott's] preaching, when I first set out in the ways of the Lord."[196] Two of Newton's disciples (Ryland and Scott) were now discipling William Carey.

Soon after, Carey began a bivocational ministry at Moulton, working on the side to support his family. Ryland asked Newton to find support for Carey's fledgling congregation, but soon Carey was off to a larger one.[197] Nor was he there long, because William Carey had caught a heart for the nations. As a result of those Baptist meetings in 1792, Ryland, Sutcliff, Andrew Fuller, Samuel Pearce, [198] and others committed to create a society to propagate the gospel. [199] The aforementioned men covenanted together to "hold the ropes for their sent-forth friend."[200]

William Carey heard the call to India, and was ready to go. There was only one problem: it was illegal for him to go there.

Although in 1792 William Wilberforce had put forth a motion in Parliament to force the East India Company "to appoint chaplains, teachers, and missionaries," the directors of the company were staunchly opposed to any such measures.[201] To keep anyone from covertly sneaking missionaries in, it was made a "high misdemeanour to enter without a licence."[202] Violaters would face fines or even imprisonment.[203] That left guys like William Carey in a bit of a pickle. God had clearly called him. Should he go without the proper documentation?

Who else would he turn to but old Mr. Newton? "What if the company should send us home on our arrival in Bengal?" he asked. The old Anglican rector, thirty-six years Carey's senior, replied, "Then conclude that your Lord has nothing there for you to accomplish. But if He have, then no power on earth can hinder you."[204]

Shortly thereafter, we find Newton penning a letter to his MP friend: "I expect that a Mr. Cary [*sic*] will shortly wait upon you, and will probably bring an introductory line from me. Though I do not personally know him, his character and business are such, that I could not refuse him this request."[205] The letter goes on to tell of Carey's character, his desire to go to Bengal, an appeal for him to be able to go over on an East India Company ship, a plea to support him financially, an inquiry as to whether he would be able to stay if he went over on a foreign ship, and finally a request that Wilberforce might give Carey fifteen minutes of his time to hear his case.

Although things did not work out with the East India Company, Carey eventually sailed over in a Danish ship. Upon approaching the coast, he boarded a small fishing boat and "slipped into the vast city unnoticed and unmolested by the company officials."[206] Newton's advice had been followed.

While the two had not known one another well in England, we find them continuing to correspond almost ten years later.[207] Clearly, Carey had become dear to Newton. In a letter to Ryland, Newton notes,

> Mr Carey has favoured me with a letter which indeed I accept as a favour and I mean to thank him for it. I trust my heart as cordially unites with him for the success of his mission, as though I were a brother Baptist myself. I look to such a man with reverence. He is more to me than a Bishop, or Archbishop; he is an Apostle. May the Lord make all who undertake missions like-minded with Brother Carey.[208]

But it was a two-way street. When missions in a pioneer land proved difficult, Carey wanted to quit. One of the gracious gifts that God used to keep him going was a letter from John Newton. With thankfulness, Carey writes,

> Yours of last year I read and must say that it not only afforded me much pleasure, but profit also: the justice of your remarks upon disappointments, and want of success, was such as struck me very forcibly, and contributed much to my support and encouragement, and I feel myself determined to go on, in the name of the Lord, even till Death.[209]

For the next thirty-five years, William Carey did just that.

But Newton's friendship addiction with promising young leaders was not always so long-distance. We find Newton, on more than one occasion, taking bright students into his home. Thomas Charles was one of them (Figure 11). On break from Oxford in the summer of 1777, Charles somehow found lodging at the vicarage in Olney.[210] He was twenty-one years old. How exactly he was introduced to Newton, we know not.[211] What we do know is that Charles and another student came that summer to study theology under Newton in his home.[212]

This kind of round-the-clock access to Newton "proved very comfortable and very profitable indeed."[213]

Figure 11. Thomas Charles.

> Having a Newton to be instructed by, both by edifying discourses in the pulpit, and by conversation in the closet, what place or situation can I be in, more pleasing and delightful? I had formed in my mind great ideas of him, but really he has exceeded my most sanguine expectations.[214]

One can only imagine what kind of conversations they had around the breakfast table, or just before retiring at night. Among other things, Charles assisted Newton by copying many of the letters Newton was compiling in order to publish his *Cardiphonia*.[215]

The summer was soon over, but the friendship had just begun. Upon receiving a letter of appreciation from Charles, Newton responded,

> I have reason to be thankful if you think the time you spent in Olney was not altogether lost, nor the views which led you thither wholly disappointed. It is certain the Lord gave me a desire, to be some way helpful to you and Mr. Mayor. . . . [The Lord] made your company very acceptable to me likewise, and as you were both to leave Olney, we felt loth to part with you, and miss you sensibly now you are gone.[216]

In response to Charles' request for Newton's guidance, Newton said,

> You would be very welcome to the results and points of my experience such as it has been; but to attempt to offer you rules and directions at large, would be too indeterminate, as well [as] too assuming a task. Let it suffice that if as occasions arise, you think proper to consult me upon any particular, I shall be ready to give you my judgment, without ceremony and without reserve.[217]

Occasions arose. A lot.

After finishing at Oxford, Charles was accepted as a deacon in the Established Church, and finally into full orders as an elder.[218] However, his heart was in Wales, and he left England in 1783 without a ministry prospect.[219] Newton helped him get an appointment to a curacy in South Wales, but it was not close enough to home for Charles' fiancée.[220] Charles asked for advice. Should he leave the Established Church to work with the Methodists closer to home?

Newton told him it would be all right but encouraged Charles to consider taking an appointment that was not necessarily in his own backyard. Charles promptly disregarded everything that Newton advised, broke with the Church, and stayed in Bala with his new wife![221] Thomas Charles had a mind of his own, but it had no ill effect on his friendship with Newton. He was his own man. That is why he became an effective leader in his own right, and that is why Newton loved him. Charles still religiously followed Newton's guidance in other matters,[222] and the two continued a dear friendship that lasted until Newton's death. In fact, twenty-two years after that summer holiday, we find Charles writing to a friend about how they still made a point to spend time together every summer. When it did not work out that year, Charles lamented, "I feel disappointed in leaving London without the usual annual interview with him."[223]

No one could have foreseen the incredible doors for ministry that God would open for Charles in Bala. Wales was a land that had been showered with revival, rich in gospel truth, but poor as dirt. And not only were they poor, many were illiterate. How were they to read the Words of Life? In his quest to answer that question, Thomas Charles would educate a generation of Welsh children.

If it took courage, determination, a deep sense of call, and a splash of naiveté for Ryland to presume to help start a worldwide mission-sending agency, for Carey to claim India for Christ, or for Charles to take on a nation's illiteracy, it must have been sheer lunacy for Richard Johnson in 1787 to board a ship with his new bride along with 750 convicts in their fleet to set sail for Australia (Figure 12). [224] Either he was crazy, or God was at work. Newton was positive it was the latter.

Figure 12. Richard Johnson.

In the seventeenth century, England had a bright idea: *If people want to commit crimes, fine. Just don't do it here.* So began the campaign to ship violent criminals overseas. When New Holland became the destination of choice, one can be sure the aboriginal peoples were thrilled.[225]

What many in Parliament saw as an opportunity to rid England of its basest riffraff, evangelicals tended to see as an opportunity for the gospel. Among those in the latter camp was one Mr. Newton. As the Eclectic Society would soon ask, "What is the best method for planting and propagating the gospel in Botany Bay?"[226] Newton seemed to already have an answer: a chaplain could go, who, while ministering to the convicts, could also reach the aboriginal peoples with the gospel.[227] But who would be fit for such a task? Newton had an idea. He recently had a young man come preach for him. He was impressed and told a friend about it: "Yesterday I put Mr. Johnson in my pulpit, (who I think gives us an earnest of a judicious good preacher)."[228]

After talking to Johnson about it, they approached Wilberforce, who in turn brought the matter to the Prime Minister, William Pitt.[229] Pitt liked the idea, and by November 15, 1786, we find Newton congratulating Wilberforce on pushing it through:

> To you, as the instrument, we owe the pleasing prospect of an opening for the propagation of the gospel in the Southern Hemisphere. Who can tell what important consequences may depend upon Mr Johnson's going to New Hollands![230]

While Newton and Wilberforce celebrated, Richard Johnson faced a daunting task. Newton realized that and encouraged him at every turn. Before Johnson ever set sail, Newton wrote him a poem:

> The Lord, who sends thee hence, will be thine aid;
> In vain at thee the lion, Danger, roars;
> His arm and love shall keep thee undismayed
> On tempest-tossed seas, and savage shores.
>
> Go, bear the Saviour's name to lands unknown,
> Tell to the Southern world His wondrous grace;
> An energy Divine thy words shall own,
> And draw their untaught hearts to seek His face.
>
> Many in quest of gold or empty fame
> Would compass earth, or venture near the poles;
> But how much nobler thy reward and aim—
> To spread His praise, and win immortal souls![231]

How Johnson needed every line! He spent nine months at sea before finally arriving at his destination,[232] where he stayed in a hut "built chiefly of cabbage trees, and tiled with rushes,"[233] while the governor had two mansions built for himself.[234] Within five years, Johnson had officiated

851 funerals, almost one every other day, in addition to 226 baptisms and 220 marriages![235] He was overworked and under-appreciated, preaching open-air to six hundred convicts,[236] needing to maintain a garden to have enough food,[237] and even overseeing the building of the chapel himself, because he was unable to obtain any governmental assistance.[238] Once, the foundation of a church building was laid, but before being finished it was converted into a jail.[239] Go figure.

Johnson needed help with the load, and Newton earnestly sought out a companion for him, telling Johnson in a letter that "The enquiry has been long and constantly upon my mind."[240] Johnson could not handle the workload on his own, so he resorted to mass communication by penning an address to all of the convicts at Botany Bay. He hoped this would be a way to reach people he could not interact with personally.[241] Newton was the one who made sure that the expenses were covered, and he was also the one who broke the wonderful news when they had finally found Johnson a helper.[242]

In letter after letter, Newton sought to encourage Johnson, comparing his plight at different times to Noah's, Abraham's, and even Paul's.[243] "Nothing can hurt you while the LORD is with you."[244] To the very end, Newton was cheering him on. In the last known letter from Newton to Johnson, the old mentor wrote, "may the good seed you are sowing, spring up to flourish for ages. Notwithstanding the discouragements you have met with, I am persuaded the Lord has not sent you so far to labour in vain."[245]

In vain it was not. In fact, some convicts once made a daring escape from Australia in a small boat. They were eventually imprisoned in England; not surprisingly, they had to answer for many things. Out of curiosity, they were asked about the chaplain at Botany Bay. The men paused at the question. "They *did not believe there was so good a man beside in the whole world*."[246] That good man, Richard Johnson, would never have come to New Holland, or stayed, if it had not been for the friend that he possessed in John Newton.

While Johnson was getting acclimated to his new ministry role, another precocious young leader was still finding his way. His name was John Campbell, and he proved to be one of the last young men that Newton ever took under his wing (Figure 13). Newton was almost sixty-five years old when they met, Campbell only twenty-three. It was 1789,[247] and Newton's influence in ministry had reached its peak. What better way to spend his declining years than in friendship with a young man who seemed to possess a kindred spirit?

Figure 13. John Campbell.

John Campbell had been orphaned when he was only six years old[248]; undoubtedly, his own experience led to his compassionate disposition. He had a heart for orphans as well as for Africa. Not surprisingly, with interests such as those, he and Newton got along incredibly well. Though Newton was in London, and Campbell in Scotland, it did not seem to slow their communication. A whole volume of their correspondence survives.[249] Campbell's biographer notes that though he had been active in compassionate ministry prior to meeting Newton, it was through their friendship that he came to an assurance of his own salvation.[250]

When Campbell was training for the ministry, Newton warned him about getting too caught up in books, and encouraged him to drink deeply of the fountain-head.[251] It is when people abide in Christ that compassion overflows.

> We should be jealous for the Lord of hosts, and compassionate to the souls of men.[252]

> Indeed, I believe, the most lively grace, and the most solid comfort, are known among the Lord's poor and undistinguished people.[253]

> Self likes to be employed in great matters—grace teaches us to do small and common things with a great spirit.[254]

Campbell's future ministry would be shaped deeply by words such as these.

Newton became his model.[255] In fact, upon Newton's death, Campbell collected all of his letters from Newton for print, as well as thirty pages of conversations with Newton that he had taken down in his journal. It is evident that Campbell hung on Newton's every word.

> Mr. Newton is nowise inferior to what he was represented. In the pulpit, I have always seen him bathed in tears. In *private*, he is a David for devotion, a Moses for meekness, a Solomon for knowledge, a Paul for zeal, and a John for love. His house may be called a Bethel.[256]

A Bethel it was! His house was constantly filled with visitors: "I have been long in the habit of seeing my friends, *at home* . . . On a Tuesday I frequently have more than Forty in the course of the day."[257]

Campbell made sure to be one of them. During Newton's last year, Campbell was constantly at his side.[258]

> I breakfasted this morning with my dear friend Mr. Newton. I cannot well say how glad he was to see me. He took me by the hand, in the midst of our crack in his study, and expressed his happiness to see me once more in this poor world. He loves me, and I am sure I love him; so our love is one.[259]

In the end, the two men saw each other many more times in this poor world. The week before he died, John Campbell visited his friend for the last time. "After going to prayer with him, he stretched out his hand, and shook mine, as if he thanked me; but he said nothing."[260]

He did not need to. His life had said it all. And so on Monday, December 21, 1807, John Newton, a great sinner who knew a great Savior, passed away in peace.

PART TWO

to change the world:
THE LEGACY OF JOHN NEWTON

CHAPTER THREE

Influencing Friends

In addition to the dozen examples given above, other remarkable friendships could have been highlighted, including Newton's relationships with Henry Venn, John Berridge,[1] William Jay, or Richard Cecil,[2] to name a few. That John Newton had a wide ranging circle of friends, over whom he yielded considerable influence, is undebatable. The question is, what made him so compelling? How did he shape such disparate people so profoundly? And finally, why is it that people who spent generous amounts of time with John Newton seem to go on, not only changed, but also called to engage in justice concerns and compassionate ministries?

Simply put, John Newton walked the talk, influencing others through both word and deed. He was a man who had been forever changed by grace. On the plaque above his desk were engraved the words, "Thou shalt remember that thou wast a bond-man in the land of Egypt, and the Lord thy God redeemed thee."[3] Even a legal document such as his will was filled with typical references to his former slavery and subsequent salvation: "I commit my soul to my gracious God and Saviour, who mercifully spared and preserved me when I was an Apostate a Blasphemer and an Infidel and delivered me from that state of misery on the coast of Africa into which my obstinate wickedness had plunged me and who has been pleased to admit me (though most unworthy) to preach His Glorious Gospel."[4]

As Timothy Keller argues in *Generous Justice*, "There is a direct relationship between a person's grasp and experience of God's grace, and his or her heart for justice and the poor. . . . As I preached the classic message that God does *not* give us justice but saves us by free grace, I discovered that those most affected by the message became the most sensitive to the social iniquities around them."[5] Exhibit A: John Newton.

As quoted above, Newton's memories of being stranded and alone on the coast of Africa stayed with him every hour for the next forty years. That Christ would save him out of such wickedness and hopelessness forever changed Newton. He had been profoundly affected by the gospel and deeply gripped by God's grace. "Amazing grace, how sweet the sound, that saved a wretch like me." He had not received God's justice—eternal damnation—and as Keller puts it, God's grace was making him just.

That said, his compassionate concern toward others was a process, to be sure.[6] Early on, Newton was still too calloused to be bothered by the barbarity of human trafficking. But the blade of grace can be seen beginning to sprout even while Newton was an active participant in the trade. While serving as captain aboard the *African*, on November 21, 1753, Newton wrote in his diary, "I cannot but think it incumbent upon me to bestow a part of my superfluities towards relieving those who are struggling under a want of necessaries."[7] He penned those words on his third and final voyage. It was the journey when not a single person died under his care, slave or free. It was "perhaps the only instance of its kind that was ever known."[8]

BY EXAMPLE

Even if he was not prepared to take on the atrocities of the slave trade just yet, by the time Newton arrived at his first pastorate, he was more than eager to meet the needs of those around him. Olney was a small town, composed mostly of poor lacemakers,[9] many too poor even to buy a Bible.[10] In fact, the only houses in the entire community with servants were his own and the home of William Cowper.[11] Newton cared deeply for his people, referring to them as his "sheep and lambs,"[12] with whom he had become "knit . . . in mutual affection."[13] John Thornton, Newton's gracious benefactor, gave Newton two hundred pounds a year to keep pace with the growing needs of the poor in the community.[14] In the winter, when food was scarce, Newton gave away bread.[15] When business was slow, Newton attempted to get the town to take a collection for those in need.[16] In 1756, Newton even appears to have purchased a lottery ticket with hopes that if he won, he would be able to give the money away to the poor![17] Though his methods may have been somewhat lacking, his desire to help the needy certainly was not.

In 1768, he joined the Society for Promoting Religious Knowledge Among the Poor,[18] and to that he soon added his concern for poor clergy. On one occasion he even raised two hundred pounds for the family of a Welsh curate who had passed away. His same care and concern amongst the least of these continued when he arrived at St. Mary Woolnoth in London. He gave his "bounden attention to the Sick & Sorrowful," visiting Newgate prison, bringing the poor into his home, delighting impoverished children with treats, and asking affluent benefactors to help deserving cases.[19] Even as late as 1803, when Newton was a feeble seventy-seven-year-old man, he could write in his journal, "In the evening visited some poor cottagers. . . for Thou art gracious to many whom men overlook and despise."[20]

BY LETTER

As time went on, Newton appears to have become more vocal in his passion for mercy and justice, and references to the subject begin to appear in his correspondence. It was not enough that he cared for the poor. He wanted others to share that concern. Early on, Newton said, "my correspondence is so large, that it almost engrosses my time."[21]

Sometimes he spent six, eight, or even ten hours a day writing letters.[22] Allusions to his former African bondage occur regularly, and every letter seems to highlight God's grace.[23]

Some of the letters rope the reader into acts of mercy, whether they desire to be involved or not. On one such instance, Newton sent money to William Bull, saying, "Be so good as to send the inclosed immediately by some careful hand at your market. Should it not be received to-morrow, several poor folks at Olney will miss their Christmas dinner."[24] When a poor blind man could no longer afford to provide for a youth under his care, it is Newton again urging Bull to get involved. "Mr. Atkins, the blind man, desired me to speak to Mr. Thornton, on behalf of the youth . . . whom Mr. Neale sent to Newport. I thought I would, but upon second thoughts, which are sometimes best, it seemed better to refer the business to you."[25] Newton knew Thornton better than Bull did; he introduced them to each other. Even so, Newton invited Bull into the benevolent act.

Some letters, such as one to John Ryland Jr., simply recount stories from Newton's life about helping a poor person who needed it.[26] At other times, Newton praised a third party who attends to the needy.[27] We find him thanking people for their generous contributions, as he did to William Wilberforce upon receiving his gift to the Society for the Relief of Poor Clergy. Newton shared how important this work is: "I shall not willingly miss any opportunity of attending the meetings of this Society." Finally, he wrapped up the letter with a veiled reference to Isaiah 58, where God promises to bless those who care for the hungry, the homeless, the naked, and the afflicted.[28]

As early as 1775, Newton's letters reflect his deep regret over his involvement in something so shameful as the slave trade, "the cry of blood, the blood of thousands, perhaps millions, from the East Indies."[29] "I now see [it] was unlawful and abominable," he wrote to John Campbell.[30] After writing his *Thoughts Upon the African Slave Trade*, he expressed his desire to Hannah More to see justice executed: "What may be done just now, I know not, but I think this infamous traffic cannot last long; at least this is my hope. But after the period of investigation, should it still be persevered in, I think it will constitute a national sin, and of a very deep dye."[31] To William Bull he shares his fears: "If the business miscarries again, I shall fear not only for the poor slaves, but for ourselves. For I think if men refuse to vindicate the oppressed, the Lord will take their cause into his own hands."[32]

BY PREACHING

Eventually, his justice concerns made the leap from private correspondence to public proclamation. He seems timid at first. In his Fast Day sermon[33] from February 21, 1781, Newton shared his scruples about the proper subjects of preaching:

> Political disquisitions, except immediately connected with scriptural principles, appear to me improper for the pulpit at all times. . . . I must, however, hint my apprehension, that acts of oppression and violence, in some parts, at least, of our widely extended settlements, have contributed to enhance and aggravate our national sin. If the welfare and the lives of thousands have been sacrificed to the interest of the few; if the ravages of cruelty and avarice, though notorious and undeniable, have met with no public censure or punishment, may we not expect that God himself will avenge the oppressed, and plead their cause, not only against their actual oppressors, but against the community that refused to hear their cries and redress their wrongs?[34]

Without ever directly saying it, as early as 1781 Newton was certainly attacking not only the traffic but also the institution of slavery in front of packed crowds from the pulpit of St. Mary Woolnoth in the center of London. He had only been pastor there for one year. When this sermon was preached, there was no parliamentary campaign against the trade. William Wilberforce had only been elected to Parliament less than six months prior, and would not experience conversion for another five years.[35] Contrary to some recent assertions,[36] Newton was publicly challenging the slave trade at a time when, by and large, the Anglican church in general, and the Clapham Sect in particular (which Newton had such a profound influence upon), had not yet formally engaged the issue.[37]

John Wesley had been vocal in his opposition to the slave trade for some time, but even so, in 1781, Newton was taking a remarkable stance for an even-keeled, respectable, non-irregular Anglican rector.[38] As late as 1788, when John Wesley preached an antislavery sermon in Bristol, he was taking his life into own hands. Wesley records the scene in his journal:

> About the middle of the discourse, while there was on every side attention still as night, a vehement noise arose, none could tell why, and shot like lightening through the whole congregation. The terror and confusion were inexpressible. You might have imagined it was a city taken by storm. The people rushed upon each other with the utmost violence; the benches were broke in pieces, and nine-tenths of the congregation appeared to be struck with the same panic.[39]

Newton's preaching against human trafficking became more pointed and more frequent as the years went by. In 1792, after William Pitt expressed his hope that Wilberforce would not bring forward his bill that year, Newton preached on the subject.[40] His correspondence to William Bull reveals that Newton had also preached against it the year before.[41] In his Fast Day sermon from 1794, Newton thundered, "I should be inexcusable, considering the share I have formerly had in that unhappy business, if, upon this occasion I should omit to mention the African slave-trade. . . . petty and partial interests prevail against the voice of justice, humanity, and truth. . . . There is a cry of blood against us; a cry accumulated by the accession of fresh victims, of thousands, of scores of thousands, I had almost said of hundreds of thousands, from year to year."[42]

We find him kicking the same horse at the end of 1797. It was a national day of thanksgiving for recent naval victories, but Newton had another victory in mind: "Oppression is a national sin. . . . I have more than once confessed with shame in this pulpit, the concern I too long had in the African slave-trade. . . . while we are delaying from year to year to put a stop to our part of it, the blood of many thousands of our helpless, much-injured fellow-creatures, is crying against us."[43]

The pulpit was a place where Newton's prophetic voice could be heard. It was from the pulpit that that Newton railed against the slave trade, and it was from the pulpit that he encouraged ministry to the poor.[44] When Richard Cecil suggested that perhaps it was time for Newton to stop preaching—he was over eighty, after all—Newton responded by saying, "I cannot stop. What! shall the old African blasphemer stop while he can speak?"[45] He could not see to read his text; on occasion his memory failed. But the pulpit as a medium to communicate divine grace, and compassionate concern, was too precious to give up.

BY WRITING

Early on, however, Newton learned that writing could reach a still larger audience than preaching. It is no surprise, therefore, that in time his concern for mercy and justice would work its way out in print. From 1771 to 1774, *Gospel Magazine* published a sampling of Newton's personal correspondence under the moniker, "Omicron."[46] In 1775, the letters were gathered and turned into a book.[47] The first letter was to an anonymous young pastor, who had recently been married. Newton's advice? Be generous to the poor.

> When I look among the professors, yea, among the ministers of the Gospel, there are few things I see a more general want of, than such a trust in God as to temporals, and such a sense of the honour of being permitted to relieve the necessities of his people. . . . 'He that hath pity upon the poor, lendeth unto the Lord'. . . . I dare stake all my interest in your friendship . . . that if you act upon this maxim . . . you shall not be disappointed. . . . You cannot, I trust, in conscience think of laying out one penny more than is barely decent; unless you have another penny to help the poor.[48]

He even advised the young man to turn away friends who had come for a visit before he would turn away someone in poverty who needed a place to stay! After all, turning away a friend is turning away a friend. But to turn away the poor was to turn away Jesus. For a man so deeply invested in friendships, Newton's words ring with strong conviction.

Late in life, Newton wrote a biography, *Life of Mr. Grimshaw*.[49] The subject was a pastor who, according to Newton, "had no good opinion of the religion of those who were not, at least, gentle to the poor."[50] Grimshaw was "careful to retrench all superfluities in himself, that he might have the more wherewith to relieve the real necessities of the poor. Nay, for their sakes, I am assured, he sometimes really straightened himself, so as to be obliged to postpone the payment of bills for articles of necessary consumption."[51] Newton reports that he even collected old shoes from friends, had them repaired, and then distributed them among the needy.[52] Needless to say, Newton thought incredibly highly of him: "He was, in some respects, the most extraordinary man I have known."[53] That is saying something, given the people Newton knew personally!

Not only did he write a biography highlighting a compassionate figure, Newton then proceeded to donate all the benefits to the poor. "I gave it entirely, with the copyright, to the Society for the Relief of Poor Pious Clergy of the Established Church, many of who are truly pious and very poor."[54]

Even so, when it came to justice and compassion concerns, it was the slave trade that received the greatest attention from his pen. Although Newton had expressed that he found the slave trade disagreeable in his *Authentic Narrative*, published in 1764, he never denounced the trade, nor his involvement in it. However, in 1793, when Newton wrote his *Letters to a Wife* (in which he published letters he had written to Mary while he served as captain over slave ships), he sought to put the matter right. He viewed this work as a "sort of commentary upon my Narrative."[55]

He did not spill much ink before addressing the issue. In the preface, Newton says that the second volume was written "after the good providence of God freed me from that iniquitous employment in which

I was too long ignorantly engaged."[56] Midway into the work, Newton makes the remark:

> The reader may perhaps wonder, as I now do myself, that, knowing the state of the vile traffic to be as I have here described, and abounding with enormities which I have not mentioned, I did not, at the time, start with horror at my own employment, as an agent in promoting it. Custom, example, and interest, had blinded my eyes. . . . I felt the disagreeableness of the business very strongly. The office of a gaoler, and the restraints under which I was forced to keep my prisoners, were not suitable to my feelings; but I considered it as the line of life which God, in his providence, had allotted me; and as a cross which I ought to bear with patience and thankfulness, till he should be pleased to deliver me from it. Till then, I only thought myself bound to treat the slaves under my care with gentleness.[57]

Newton seems somewhat burdened, even at this late date, to set the record straight; at one and the same time he attempts to communicate both his good conscience while participating in the trade and his shame over being involved in it for so long a time.

But in truth, Newton had already done that five years earlier, in January of 1788, when he published his *Thoughts Upon the African Slave Trade*. The Parliamentary campaign against the trade was just beginning, and Newton was not about to keep quiet. He wrote "from a conviction that silence, at such a time and on such an occasion, would, in me, be criminal."[58] The month before, Wilberforce had made public his intentions of introducing an Abolition Bill. When Newton's work was released on the heels of such news, it immediately became a bestseller in spite of the "expensive price of one shilling."[59]

Though Newton was no politician ("I am neither Whig nor Tory, but a well wisher to both"[60]), he was savvy. He understood that compassion was not the utmost concern of many in Parliament, but rather, national interest. Therefore, with his "old shipboard diaries" at his side,[61] Newton began his work by writing about the terrible loss of life among British subjects who worked in human trafficking. Newton reckoned that some fifteen hundred sailors lost their lives each year at this employment.[62] Hardened and calloused consciences should also concern Parliament, Newton said.[63] It was bad for English society. One sailor threw a baby overboard for crying too much.[64] Surely England would not want to become a nation full of people that would offend finer sensibilities. That would be terrible.

It was only after Newton made these first two points that he began to recount the atrocities and inhumanity that trafficking unleashed on slaves. The Africans, contrary to popular belief, were not savages, but kind, honest, and gentle people. The real savages were those ripping families apart by capturing and selling people:

> When the women and girls are taken on board a ship, naked, trembling, terrified, perhaps almost exhausted with cold, fatigue, and hunger, they are often exposed to the wanton rudeness of white savages.[65]

The slaves were packed in like books on a shelf,[66] and "the heat and smell . . . would be almost insupportable to a person not accustomed to them."[67] On average, a quarter died from disease, but it was not uncommon to lose a third, or even a half of the slaves on board.[68] He asked, "Can sound policy suggest any effectual expedient, but the total suppression of a trade, which, like a poisonous root, diffuses its malignity into every branch?"[69]

This trade was nothing less than flagrant sin against a holy God:

> Though unwilling to give offence to a single person in such a cause, I ought not to be afraid of offending many, by declaring the truth. If, indeed, there can be many, whom even interest can prevail upon to contradict the common sense of mankind, by pleading for a commerce so iniquitous, so cruel, so oppressive, so destructive, as the African Slave Trade![70]

This publication took a man who only received formal education until he was ten and landed him in a room full of the most powerful men of the most powerful nation in the world. A week after publication, the Society for Effecting the Abolition of the Slave Trade decided to send a copy of Newton's work "to every member of of both Houses of Parliament."[71] Two weeks later, Newton received an invite from the

Privy Council, "a group of senior royal advisors and Ministers of the Crown, headed by the Prime Minister."[72] They wanted to hear his account firsthand.

BY TESTIMONY

So began John Newton's political career.[73] "When the clerk called out, 'The Reverend John Newton,' the committee members rose to their feet while the venerable pastor entered the council chamber, escorted to his place by William Pitt."[74] Newton gave testimony to the council, speaking specifically to the attitudes and behaviors of the African people who were being kidnapped. His testimony was followed up with a "supplementary letter" to the council.[75] That summer, Newton also wrote to the leader of the Anti-Slavery Society, Richard Phillips, giving him further details about the trade that he had withheld when he published his *Thoughts*.[76] Two years later, Newton was testifying again, this time answering eighty questions in front of a committee from the House of Commons. Only ten people were asked for testimony in both hearings; Newton was one of them.[77]

As William Jay notes, John Newton was not struck at first by the wickedness of the slave trade,

> yet, when led to just reflection upon that subject, no one could think worse of its enormity, or bewail himself more for the share he had had in it. To this, also, he often referred; and one day, as a person told him that the Americans had dubbed him D.D., he said, "I always resolved I would accept of no diploma, unless it came from the poor blacks."[78]

On those rare occasions when slaves became free, they were often still trapped in utter destitution; to help remedy the problem, Newton was made a director of the Sierra Leone Company—the dream of a place where freed Africans could have a fresh start.[79] He talked about slavery and his involvement in it until the day of his death.

One can only imagine how overjoyed Newton was to hear that on February 23, 1807, the House of Commons voted 283 to 16 to abolish the slave trade.[80] He had published his *Thoughts Upon the African Slave Trade* nineteen years earlier. The trade that he had formerly helped along he had now helped destroy. Ten months later, Newton's work on this earth was done.

John Newton was profoundly aware of the grace that he had received. Of his life, he could say:

> I am ready to take it for granted, and to think all who know me must allow, that my case is a unique, not to be matched by anything, as yet, recorded in the annals of the church of Christ. Few at the same age, have gone equal lengths with me, in wickedness; few have sunk into equal depths of wretchedness; fewer still have been spared and reclaimed; and perhaps not one of these few has attained to preach the Gospel—especially in such a situation as mine, exempted from want, abounding in comforts, honoured with acceptance, and surrounded with friends. It was the Lord's doing; it has been wonderful in the eyes of many. Oh how wonderful ought it to be in my own eyes![81]

The crescendo of God's grace towards John Newton was to surround him with friends. He had not only been saved, washed clean, called to ministry, and blessed materially; he had also been given the gift of friendship. These friendships he cherished, nurtured, and sustained. These he embraced as a careful steward. And though his life is pockmarked with folly, even at times in his pastoral career, no one can question the loyalty that John Newton exhibited in his friendships, nor question that those friends constantly heard about Newton's experience of grace.

That grace was contagious. It was magnetic. Everyone needs grace.

Meanwhile, God's grace was at work in Newton's life. As Keller notes, "People who come to grasp the gospel of grace and become spiritually poor find their hearts gravitating to the materially poor."[82] And so as people flocked to Newton's parlor, ministered alongside Newton, traded letters with him, listened to him preach, read his writings, and watched his life, they witnessed a man who did justice and loved kindness and walked humbly with his God.

Someone smart once said that students tend to become like their teacher, and so, not surprisingly, history honors the second half of each story, each friendship recounted above. William Wilberforce eventually gets over himself, gets over his fear, contacts Newton, and the two embark on the abolition trail. The sphere of politics is changed. William Cowper picks up his pen again, leveraging literature for the cause of the oppressed. Hannah More and Thomas Charles take up the cause of educating illiterate children. Yet it is not only society that is altered; the church is changed as well. The former heretic Thomas Scott becomes a chaplain to prostitutes, while Charles Simeon creates space for evangelicals in the Established Church. Dissenting church pastors such as William Bull and John Ryland Jr. exhibit a warmth of theology infused with compassion. And the reach is global. William Carey and Claudius Buchanan help to transform India while Richard Johnson serves prisoners in Australia and John Campbell seeks the welfare of Africa.

The extent to which these friendships left lasting impact is simply astounding. It would not be hyperbole to say that as one traces the trajectory of these friendships and what took place as a result, justice rolled down like waters and righteousness like an ever-flowing stream.

Simply put, these were friendships that changed the world.

CHAPTER FOUR

To Change Society

POLITICS

The chill of a late November evening was the furthest thing from his mind as William Wilberforce walked aimlessly through the streets. "I thought seriously this evening of going to converse with Mr. Newton—walked in the night—obliged to compel myself to think of God."[1] "Dec. 2nd. Resolved again about Mr. Newton. It may do good; he will pray for me; his experience may enable him to direct me."[2] Little did Wilberforce know how true those words would be for him. That same day in 1785, he mustered up the courage to write a letter to John Newton, a man he had not seen since he was a child:

> Sir,
>
> There is no need of apology for intruding on you, when the errand is religion. I wish to have some serious conversation with you, and will take the liberty of calling on you for that purpose, in half-an-hour; when, if you cannot receive me, you will have the goodness to let me have a letter put into my hands at the door, naming a time and place for our meeting, the earlier the more agreeable to me. I have had ten thousand doubts within myself, whether or not I should discover myself to you; but every argument against doing it has its foundation in pride. I am sure you will hold yourself

> bound to let no one living know of this application, or of my visit, till I release you from the obligation.
>
> P.S. Remember that I must be secret, and that the gallery of the House is now so universally attended, that the face of a member of Parliament is pretty well known.[3]

There is no doubt about it. The Cambridge-educated rising star of Parliament was wrestling with God. The obvious man to turn to during this time was John Newton. One can only imagine Newton's joy, not to mention amusement, at receiving such a clandestine invitation. It appears that Wilberforce could have made a decent spy. After walking around the block a couple of times to make sure that no one would see him enter Newton's house, Wilberforce laid his heart bare before his old friend. The counsel that he received in that meeting would change his life forever. Wilberforce was contemplating entering the ministry, but Newton advised him to stay where he had been planted—in politics.[4]

Newton had held out hope that such a reunion would occur,[5] and when it did, he lost no opportunity to invest in the young man. During this season, Wilberforce was experiencing, as he put it, his "Great Change." Everything was turning. His own distinction was no longer his "darling object."[6] In short order, Wilberforce moved closer to Newton's church,[7] and the two immediately began to enjoy extensive interactions with one another. Their reunion occurred on December 6, 1785.[8] We find Wilberforce at Newton's church the following Sunday (the 11th),[9] journaling about reading Newton's *Authentic Narrative* on the 13th,[10] and visiting Newton's house twice more before the 19th.[11] Clearly, John Newton was an extremely significant influence on William Wilberforce during this period.

Only three and a half months into their renewed friendship, we find Newton making a provocative statement: "whenever you can call you will be a welcome guest. Great subjects to discuss, great plans to promote, great prospects to contemplate, will always be at hand. Thus employed, our hours, when we meet, will pass away like minutes."[12] One can only suppose what may have been the precise content of these great subjects, plans, and prospects. However, given the fact that, a year and a half later, after spending another day with John Newton, William Wilberforce wrote in his diary with grave conviction, "God Almighty has set before me two great objects, the suppression of the slave trade and the reformation of manners,"[13] it is more than reasonable to suggest that Jesus and justice were the primary conversation pieces.

After all, Newton was the man who constantly reminded Wilberforce that God had placed him in Parliament: "It is hoped and believed that the Lord has raised you up for the good of his church, and for the good of the nation."[14] "May the wisdom that influenced Joseph and Moses, and Daniel rest upon you."[15] "I hope, great usefulness to the public, and to the church of God, will be your present reward."[16] "Who knoweth but God has raised you up for such a time as this!"[17]

According to Wilberforce's own sons, it was John Newton who first described the horrors of slavery to their father:

> For we are not left to gather from mere probability that Mr. Newton spoke upon the subject. Remorse for his own early share in its iniquity kept it so constantly before that holy man, that Mr. Wilberforce frequently declared that 'he never spent one half hour in his company without hearing some allusion to it.'[18]

In fact, it is possible that Newton, the overweight pastor who preferred his old blue sea jacket to traditional ministerial garb,[19] shared his regret over the slave trade way back when he entertained William as a boy with stories of his adventures on the high seas. How else would one account for Wilberforce, "not more than fourteen," writing a letter to the editor expressing his hatred of the trade?[20]

Not surprisingly, when this young, pious, intelligent member of Parliament essentially asked to be mentored, Newton could not resist. Of course he would; this was Newton's bread and butter. It appears that John Newton always had great subjects to discuss, plans to promote, and prospects to contemplate. Wilberforce responded to Newton's challenge to be a statesman and a Christian with great vigor.

When Wilberforce wondered how far he could accommodate others in his attempt to win them over and help him promote a good cause, Newton provided guidelines to navigate those waters. He advised being accommodating without (1) being ashamed of Christ, (2) becoming disconnected from a local body of believers, (3) participating in a church where the gospel is not proclaimed, or (4) joining with others in ungodly activities, even if they could help to advance the cause.[21] That advice Wilberforce heeded for the rest of his life.

The day after those two great objects were etched into Wilberforce's journal, he hurriedly dispatched a letter to the Society for Effecting the Abolition of the Slave Trade, seeking collaboration and assistance.[22] The struggle would consume the remaining forty-five years of his life. That part of Wilberforce's story is relatively well known. However, "a major reason why a legislated end to the slave trade was possible was the flowering of Wilberforce's second great object: the reformation of manners."[23]

In this effort, Wilberforce attempted to curb the flagrant immorality in society by getting King George III to republish "The Proclamation for the Encouragement of Piety and Virtue and for the Preventing of Vice, Profaneness and Immorality." To reinforce the proclamation, Wilberforce began forming societies led by famous and influential people to promote the monarch's decree. In short, the societies gained popular appeal, making morality trendy. "It was a subversive and politically brilliant strategy."[24]

As the Bishop of London put it, the idea was to "obtain if possible the assistance of the principal and most respected characters among the Nobility, Clergy and Gentry in and about London and afterwards throughout the Kingdom."[25] When invited to lead one of these societies, many would feel compelled to join in, subsequently forcing them to take stock of their own behavior![26] Over time, the nation began to develop a social conscience, which may very well have been the fulcrum that gave Wilberforce such leverage in his lifelong pursuit against the slave trade.

However, while Wilberforce's efforts for the reformation of manners seemed to gain traction rather quickly, the fight to abolish the slave trade proved to be another matter. The two friends got off to a quick start. Within three months of their historic meeting at the end of October 1787, Newton had already published his *Thoughts Upon the African Slave Trade*, and Wilberforce planned to introduce a new motion to Parliament.[27] Yet, between Wilberforce's sickness and opposition from the West Indian party, the work slowed to a crawl. With William Pitt's assistance, Parliament agreed to an inquiry concerning the treatment of slaves but was unwilling to consider abolition without voluminous investigation upon the topic at hand.[28] The cruelty of slavery, without extensive proofs, was simply denied.[29]

Wilberforce and a slew of allies began working tirelessly, regularly putting in nine hours a day, with plans of pulling a weekly all-nighter to pore through various documentation.[30] In time, Wilberforce's devoted circle of evangelical activists would come to be known as the Clapham Sect, since several of them relocated to Clapham Common together, on the edge of London, for fellowship and collaboration. To be sure, other than Newton's book, preaching, and rare testimonials before Parliament, Newton's involvement in the campaign was behind the scenes. Wilberforce and others were clearly at the fore, taking the brunt of the resistance and hostility to the effort.

What Wilberforce needed was encouragement, someone who would continually pray for him, point him to truth, to the value of his work, and to the One who could sustain him through the battle. John Newton served that purpose admirably. Wilberforce basically said as much:

> I believe I can truly declare, that not a single day has passed in which you have not been in my thoughts, and at those seasons too when the mind abstracts itself . . . and fixes its consideration on what it most esteems and loves.[31]

In the thick of the abolition campaign, Newton was constantly on Wilberforce's mind. "O my Dear Sir, let not your hands cease to be lifted up, lest Amalek prevail—entreat for me."[32]

In 1791, Wilberforce's bill finally came to the floor of Parliament.[33] It was opposed, with almost two votes against it for every one in favor.[34] In 1792, Wilberforce made another push, but the momentum failed when one MP suggested that the trade should be abolished gradually. Others agreed, and Parliament voted to abolish the trade by 1796.[35] However, the next year, "the House of Commons refused to confirm the 1792 vote for gradual abolition."[36] Opposition mounted, and by 1795, Wilberforce had received multiple death threats.[37]

Even so, Wilberforce's efforts continued to gain steam, and a victory was within reach in 1796. However, when it came time for the vote, some of his opponents from the West Indian party gave several of Wilberforce's supporters free tickets to the opera. Wilberforce wrote in his diary:

> My Slave Bill was thrown out by 74 to 70. . . . Ten or twelve of those who had supported me [were] absent in the country, or [away] on pleasure. Enough were at the Opera to have carried it. [I am] very much vexed and incensed at our opponents.

[38] The defeat of the motion in 1796 was devastating.

It was at critical moments like this when Newton seemed to shine brightest. From the very beginning, Newton's voice provided calm assurance to a man navigating new and dangerous waters. When the epithet, "Methodist," was first cast in Wilberforce's face, Newton professed, "Nothing more than attention to the cause of Justice, Truth and Humanity, seems necessary at present, to fix the imputation of Methodism upon the most unexceptionable characters." [39] After Wilberforce's bill was opposed the first time, Newton empathized, "Both the importance and the difficulties of your station, superadded to my regard, entitle you to a double portion of my thoughts and prayers."[40]

When the abolition of the trade was still in the distance, Newton was the man who reminded Wilberforce of all the good that had already been accomplished.[41] When the question came up as to whether Christians should boycott West Indian products, Newton sought out Wilberforce's stance so that he could publicly support Wilberforce's position.[42] After engaging in the struggle for eight years with no apparent success, Newton reassured Wilberforce, "You have acted nobly, Sir, in behalf of the poor Africans. I trust you will not lose your reward."[43] When ongoing failure would make a person want to abandon ship, Newton again stood in Wilberforce's corner: "But you are in your appointed post, and the Lord supports you in it. You live like the young men, and Daniel in Babylon, preserved in the midst of flames and lions; because the Lord is with you."[44]

But when those from the West Indian company thwarted Wilberforce with opera tickets and underhanded tactics, he had had enough. William Wilberforce wanted to quit. "Severe fever," "intestinal troubles," and a "nervous breakdown" ensued.[45]

John Newton came to his aid as only a long-time friend could:

> We have powerful motives to fidelity and diligence in our posts. . . . But we are not responsible for the success of our attempts. . . . God accepts people, not according to what they have actually done in his service, but according to what they would have done, had they been able. . . . Your efforts in favor of the poor Africans, have again been counteracted. But it was well it was in your heart to relieve them from oppression. I was grieved to hear the bill was thrown out of your house. . . . This life, my dear Sir, is like a turbulent boisterous sea. But we have a peaceful port in view, a happy shore, where the storms of trouble are unknown.[46]

Those words, as encouraging as they were, did not curb the despair Wilberforce was feeling. He still wanted to throw in the towel. Serving Christ and championing the cause of the oppressed in the political sphere was a bloody battle and heartbreaking venture that had taken a toll on Wilberforce. He wanted to retire. He wanted to rest. He asked Newton if he should leave politics.

Newton's response changed history:

> Some of [God's] people may be emphatically said, Not to live to themselves. May it not be said of you? Would you not be glad to have more command of your time, and more choice of your company, than your situation will admit? You meet with many things which weary and disgust you, which you would avoid in a more private life. But then they are inseparably connected with your path of duty. And though you cannot do all the good you wish for, some good is done, and some evil is probably prevented, by your influence, and that of a few gentlemen in the House of Commons, like-minded with yourself. It costs you something, many hours, which you could employ more to your known personal satisfaction, and exposes you to many impertinencies from which you would gladly be exempted; but if upon the whole you are thereby instrumental in promoting the cause of God, and the public good, you will have no reason to regret, that you had not so much leisure, for more retired exercises, than some of us are favoured with. Nor is it possible at present to calculate all the advantages that may result from your having a seat in the house, at such a time as this. The example, and even the presence of a consistent character, may have a powerful, though unobserved, effect upon others. You are not only a Representative for Yorkshire. You have the far greater honour of being a Representative for the Lord, in a place where many know him not, and an opportunity of showing them, what are the genuine fruits of that religion which you are known to profess.
>
> Though you have not fully succeeded in your persevering endeavours to abolish the slave trade as yet, the business is still in train, and since you took it in hand the condition of the slaves, already in our Islands, has been undoubtedly meliorated.[47]

For the second time, Newton's influence kept Wilberforce planted in politics. Wilberforce took courage, and he resolved to keep going. In fact, it was after this defeat that Wilberforce seemed to catch his breath and get a second wind. His self-described manifesto, *A Practical View of Christianity*, was published in 1797, after eight years of working on it.[48] This was also the year that William Wilberforce was married. He was thirty-eight years old, and had seemingly come to terms with his "solitary state."[49] Barbara Spooner was only twenty. Six weeks after their first meeting, the two were wed, and they enjoyed each other for the next thirty-six years. They had six children together, four boys and two girls.[50] Wilberforce defied the social norms of the day, enjoying rich relationships with each child.[51] When Robert and Samuel grew up to write a biography about their father, they boasted that he "was beloved in general society; but if he sparkled there, he shone at home."[52] Though Wilberforce poured himself out while fighting for the abolition of the slave trade, family life kept filling him up.

Wilberforce continued to push the cause forward. In the next few years, his motion was defeated three times, then postponed three other times.[53] It was not until 1807 that the slave trade would finally be abolished. The conscience of a nation had lately come into bloom, and on that day on the Parliament floor, one person after another gave speeches praising the decision, until, at the end of the evening, Sir Samuel Romilly compared William Wilberforce with Napoleon Bonaparte. Napoleon would come home, at the end of the day, with power and luxury, but with a conscience ridden with guilt. Wilberforce, on the other hand, would go home to a beloved family, with peace of mind, because he had saved millions of lives.[54] "The House of Commons rose nearly to a man, turned to Wilberforce, and began to cheer. The chamber was swept again and again with sustained applause. Wilberforce sat with his head bowed and wept."[55]

When the victory was all but in the bag, the elderly Newton applauded Wilberforce on his upcoming triumph:

> Though I can scarcely see the paper before me, I must attempt to express my thankfulness to the Lord, & offer my congratulations to you for the success which he has so far been pleased to give to your unwearied endeavours for the abolition of the slave trade.[56]

Though Newton knew he may not live to see it come to pass, "the hopeful prospect of its accomplishment will, I trust, give me daily satisfaction so long as my declining faculties are preserved."[57] Wilberforce responded with a request for prayer, adding, "I shall ever reckon it the greatest of all my temporal favours, that I have been providentially led to take the conduct of this business."[58]

Providentially led, he certainly was.

Providentially, William Wilberforce met a former slave ship captain-turned-preacher when he was only a boy. Providentially, he found his way into Parliament, though not for any benevolent purpose, and became best friends with the soon-to-be Prime Minister, William Pitt. Providentially, he resumed correspondence with the old preacher during his struggle in coming to faith. As Providence would have it, that man encouraged him to stay in Parliament when he considered leaving to pursue vocational ministry, and again when he was ready to quit politics for a quieter life. Providence so ordered things that the preacher died within the year of the abolition of the slave trade, and the politician, within the week of the abolition of slavery itself.

God's providential hand is evident all over the life of William Wilberforce, as well as the events that led to abolition in the British Empire.

Yet, in God's providence, neither this effort, nor any of the "sixty-nine separate groups dedicated to social reform" in which William Wilberforce was involved, were done alone.[59] Not only would it take more than just one person; it would also take more than just political action to change the world.

LITERATURE

Changing society is more than a one-man job. Fortunately, John Newton was friends with just about everybody. Moreover, he was willing to use every tool possible to effect change, and pull others into the orbit of his agenda; political measures alone would hardly do. No, Newton knew better. The cause of compassion and justice required the involvement of the masses. The obvious way to engage them was through the power of the pen.

Ironically, the man who is now viewed as "one of the most powerful teachers of the English people" through his writings, was hardly an accomplished author when his friendship with Newton commenced.[60] William Cowper's own biographer suggests that Newton "wakened

Cowper's literary impulse" by inviting him to collaborate on the *Olney Hymns* project.[61] Prior to that time, Cowper had not written anything of substance.[62]

However, writing seemed somehow to ease Cowper's depression,[63] and after Newton moved away to London, poetry appears to have become Cowper's close friend.[64] Newton found Cowper a publisher[65] and even wrote the introduction to his first work. However, the publisher felt that it would have a wider readership without an overt appeal to Christianity in the introduction, so the idea was scrapped.[66] The compilation of poems hit the shelves in 1782. Cowper later remarked that the last poem, "Expostulation," sounded very much like one of Newton's later Fast Day sermons[67]; both denounced injustice and infidelity. This preachy tone is the likely reason that his first book received mixed reviews, but, among others, Benjamin Franklin praised it, which helped its reception immensely.[68] In "Charity," Cowper laments:

> But ah! what wish can prosper, or what prayer,
> For merchants rich in cargoes of despair,
> Who drive a loathsome traffic, gauge, and span,
> And buy the muscles and the bones of man?
> The tender ties of father, husband, friend,
> All bonds of nature in that moment end;
> And each endures, while yet he draws his breath,
> A stroke as fatal as the scythe of death.[69]

As others have observed, "one can see Newton's passion for social reform mirrored in Cowper's thought."[70] This is not Cowper jumping on the abolition campaign bandwagon; that wagon had not yet pulled out of the barn in 1782. Even so, behold Cowper, a depressed recluse that barely left his own property, addressing injustices taking place around the world! Cowper told Newton, before "Charity" was published, that he had written it

> in hopes to do good; and if the reviewer should say 'to be sure, the gentleman's Muse wears Methodist shoes; you may know by her pace, and

> talk about grace, that she and her bard have little regard for the taste and fashions, and ruling passions, and hoidening play, of the modern day; and though she assumed a borrowed plume, and now and then wear a tittering air, 'tis only her plan, to catch, if she can, the giddy and gay, as they go that way, by a production on a new construction. She has baited her trap, in hopes to snap all that may come, with a sugar-plum.' His opinion in this, will not be amiss; 'tis what I intend, my principal end; and if I succeed, and folks should read, till a few more are brought to a serious thought, I shall think I am paid, for all I have said.[71]

Cowper did not simply write. He fished. He hoped that some would come to faith, and others to a new appreciation of the horrors of slavery. Two years after "Charity," Cowper wrote another poem, "The Task," without even telling Newton about it.[72] This time he specifically put all of the "religious material" at the end of the work because he did not want to lose readers before he had a chance to snag their interest and sympathy. His hope was that, through poetry, he could reach an audience that would never listen to plain prose.[73]

Later, when Cowper left off composing original work in order to translate Homer, and then, to edit Milton, Newton appeared vexed: "I am sorry to see the author of *The Task* degraded into a mere editor."[74] Newton had hoped that he would write something specifically on the Christian life.[75] Cowper refused.

However, when Richard Phillips, of the Anti-Slavery Society, asked Newton to convince his friend to help out with the campaign by contributing a poem, Newton obliged.[76] At first, Cowper did not want to, but he came around in time. In the spring of 1788, just months after Newton's *Thoughts Upon the African Slave Trade* was published, Cowper issued five poems to be used in the abolition efforts.[77] "The Negro's Complaint" was set to music, and became the "campaign anthem."[78] The correspondence between the two men make it clear that Cowper had read and appreciated Newton's *Thoughts* before penning these poems.[79] However, even without the extant correspondence, when one compares the two works side by side, the echo of Newton's voice is striking in Cowper's poetry.

Newton's *Thoughts*:

> I have seen them sentenced to unmerciful whippings, continued till the poor creatures have not had power to groan under their misery, and hardly a sign of life has remained. I have seen them agonizing for hours, I believe for days together, under the torture of the thumb-screws; a dreadful engine, which, if the screw be turned by an unrelenting hand, can give intolerable anguish.[80]

Compare the "The Negro's Complaint":

> Think, ye masters iron-hearted,
> Lolling at your jovial boards,
> Think how many backs have smarted
> For the sweets your cane affords.
>
> Is there, as ye sometimes tell us,
> Is there One who reigns on high?
> Has He bid you buy and sell us,
> Speaking from his throne, the sky?
> Ask him, if your knotted scourges,
> Matches, blood-extorting screws,
> Are the means that duty urges
> Agents of his will to use?[81]

Cowper's poetry had dramatic effect. One can hardly read his "Sweet Meat has Sour Sauce: or, the Slave Trader in the Dumps," without the thick sarcasm piercing the conscience:

> Here's padlocks and bolt, and screws for the thumbs
> That squeeze them so lovingly till the blood comes
> They sweeten the temper like comfits or plums
> Which nobody can deny, deny
> Which nobody can deny![82]

By the time of his death in 1800, Cowper's poetry had reached high and low, penetrating thousands of homes that otherwise would never have been influenced in other ways. It has been claimed that "In Cowper the poetry of human wrong begins, that long, long cry against oppression . . . which rings louder and louder through Burns, Coleridge,

Wordsworth, Shelley, and Byron." [83] Another has asserted that evangelicals "found in him their first clear voice."[84]

William Cowper may very well have been evangelicalism's "first clear voice." But he certainly was not their last. In fact, upon Cowper's death we find John Newton breaking the news to another writer, a common friend who wielded the pen to great effect. On May 24th, 1800, John Newton scribbled the words, "My most dear and intimate friend, William Cowper, has obtained a release from all his distresses."[85] One can only wonder how Hannah More took the news, knowing that on one hand, Cowper was now free forever from his tormenting conscience, but on the other, she had just lost a valuable ally in the world of literature.

Unlike Cowper, More had already established herself as a writer among London's upper crust before she met John Newton. Her play, *Percy*, had been wildly successful in the winter of 1777. Moreover, about the same time More was making Newton's acquaintance, she had also received a request to meet the Prince of Wales.[86] Hannah More was clearly well connected.

Even so, after reading Newton's *Cardiphonia*, and coming to saving faith, the affections of her heart began to change. In short order, so did the direction of her writings. Over the next forty-plus years, Hannah More's writing career seems to have gone through several phases. At first she moved from writing for the stage to writing books and poetry on biblical themes. In the late 1780s and early '90s, More published her *Thoughts on the Manners of the Great*, as well as *An Estimate of the Religion of the Fashionable World*, both of which served as critical commentaries on the state of the church, particularly in high society. In an about-face, More churned out massive numbers of "improvement tracts" in the late '90s, aimed directly at those who were excluded from England's higher classes. In time, tracts seem to have no longer grabbed her attention, and by the turn of the century, More chose to focus her efforts on writing about women's issues. Finally, at the end of her life, More settled down to write works meant to foster spiritual formation.[87]

It is obvious that Hannah More had a successful writing career apart from John Newton. Yet, it quickly becomes just as obvious that More, after being introduced to Newton, began to write in hopes of influencing others for good. Hannah More, as a new creation, also became a new writer, with Newton guiding her along the way.[88] Before even meeting him, she told a friend how she liked *Cardiphonia* "prodigiously," and after finishing it, she set out to read the books that Newton had recommended within its pages. When the two finally met face to face, they began to make it a habit to send one another copies of what they wrote. Upon receiving More's *Manners* and later, her *Estimate*, Newton immediately and warmly encouraged More in her literary efforts.[89]

It is not altogether surprising then, that when Newton sent More his *Thoughts Upon the African Slave Trade*, she, like William Cowper, decided to compose her own work to contribute to the abolition movement.[90] The result was "Slavery, A Poem":

> Thy followers only have effac'd the shame
> Inscrib'd by SLAVERY on the Christian name.
> Shall Britain, where the soul of freedom reigns,
> Forge chains for others she herself disdains?
> Forbid it, Heaven! O let the nations know
> The liberty she loves she will bestow;
> Not to herself the glorious gift confin'd,
> She spreads the blessing wide as humankind;
> And, scorning narrow views of time and place,
> Bids all be free in earth's extended space.
> What page of human annals can record
> A deed so bright as human rights restor'd?[91]

That Hannah More would speak of human rights at a time when thumbscrews and "instruments for wrenching open the jaws"[92] were regularly employed betrays the truth that More was a woman ahead of her time.[93] In her involvement for abolition, More became close with Wilberforce and the rest of the Clapham Sect, eventually becoming "the most influential female member of the Society for Effecting the

Abolition of the African Slave Trade."[94] Later writings, including "Sorrows of Yamba," were also dedicated to the cause.

Perhaps More's most read writings were her *Cheap Repository Tracts*, with over two million sold in the first year alone.[95] They were cheap booklets—114 to be exact[96]— that were meant to provide alternative reading for the masses of English folk who consumed the typical vulgar and crass booklets that circulated like wildfire, especially among the poor. Though More was the main author of these stories and songs, Newton lent his pen as well, and before they were done, enough had been printed for one out of every two people in Britain.[97] Though many of the tracts are condescending in tone,[98] William Pitt himself was pleased to hear that "this sort of reading was gaining ground."[99] Hannah More's posture toward those in poverty is certainly paternalistic to a modern reader, but one would think that had she been terribly off-putting to her audience, sales would have slowed, and the readership would have diminished. It did not. The tracts were moralistic, but also promoted service to the poor, as well as the transforming power of the gospel.[100] The undisputed fact is that the general public consumed them.

Newton encouraged More not to "try to frighten men out of their sins," instead encouraging her to win people over by demonstrating the incredible love of Christ.[101] By the time More came to write her later works on the spiritual life, mercy was the natural overflow of pursuing holiness, and charity expressed itself in compassion.[102] To be sure, she did not simply write about these things. In fact, when More died, she left thirty thousand pounds to "charity and religious societies," totaling several million dollars in today's currency.[103]

But Hannah More did more than write about justice and throw money at problems. She rolled up her sleeves and got to work.

EDUCATION

When William Wilberforce observed the dire poverty in an area known as the Mendips, he said to his friend, "Miss Hannah More, something must be done."[104] He turned to the right person. In short order, Hannah, along with her sister, Patty, decided to start a school to help educate and empower the poor. The Thornton family funded it, as they did so many of the compassionate efforts of Newton and his circle, and with 120 students, the school was launched on October 25, 1789, within four months of More's initial conversation with Wilberforce![105]

Despite Hannah More's disparaging attitude toward the poor in some of her writings, she had still come to embrace John Newton's heart for the least of these, telling him,

> One great benefit which I have found to result from our project is, the removal of that great gulf which has divided the rich and poor in those country parishes, by making them meet together; whereas; before, they hardly thought they were children of one common father. Oh! how glad I should be to get you to preach to a little colony of colliers we have raised up.[106]

The school was free, offering both Christian education on Sundays, as well as reading and job skills classes during the week, including sewing and spinning.[107] Perhaps what made this school attractive to some was that students actually got paid for the work accomplished. Within a year, a second school was started on the same principles; a decade later, there were eleven.[108] In 1796, More wrote to Newton, "You will be glad to hear that our work rather increases. I think our various schools and societies consist of about sixteen or seventeen hundred."[109]

On multiple occasions, More asked if Newton had any particular books or sermons that would communicate well to her students.[110] Once Newton suggested that the poor tended to appreciate John Bunyan's *Pilgrim's Progress.*[111] She apparently liked the suggestion, writing her own version, "The Pilgrims. An Allegory," in one of her *Cheap Repository Tracts.*[112]

Even if More's condescending posture is not worthy of emulation, her creativity in tackling issues of poverty is well worth our attention. In addition to training unskilled workers with job skills, More's fictional account "The Cottage Cook," from one of her *Cheap Repository Tracts,* reveals some of her other real-life strategies. A baker who cheats his clients by selling smaller loaves for the price of a large one is confronted and reprimanded. The rich in a town are lobbied to buy expensive cuts of meat for their soups so that the cheaper cuts are left for poor; otherwise the rich buy the cheap cuts, and the poor are left with no meat that they can afford.[113]

Clearly, these relief efforts, not to mention the schools themselves, could have become all-consuming for More. Yet, in the midst of all the bustle, John Newton reminded her not to neglect her important work as an author.[114] He advised More in other ways as well, visiting in 1791, and preaching at her Sunday school.[115] He was so impressed by the work that was taking place that he later told Wilberforce how he felt like the Queen of Sheba at Solomon's court![116] Reports of More's schools failed to convey the enormity of her accomplishment.

In 1801, when More came under attack in a political periodical for establishing her schools, Newton quipped, "I am more disposed to congratulate than to condole with you on the unjust and hard treatment you have met with," and he encouraged her to keep going.[117] After all, he had long been a supporter: "The strong, Almighty arm of the Lord is with you, and therefore you do wonders. . . . May his presence comfort your heart, and his blessing crown all your labours of love for his sake."[118] "May the lights on Cowslip Green illuminate the whole country, and may they long continue to burn and shine."[119]

The lights did long continue to burn and shine. In fact, three of Hannah More's schools operated for well over one hundred years.[120]

Yet Hannah More was not the only one of John Newton's friends who changed society through education. Thomas Charles was an educator as well, though he came at it from the back door. To set the record straight, Charles was a preacher first, and a good one at that. The summer he had spent living with Newton whetted his appetite to see revival in his own land of Wales. After leaving the Anglican church, Charles became part of the Methodist movement, seemingly facing crowds of both hungry listeners and angry mobs wherever he preached.[121]

The problem that Charles began to see, however, was that the effects of his preaching wore off quickly because very few of his audience could read the Bible once he moved on to a new locale.[122] In many rural Welsh villages, only two or perhaps three of the most wealthy children could afford to be sent to a neighboring town in order to learn to read English.[123] That simply would not do, and so Thomas Charles came to the conviction that every child in every place needed to learn how to read in their mother tongue.

Griffith Jones, a remarkable man in his own right, had started a number of circulating schools throughout Wales for the same purpose, but had passed away when Thomas Charles was only a small child.[124] In time, his schools were shut down, and by the time Charles came of age, an entire generation had grown up in complete illiteracy. Thomas Charles picked up Jones' mantle, and in 1787 began establishing circulating schools.[125] His schools remained in one place for nine months at a time,[126] and all ages were welcome.[127]

During his summer stay with the Newton family, John had introduced Thomas Charles to Thomas Scott, the neighboring pastor who was just starting to come around to an orthodox faith. Newton routinely did this, networking his friends together, which, in the end, served to strengthen and propel each one on to even greater heights. This occasion was no exception. Over the years these men kept up a lively friendship, Scott becoming one of Charles' biggest supporters. Scott, in fact, was the recipient of Charles' earliest extant letter giving details about the charity schools:

> When I came a little acquainted with the country, I was surprised and grieved to find so many totally illiterate and not able to read a word in [the] Bible in their Mother's Tongue. I have attempted and succeeded far beyond my expectations in setting up charity schools, with a view <u>only</u> of teaching poor children and young people to read [the] Bible in a language they understood, and teach them [the] principles of [the] christian Religion by catechising them . . . by these means we are able to teach [the] whole country with no great expense. I visit all [the] schools myself as often as I can. . . . I have been often, in my journeys through different parts of

> [the] Country, questioned whether I knew where a Welch Bible [could] be bought for a small price? and it has hurted my mind much to be obliged to [answer] in [the] negative.[128]

Like Hannah More, Charles provided the schools free of charge, paying teachers out of his own pocket. His salary from the church was dedicated entirely to the work, and he relied completely on his wife for income.[129] As the word began to spread, so did the gospel. A powerful revival broke out in Bala in 1791, the reports of which made their way throughout Scotland and England.[130] Interestingly, John Campbell heard about the Spirit's work in Wales, and asked Newton what he thought about it. Newton told Campbell to thank God for it, and recommended that he ought to connect with Thomas Charles directly. Another connection had been made. As he had with Scott, Charles also began corresponding with Campbell, helping to spark revival in Scotland as well.[131]

Though some opposed Charles's efforts, especially of the Sunday schools, seeing it as a violation of the Sabbath,[132] the work began to thrive. Within two years, "some thousands" had been taught to read Welsh.[133] By 1799, over one hundred Sunday schools had been established in various Welsh villages and towns, in addition to numerous literacy schools.[134]

Soon, however, Charles realized that people needed more than schools. They needed books at the schools. Charles described the obstacle he was facing: "there are thousands of poor children in our country whose parents cannot afford a penny to buy an A. B. C."[135] To fix the problem, Charles brought a press to Bala, wrote a spelling primer himself, and even put together a Welsh Bible dictionary.[136]

He was a man acutely aware of social injustices, viewing the poor often as prey of rich and corrupt clergy, kept "in ignorance for that purpose."[137] His life was a determined effort to reverse such fortunes. He lobbied the Society for Promoting Christian Knowledge (SPCK) to print some Welsh Bibles, but when it took them seven years to print only a fraction of what was needed,[138] he turned to other friends for help. The

SPCK was an Anglican organization, with little desire to promote the work of a Methodist educator. Newton's circle of (mostly Anglican) friends were much more generous in their associations. Newton himself opened up his church for a fundraising event to support the charity schools,[139] and on numerous occasions Thomas Scott sent along any Welsh Bibles he could get his hands on from the SPCK.[140]

However, as a result of the SPCK's reticence, in 1804 the British and Foreign Bible Society was formed with the help of several laymen, including William Wilberforce,[141] who also financially supported the charity schools.[142] When the first batch of new Bibles came out two years later, droves of young people reportedly stayed up all night to read the Bible.[143] Many Welsh people had been starved for truth, walking great distances to be able to be able to read a Bible for themselves.[144]

The story of Mary Jones is perhaps one of the most heart warming. For six years, she regularly walked two miles to a neighboring farmhouse to read a Welsh Bible. When she had finally saved up her money, this sixteen-year-old girl walked twenty-five miles barefoot to Thomas Charles' home in hopes to buy one. Upon hearing that all of the Bibles in his latest batch were either gone or already spoken for, she burst into tears. Moved by her desire to have a copy of the Bible, Charles gave her one that had been reserved for a friend.[145]

By 1819, this new society had given out two and a half million Bibles in Great Britain, publishing the Scriptures in Welsh plus 127 other languages on four continents![146]

In the end, Thomas Charles seems to have become much like the man he claimed was "one of [the] most eminently pious Gospel Ministers now in [England]."[147] Charles constantly had a house full of visitors, as well as children's meetings, much like Newton had during the summer he spent with his mentor in Olney back in 1777 as a divinity student. [148] Likewise, he shared Newton's compassionate heart; his ministry to the poor and disadvantaged children of Wales lends abundant evidence to this fact. Even his final words sound like an echo from John Newton's famous line: "My memory is nearly gone; but I remember two things: That I am a great sinner, and that Christ is a great Saviour."[149] Shortly before Charles died, after some ten thousand Welsh children had learned how to read,[150] he would claim, "Charles is a great sinner; just a poor and unworthy sinner."[151] Just an unworthy sinner who quietly enlightened both mind and soul of thousands in his native land.

CHAPTER FIVE

To Change the Church

THE ESTABLISHED CHURCH

After writing to Thomas Charles to assure him that Welsh Bibles were on the way, Thomas Scott finished his letter with a request for prayer:

> Pray for a Blessing upon this and all other Attempts of [your] poor Brethren in London, and tho we are so distant in our Situation, yet being all engaged in one Warfare under one Captain, against one common Enemy, we may be helpful to one another by Prayers, Exhortations, Encouragements, &c.[1]

Make no mistake: Scott needed prayer. He was biting off one of the greatest challenges of his life.

From a sleepy country curacy, Scott's plunge into urban ministry must have come as a shock. Earlier, his biggest concern had been following in John Newton's footsteps as the curate at Olney. It had been his express goal: "I would wish to tread in the steps of Mr. Newton."[2] He had felt embarrassed that he could not give as generously to the poor as Newton had been able to because of John Thornton's financial backing,[3] and never was terribly popular there. In time, however, Scott found his own way, and completed a five-year stint preaching in the Olney church.[4]

However, when an invitation from the fashionable chapel connected with Lock Hospital arrived in September 1785, Scott was intrigued with the possibility.[5] After all, Newton had preached there from time to time,[6] it afforded a great opportunity to be involved in compassionate ministry at the Hospital, and more than likely, it was Newton who put Scott's name forward as the best candidate for the job.[7] Moreover, moving to London to be close once again to his long-time mentor must have had some appeal. Scott went through the application process, and landed the job. Little did he know that it would be the most difficult season of his life.[8]

At the time, "No less than 25 percent of all unmarried women in London were prostitutes," the average age being only sixteen years old. Some brothels advertised working girls under the age of fourteen.[9] It was for these souls that Scott's heart broke. He saw young girls who came to London:

> just in the light I do upon the cattle that come to Smithfield market; they come to be a prey to the inhabitants. I wonder that any of those who have not very prudent and friendly connections escape prostitution. . . . At every offence girls are turned out of door with a month's wages, often in the evening, and at an hour's warning. They have lodgings to seek; a set of wretches let lodgings, who make it their study to betray them into situations from which few escape. Often their clothes are stolen; if not, they are pawned for money to pay expenses, and in a few weeks they are thus stripped of apparel, and can go to no place at all. In short, dangers are innumerable, and the number that without any such previous intention, are seduced, and become prostitutes, and perish without any regarding it, is incredible. It is shocking to me beyond expression.[10]

Shocking indeed, and Thomas Scott felt that something must be done. Here was an opportunity. Lock Hospital was designed specifically to treat those who had contracted sexually transmitted diseases.[11] Though the congregation at the chapel initially had over three hundred people, his unpopular preaching soon whittled it down to half the size.[12] Even so, this post allowed Scott to be involved in ministering to the least of these. He regularly went through the wards, visiting the patients, and preaching the gospel. This part of the work was his greatest joy.[13]

Unfortunately, this was not the norm in the Established Church of the day. Others would preach in the chapel services, but none walked the halls:

> Mr. Scott was the first clergyman who could be got to do this work, the nature of which may be inferred from the fact that the patients belonged, for the most part, to the lowest class of society, that they were suffering from a frightful, loathsome and most contagious disease, manifesting itself in hideous disfigurement of the features, and offensive to other senses than that of sight.[14]

Speaking of lepers in St. Francis' day, Donald Spoto writes, "Everyone kept a distance from lepers, for their condition was considered both highly contagious and a sign of dreadful sinfulness."[15] Perhaps the same could be said of those infected with STDs in Scott's day. Though many Anglican clergy (including Scott, prior to his conversion) saw the pastorate as little more than an easy paycheck, Thomas Scott provided an alternate vision of what ministry in the Established Church could be.

Once Scott came to evangelical convictions, his whole understanding of pastoral ministry changed. Working faithfully and selflessly was no longer in question. The question he did begin to ponder, however, is what would become of these girls once they got better?

> Betwixt 500, and 600 every Year of Men and Women are cured in it, who are generally the most profligate and ignorant of the People. . . . But the Women being most of them prostitutes, have scarce any Alternative, but returning however reluctantly to their old Occupation.[16]

And so, it was that Thomas Scott begged Thomas Charles for prayer. A month before, he had decided to start the Lock Asylum, an institution that would pick up where the hospital left off. He had already been taking in select patients to live with his family for five weeks at a time so that he would not have to turn them out on the streets again.[17] That simply was not enough, and so in July 1787 the first two houses were opened.[18] Four months later Scott wrote, "Twenty-eight have been admitted."[19] Daily, Scott led family worship in the homes,[20] served selflessly, and prayed for the day when these young women would be able to "be restored either to their friends, or the community at large, in a way of industry according to their ability."[21]

Thomas Scott seems always to have been a bit prickly, and his ministry appears to have been riddled with relational tension. Even so, his heart for the poor and oppressed shines bright. For instance, once at a very nice dinner, he announced to all in attendance that such opulent meals were inconsistent with the gospel, and that instead they should be feeding "the poor, the maimed, the lame, and the blind." He was not invited back.[22] Scott was also known to hate slavery.[23] He held strong opinions, and felt slighted by his meager pay,[24] but all in all, Thomas Scott was a man with a warm, compassionate heart, serving faithfully at Lock Hospital for seventeen years.[25] His Asylum, however, continued to protect girls from subjecting themselves to prostitution for roughly a hundred and fifty years after his departure.[26]

As time wore on, Scott's friendship with John Newton continued strong. Both were active in the Eclectic Society until 1804,[27] by which time Newton had become quite feeble and almost blind. Over the years, this group prayed together, discussed theological concerns, and planned ways to spread the truth of the gospel. When the Church Missionary Society was born out of those meetings in 1799, Scott served as the honorary secretary of the group,[28] while Newton served on the original committee. But without a doubt, the man who had most promoted the cause of missions in the Established Church prior to the formation of the Church Missionary Society was a young pastor from Cambridge, Charles Simeon.[29]

Simeon had been appointed to his post at Trinity Church when he was only twenty-four years old. However, the parishioners staunchly opposed his leadership, locking their pew doors, and refusing to attend services. Those who did wander in were left to stand in the aisles. Once, the congregation even locked Simeon out of the church building![30] No wonder he sought out Newton for some advice.

Newton was eager to encourage him:

> The Lord sees fit to fix you in a noble stand indeed. Were I a Collegian, I think I should prefer a church in one of our Universities (and perhaps Cambridge especially) to any station in the Kingdom. And yet I overrate myself in thinking I would dare to make such a choice, were it in my power. . . . He has chosen you, and on Him therefore you may confidently rely for all that patience, fortitude, and meekness of wisdom which you will need, especially in a place where so many eyes will be upon you, so many tongues ready to circulate every report to your prejudice, and so many ears open to receive them.
>
> Your sense of His great goodness, and the strong impression you have received of the power and reality of unseen things, have inspired you with a commendable zeal. Shall I advise you to repress your zeal? Far from it. . . . Yet there is such a thing as true Christian prudence. . . . Particularly the spirit and conduct of our Lord in the days of His humiliation furnish the best model. His manner, His gentleness, His patient attention to the weakness and prejudices of those around Him, we cannot imitate too closely. . . . I have seen some frozen into mere lifeless images of their former selves, and some have not even retained a resemblance of what they were. So I have almost by habit a fear and jealousy over those who are remarkably warm and active at their first setting out. . . . Believe me to be, dear Sir, Your affectionate friend and servant, John Newton.[31]

When a pastorate starts out that rocky, a fifty-four year tenure should be considered as nothing less than miraculous.[32] But that is exactly what happened. In fact, over time, Simeon's influence at Cambridge became incredible. First of all, as a lifelong bachelor, he required very little to live on. As such, when he inherited a great sum of money from his brother, he distributed it generously among the poor.[33] He also began the habit of buying up advowsons,[34] which gave him the right to place evangelical pastors into vacant Established Church pulpits. By the end of his life, some fifty to sixty livings were in his possession.[35] What made this particularly strategic was Charles Simeon's position as a dean and later vice-provost at Cambridge.[36] He made it his aim to train men in divinity who would eventually become pastors of churches where he owned the rights of appointment![37]

Over time, Simeon would see to it that evangelicalism had a place within the Established Church long after his own ministry came to an end. Simeon certainly deserves credit for his innovative approaches to ministry, but Newton's critical role in bridging the gap between the earlier evangelists such as George Whitefield and John Wesley with the younger generation of leaders, including Simeon himself, should not be glossed over. Though it has been said that "Newton's kind of acquiescent piety was increasingly out of step with the new possibilities open to evangelicals in the public sphere,"[38] juxtaposing Newton as a less sophisticated forerunner to Simeon, it is better to see Newton as a man laying the groundwork for such new possibilities.

Simeon must have felt lonely as an evangelical in a hostile environment when he first arrived at Cambridge, but Newton deliberately lent his support. Simeon received encouragement by participating in the evangelical network of pastors that Newton had begun, the Eclectic Society. At a time when the evangelical wing of the Established Church was a significant minority and the cause of missions in Anglicanism was not being advanced with the zeal or faithfulness evangelicals deemed appropriate,[39] Newton's circle became the incubator for something new. Newton was excited about the prospect: "We are forming a Church of England Missionary Society. It is at present in the Egg, but I hope the Egg will be hatched about the 23rd of this month."[40] If it were not for Simeon's urging, it may not have hatched at all. As early as 1787, Simeon had become involved in a project to reach India with the gospel,[41] and three years before the Church Missionary Society was established he had pitched the idea of forming a new mission agency to the Eclectic Society.[42] It took some time to become a reality, but in due course the new work came to fruition with a concern for justice as well as evangelism.[43]

One of Simeon's biographers notes that both his attitude toward high society as well as his views on controversial matters were deeply influenced by John Newton.[44] Simeon tells us himself that he wanted to finish strong, as Newton had.[45] That he did, in remarkably similar fashion. As an old man, Simeon noted,

> I remember the time when I was quite surprised that a Fellow of my own College ventured to walk with me for a quarter of an hour. . . . But now, on my open days, when I receive visitors to tea, frequently more than forty (all without invitation) come.[46]

As John Newton did before him, Charles Simeon opened both his heart and his home to a cadre of churchmen who would carry the evangelical baton into the next generation.

THE DISSENTING CHURCH

As committed as John Newton was to the Established Church, there is no question that the man was, as William Bull commented, a "speckled bird."[47] Though he jumped through numerous hoops to ensure his own ordination within the Anglican fellowship, he was by no means tied to his denomination. His orbit went well beyond the bounds of his own church because he extended the right hand of fellowship to all pastors who called on the name of the Lord Jesus. The lasting impact that he left on the Dissenting church as a result is impressive.

William Bull's friendship with Newton illustrates the point. While Bull encouraged Newton to read the mystics, being particularly fond of Madame Guyon,[48] in reciprocal manner, Newton exerted his own influence through his constant chattering about visiting prisoners,[49] the injustice of oppression in the East Indies,[50] or his poor flock at Olney.[51] Newton was less than shy in reminding Bull that Jesus "comes to the poor as readily as to the rich."[52]

In time, this too would become a theme of William Bull's message, first to those most dear to him, including his own son, Tommy. Newton became quite fond of Tommy as well, once warning William jokingly, "I charge you upon your allegiance to bring Tommy with you, and not venture into my presence without him."[53] Frankly, William Bull wanted

Tommy to grow up to be just like John Newton.[54] Specifically, he hoped that his son would grow into a man with a compassionate heart, praying that Tommy would

> be inflamed with love to a precious Jesus, and with incessant delight in Him . . . that you may never be unmindful of the poor—visit them, pity them, relieve them, pray for them; and be in everything the very pattern of the Lord Jesus Christ.[55]

Many of these Christ-like attributes were qualities Bull had observed in Newton.

On the day that Tommy was ordained to become co-pastor with his father, William Bull reiterated this hope, charging him with these words:

> Be always humane and tender. Pity the poor, and do them all the good you possibly can. No money is so well laid out as that which is given to the poor, and when your own circumstances will go no farther, use your interest with others that they may assist you in this good work. Visit the afflicted, and help them to bear their burdens. Never think yourself above the meanest of your hearers in their afflictions.[56]

Thomas heeded the admonition. Years later, when he co-pastored the independent church at Newport Pagnell with his son, Josiah Bull, the church operated four cottages which were used as free housing for the poor of the community.[57]

It would be natural to assume that if Bull charged his son with a call to compassionate ministry, he would do no less with each young man under his tutelage at the Newport Pagnell Evangelical Institution for the Education of Young Men for the Christian Ministry. Given the fact that the Bible school was essentially John Newton's brainchild, it is difficult to imagine otherwise. Back in April of 1782, Newton had written to Bull:

> Mr. Clayton lately called upon me, to tell me that many persons are seriously thinking of establishing a new academy, upon a liberal ground, for preparing young men for the ministry, in which the greatest stress might be laid upon truth, life, spirituality, and the least stress possible upon modes, forms, and non-essentials; that it must be at a moderate distance from London; that, in fact, Newport Pagnel was the place fixed upon, for

> the sake of one Mr. Bull, who lives there, and who, it was hoped, would accept the superintendency. He then said it was his request, and the desire of many of his friends, that I would draw up a plan for the formation of such an academy, and likewise that I would write to you upon the subject.[58]

A month later, Newton wrote again,

> This will seem an awkward business all round to some persons. What apology can Mr. Clayton make to many dissenters for applying to a[n] [Anglican] clergyman for a plan of an academy? And what can the poor [Anglican] cleric say to some people in his line, for chalking out the plan of a dissenting methodistical academy? . . . I think this poor speckled bird will be pecked at by fowls of every wing.[59]

However, the speckled bird was not deterred. The Anglican cleric sketched out his utopian ideal for a Dissenting Bible college.[60] Eight students at a time would be taken into Bull's care, and the course of study would last four years.[61] After the school was up and running, Bull let his good friend know that one of the texts commonly used was Newton's very own *Messiah*: "It is read three times a week by the students in turn."[62] For the next twenty-seven years until Bull's death, Bull served as superintendent while John Thornton funded the school.[63] In the end, one hundred men were sent into Dissenting pastoral positions,[64] until the academy eventually merged with Cheshunt College in 1848, over sixty-five years later.[65]

As odd as it was that Newton had his hand in shaping one Dissenting Bible college, it seems extraordinary that he would have substantially shaped two. Newton had no direct influence on the founding of Bristol Academy (later, Bristol Baptist College), as he did with the school in Newport Pagnell, but he had certainly influenced the president of the college, John Ryland Jr., since his teenage years. Ryland, the son of an accomplished Baptist leader, cut his theological teeth on High Calvinism, stressing divine sovereignty so much that human responsibility was downplayed, and general calls for sinners to repent were frowned upon. After interacting with Newton, however, Ryland's position on the matter changed. Newton, after all, likened his Calvinism to sugar in his tea cup—something that sweetened every book and sermon, but never served in full lumps.[66] In one of their exchanges, Newton wrote,

> You speak of the negative and the affirmative side of the 'modern question.' Which is which, I do not well understand. The expression is rather obscure. However I can understand that you have changed sides, and I think much for the better.[67]

Newton persuaded Ryland to adopt a warmer and more evangelistic Calvinism; Ryland in turn passed this thinking on to many more.[68] For instance, Ryland encouraged Andrew Fuller to be sure to read Jonathan Edwards, hoping that the latter would convince Fuller to change his position as well.[69] It worked, as both Ryland and Fuller, along with others such as William Carey, formed the Baptist Missionary Society, clearly promoting the use of means for the conversion of the heathen.

Fuller was not the only one who benefitted from Ryland's new views. As president of the only advanced Calvinistic Baptist theological school in England,[70] two hundred future pastors would be trained during the course of his thirty-one-year tenure.[71] Providentially, his presidency of the school and the establishment of the Baptist Missionary Society commenced within a year of one another; naturally, twenty-six of his students were sent to the mission field through the new mission agency.[72] Moreover, the school seemed to exhibit Newton's gracious tone. Through the years Newton had warned Ryland about people who carried themselves in theological discourse with "an angry and self-important spirit."[73] Ryland apparently imbibed the sentiment, counseling his students, "In the exercise of your ministry be careful to unite a gentleness of manner with a decided attachment to the truth."[74]

Ryland travelled extensively to promote the cause of missions, logging some 36,000 miles to raise funds and awareness,[75] yet Newton was never far out of the loop. When the missionary society wondered how they should navigate some difficulties concerning the Indian caste system and the Lord's Supper, Newton helped guide the way.[76] When the Baptists hoped to get their missionaries into Sierra Leone, Newton interceded on their behalf to Henry Thornton,[77] William Wilberforce, and Zachary Macaulay, the governor of the African colony.[78] As the society struggled over the question of whether their missionaries should be allowed to work as tentmakers in their new country, it was Newton's go-ahead that tipped the scale.[79]

Just as remarkable was Ryland's stance on issues of justice. For instance, according to Stephen Tomkins, by and large, Dissenters did not get overly involved in the abolition movement until as late as 1824.[80] Ryland, however, had been hearing about it years before from Newton.

> As you are a friend to liberty and mankind, you will not be sorry to hear that I have a pamphlet in the press . . . upon the African Slave trade. On this subject I can write as an eyewitness, and something more, for I was myself, too long actively engaged in it. As the business is now coming before Parliament; I thought myself bound to declare what I know.[81]

Interestingly, in this one letter, John Newton mentions three different causes: (1) abolition, (2) the Society for Promoting Religious Knowledge amongst the Poor, and (3) the Sunday School Society, which was concerned with the illiteracy rates amongst poor children who worked in factories and mills. Newton's compassion was contagious. Though other Dissenters may have been late in speaking out for abolition, when the Baptist Missionary Society commissioned their first missionaries to Sierra Leone in 1795, Ryland condemned the trade, calling the ships full of slaves "floating hells," and charging the missionaries to live lives of bold relief to the slave traders who perpetuate war and murder.[82]

When the freed slave David George ended up in England, he became almost a celebrity in Baptist circles, "but Newton was troubled by the way the Baptists were parading George around and wrote to Ryland to express his concern."[83] Newton seemed to display a sensitivity to issues of race well before his time. David George was not a curiosity, but a man worthy of dignity and respect. These and similar views were passed from Newton to Ryland. It appears that they were also passed along from Ryland to his parishioners, his students, and the missionaries whom he devoted his life to sending out.

For instance, one of the members of Ryland's church, William Knibb, was set on going to the mission field. The Baptist Missionary Society, however, was not so sure that he was fit for the task. Ryland came to Knibb's defense, and in the end, he was sent to Jamaica.[84] This man, in turn, convinced the Baptists to unite against slavery, becoming a major force for abolition in Jamaica.[85] As another has noted,

> It is no coincidence that the same John Ryland, Jr., who thirty-nine years earlier immersed William Carey, now baptized William Knibb. . . . The two early spheres of the Baptist Missionary Society's work were Carey's India and Knibb's Jamaica, a providential honor that Ryland knew only in part.[86]

An honor indeed, for John Ryland Jr.'s vision went well beyond the bounds of England. His heart, like that of John Newton's, was for every tribe, tongue, and nation.

THE GLOBAL CHURCH

In April of 1803, John Newton wrote his last letter to John Ryland, Jr. Within a day of receiving it, Ryland sent a copy of it to William Carey in India.[87] It may have been because Ryland thought that Carey would be encouraged by Newton's musings on prayer:

> I believe in the communion of saints; that the living members of that body of which Jesus is the living head, have fellowship one with another, and are reciprocally helped by the prayers of many whom they will never see in this world. But there is something in the subject which is beyond my feeble comprehension. Local distance cannot restrain thought. I can thus converse with, and pray for, a friend in Bristol or in Indostan, as readily as if he lived in the same street with me.[88]

Perhaps Ryland wanted to remind Carey that the distance between them was not so far, and that John Newton was praying for them both.

It may have been that Ryland knew that neither he nor Carey would ever tire of hearing Newton recount the story of God's amazing grace in rescuing him from sin:

> O what a horrid wretch was I when on board the *Harwich*, on the coast of Africa, and too long afterwards. Surely no one who did not finally perish was ever more apparently given up to a reprobate mind! I am singular and striking proof, that the atoning blood of Jesus can cleanse from the most enormous sins, that His grace can soften the hardest heart, subdue the most obstinate habits of evil, and that He is indeed able to save to the uttermost. Lord, I believe, O help me against my unbelief. I have been, yea to this day, I am a chief sinner, and yet I am permitted to preach the truth I once laboured to destroy.[89]

Maybe Ryland wanted to remind Carey that God could save anyone, even the people that Carey was reaching out to in India.

Or it may have been that Ryland loved Newton and knew that Carey did as well. The final letter from such a friend would definitely be something he would want to see: "I have received several very kind and friendly letters from you, and now if the Lord permits, and my eyes will hold out, you shall have one from me, which perhaps, or rather probably will be the last I shall send to you."[90] Whatever the motivation, forwarding this correspondence seemed valuable enough to Ryland that he dare not put it off. Years had passed since Carey was a young cobbler, stitching together a globe with patches of colored shoe leather.[91] The enthusiasm and excitement of reaching the world had lost some of its luster as the difficulty of ministering in India had set in. A letter from old Newton was a sure tonic for a discouraged heart.

Carey had shared his hardships with Newton over the years: one of the few converts that they actually had, a Hindu man, committed adultery after professing faith in Christ.[92] Another time, Carey broke the news, "One of our Hindoo friends was murdered some time ago. . . . weakened our hands."[93] Carey even admitted once to Newton,

> Was it not that duty requires me to write to my dear friends in England I should certainly be discouraged from it by the strong conviction which I

> have of being unworthy of the respect, or friendship of every true Christian.[94]

Newton cherished these letters and returned them with his characteristic prayers and words of encouragement. When John Fountain prepared to join Carey in his work, Newton made sure to meet with him beforehand, sending him off with a letter of recommendation to one of the East Indian chaplains.[95] Three years later, Newton was advising four more missionaries on their way to support Carey in his work, praying for them, and sending them off, again, with a letter of introduction written in his hand. [96] Newton was delighted to use whatever influence he had to pave the way for others.

It should come as no surprise that Newton and Carey also corresponded over compassionate ministry that was taking place in India. Just like Newton, Carey was appalled by the slave trade.[97] In fact, in many ways, his compassion and justice efforts were the bright spots in Carey's life: "a School which was begun some years ago for the children of the Poor, is in a very flourishing state, and that the translation of great part of the Bible is accomplished, and I hope the whole will be translated in another Year."[98] Frankly, that was only the beginning of Carey's accomplishments. Hardly any one man has been so effective in bringing about cultural transformation.

In opposition to the Hindu practice of burning lepers in hopes that a violent death would bring about a purified reincarnated life, Carey campaigned for their humane treatment.[99] He fought for women's rights, opposing polygamy, female infanticide, child marriage, widow burning, euthanasia, and forced female illiteracy.[100] Though many are aware that slavery was abolished in England in 1833 due to a decades-long battle led by William Wilberforce, few realize that four years prior widow-burning was banned in India after a twenty-five year struggle in which William Carey played a significant role.[101] His English journal, "Friend of India," as well as his newspaper, his role as professor at Fort Williams College in Calcutta, and the published reports of what was taking place, all contributed to raise public awareness and to influence upcoming leaders to oppose the abhorrent practice.[102]

In addition, Carey began dozens of schools for Indian boys and girls of all castes, introduced the first steam engines and lending libraries to the nation, built the largest printing press in India, set forth the idea of a savings bank to fight usury, and published and/or translated portions of the Bible in forty different Indian languages![103] More could be delineated, but let it suffice to say that William Carey was a lightning rod of social transformation efforts. To think that Carey might not have been in India at all apart from the initial push and ongoing support of people like John Newton!

Interestingly enough, one of Carey's co-laborers in India came directly from St. Mary Woolnoth in London. After Newton waited four years for Claudius Buchanan to graduate from Cambridge so that he could come back and serve as Newton's curate, Buchanan ended up only sticking around for about nine months.[104] This was not a complete surprise, in that Buchanan had expressed his desire to go overseas early on in his college career, telling Newton:

> From hearing various accounts of the apostolic spirit of some missionaries to the Indies and of the extensive field for preaching the Gospel, there opened, I was led to desire that I might be well qualified for such a Department, in case the Lord should intend me for it.[105]

Charles Grant, chairman of the East India Company, just so happened to be a member of the Eclectic Society.[106] Being Newton's curate surely helped pave the way for Buchanan's appointment as a chaplain to the East India Company only six months into his first pastorate.[107] Before the arrangements had been made, it is clear that Newton would have loved to keep Buchanan around. Speaking of Buchanan, Newton mused,

> From the Lord's wonderful leadings of him, I apprehend he has designed him for important services. I hope I shall be willing to part with him at the

> Lord's call; but should he be permitted to supply my lack of service . . . I shall have cause to be thankful, as he is one in whom I may full depend.[108]

However, when it became clear that God was in fact calling Buchanan on to missionary work, Newton was not the type of man to stand in the way. To the same correspondent, a month later, Newton said, "I saw his call clear, and gave him up without reluctance, though he was to me as a right hand."[109]

The two had always shared a sense of being kindred spirits, both having lived lives of wild abandonment prior to their conversions. Buchanan even went so far as to suggest that most could not read Newton's autobiography rightly, the way that he could, because of their analogous histories.[110] Naturally, Newton was the last one to receive a letter upon Buchanan's departure from England as well as being Buchanan's "only faithful correspondent" once he arrived in Calcutta.[111]

That is an unfortunate fact, because ministry in India was difficult for Buchanan as it was for Carey. He suffered from serious health concerns during the first three years of his appointment[112] and only had a handful of listeners to attend his preaching at the only place he could find to do so, the hospital.[113] But his friendship with Newton proved to be a strong support. Their correspondence covers a wide range of subjects; Newton even helped Buchanan work through some girl problems.[114] One assumes that the advice was helpful—Buchanan was married soon after![115] Though his usefulness was limited in his early years overseas, his fortunes soon changed. Once, Buchanan had an opportunity to preach to an audience including Lord Mornington, the governor-general, who was so impressed by the sermon that he appointed Buchanan vice-provost of Fort William College. The Anglican Buchanan convinced Mornington to hire the Baptist William Carey as well. [116] Ironically, in the past, Buchanan found both preaching[117] and schoolwork[118] quite difficult. No longer.

In time Buchanan became quite the scholar, and after the death of his wife he left his post at Fort Williams College for a time to research and write an account of the state of Christianity in Asia. Throughout 1806-1807 he travelled extensively over the continent, taking copious notes about customs, religions, and the state of Bible translation in Asia.[119] His *Christian Researches in Asia* earned high acclaim. The review from the *Christian Observer* in 1811 boasts,

> We should be afraid of appearing extravagant to our readers were we to say all we think respecting the importance of this Work. But we wish them to judge for themselves whether we exceed the bounds of moderation, when we rate *its value above that of any other work connected with our Oriental Empire which we have seen.*[120]

The breadth of his travels are impressive, especially given the fact that Buchanan did it without the benefit of modern transport.

And what he found, simply put, shocked him.

He found that within thirty miles of Calcutta, 115 widows were burned alive on their husbands' funeral pyre in a six-month period.[121] Buchanan called the "Proprietors of India Stock" on the carpet for having "done nothing towards the suppression of this enormity." [122] He promised, "THE AUTHOR WILL NOT CEASE TO CALL THE ATTENTION OF THE ENGLISH NATION TO THIS SUBJECT," with hopes that the practice would soon be abolished.[123] He told of idol-worship and human sacrifice.[124] He recounted how he found poor children, homeless, sitting on the ground next to their dying mother, while dogs and vultures paced and waited impatiently nearby. His horror at the sight jumps off the pages: "O, there is no pity at Juggernaut! no mercy, no tenderness of heart in Moloch's Kingdom!"[125]

Buchanan also found that the Inquisition was alive and well in India (yes, *that* Inquisition), even gaining an audience with the Inquisitor himself, though he was denied the opportunity to see the dungeons firsthand. According to his sources, supposed heretics were being burned to death.[126] The thought outraged him, compelling him to say that "the English nation ought . . . 'to abolish the human sacrifices of the Inquisition;' and a censure is passed on our Government for their indifference to this subject."[127] The practice was finally abolished in 1812, soon after Buchanan's publication of his findings.[128]

Upon his return to Calcutta in March of 1807, Buchanan found that the college had been scaled down, and there was no longer a provost position for him to resume.[129] This prompted a return to England, but Buchanan determined to make stops all along the way to keep collecting information on mission work.[130] When he finally arrived home, his first stop was to go visit John Newton, only to learn that during his journey Newton had passed away.[131] Even so, the next few years found Buchanan continually promoting missions, Bible translation, and social justice. At one point, on a visit to Simeon at Cambridge, he preached, railing against both widow burning and the Inquisition, likening them both to the slave trade.[132]

Another trip, this time to the Middle East, was planned, so that Buchanan could continue to gather information about the state of global Christianity, but a stroke prevented him from ever returning to the mission field.[133] He died at only forty-nine years of age in 1815. Two years later, speaking of Buchanan, Charles Simeon told a friend:

> There seems to have been in him a certain dignity of character very uncommon in religious men. His independence, and generosity, and capacity to adapt himself to all persons of every station, yet accompanied with such a surprising simplicity of mind, cast an air of nobleness and majesty around him, that I have never met with in any other man. He was formed for great things both by nature and grace; and great things he lived to accomplish. As compared with pious ministers in general, he shines *velut inter ignes Luna minores*.[134] Many equal him in what we should call piety; but there is a luminousness and a grandeur about him that is very uncommon.[135]

Claudius Buchanan did shine; of that there is no doubt.

His wife, Mary Buchanan, also had no doubt in her mind about the person who had most shaped her husband to become the man he was. Though the two were married in India, and though she had never met John Newton, she felt compelled to send her deep appreciation:

> I have long wished to acknowledge the debt I owe you for your valuable works. They have been blessed to many, and I trust will also be blessed to me. But I believe I am still more indebted to you as the friend, father, and instructor of my beloved husband; as such, I must consider you as the instrument, under God, of my present happiness.[136]

Though it would be difficult to find a sweeter commendation of his legacy, Newton's global influence did not stop in India. Another missionary deeply indebted to him was Richard Johnson, the first chaplain to Australia. Many evangelicals in Britain had dreams of reaching the aboriginal peoples of New South Wales with the gospel, but Newton seemed to understand more than most of his fellow Englishmen many of the drawbacks of missionary colonialism. He joked that he preferred to send missionaries in on balloons, rather than with all the trappings of being part and parcel of a new British settlement.[137] But since colonialism was a reality in Botany Bay, Newton ensured that a chaplain would be sent to the new penal colony as well. Richard Johnson was hand-picked by Newton to be the lucky guy.

As Johnson's troubles seemed abundant and ongoing, so did Newton's encouragement; one letter after another carried Newton's prayers, empathy, and support.[138] Carving a new life into the wilds of untamed Australia proved to be an immense challenge to a group of transplanted Englishmen. Disease and death spread through the territory at an alarming rate. Though Johnson never had the occasion to make missionary outreach to the Aboriginal peoples his primary undertaking, he had more than ample opportunity to do prison ministry, visiting those who were poor, sick, starving, and dying. One person testified that had it not been for Johnson sharing his own food rations, he and others would have died during a famine.[139]

Before Johnson set sail, Newton helped raise 220 pounds,[140] part of which was designated for "kind offices to such of the convicts as might appear deserving" as well as for "the relief of the convicts."[141] One kind office that Johnson found himself doing was caring for orphans. Death was commonplace; once Johnson recounted losing sixty people in a month.[142] In addition to losing parents to death, many other children were simply deserted.[143] The result was a swelling population of children without parents, living in an underdeveloped society. It was a major social concern toward which Richard Johnson could not turn a blind eye. In the end, orphan care would be Johnson's final undertaking before health concerns prompted his return to England.[144]

Samuel Marsden, the second chaplain to be appointed in Australia and co-worker with Johnson, wrote,

> There are, I believe, upwards of eight hundred children in the Settlement. Some of these children were born on passage to this Country, others after the arrival of their parents. Their fathers, in general, are either sailors, soldiers or prisoners. The former quit the country with the respective ships they belong to; and the two latter have seldom either inclination or ability to provide for their children. In addition to these, some are orphans in the strictest sense, others relinquished by their unnatural mothers.[145]

Richard Johnson and Samuel Marsden began pleading for the government to step in and help. Both Newton and Wilberforce used their connections as well, and in 1800 the government acquiesced. Two orphan schools were opened, one housing sixty girls, and the other seventy-five boys.[146]

Johnson referred to his ministry in Australia as "my long and painful services fourteen years, as the first Chaplain appointed and sent to that distant infant Colony."[147] His own pain and misery was evident; the guy never seemed to catch a break. His house was ransacked.[148] He could not get a church building erected for years. When it finally did happen, somebody burned it down. He had paid for many of the costs out of his own pocket, and when he tried to reimburse the expenses, it took four more years to finally be approved.[149] Church services were interrupted by the rotation of the guards and other military movements. At times, his ministry and position were belittled by the colonial government.[150] It was a difficult post, no doubt.

Yet, when it was time for Johnson's return to England, the orphan school committee thanked him for "his attention and assiduity in the concerns of the orphans in this Colony," asked for his continued help by raising funds for the ministry back in England, and made plans for "rescuing nine hundred and fifty-eight children from the future misery" that was surely theirs.[151] It would seem that during his long voyage home, the comforting thought that 958 children would be relieved of misery must have been well worth some of his own.

Richard Johnson was not the only one of Newton's friends who had a soft spot in his heart for orphans. John Campbell also did, in no small part because at six years old he himself became one. That would account for why Campbell, a young man without any peace of mind concerning his own salvation,[152] was still so eager to minister to the orphans of his hometown, Edinburgh.[153] When he met John Newton in 1789, not only did he find a man with a kindred spirit, as well as a mentor, he also found the instrument God would use to bring him to a settled assurance regarding his eternal destiny. In time Campbell would say, "Mr. Newton I make my chief counsellor, almost indeed my only one in matters of great importance, and I always found him the best."[154]

When the two met, John Campbell was a businessman with a heart for ministry. He was a constant fountain of new ministry initiatives. First, he began to care for the poor and sick, frequently offering compassionate benevolence.[155] Eventually he started two societies for the sick and dying.[156] He also began a Sunday school for the poor children of Edinburgh, which soon turned into several. Before long, sixty of these schools were formed, one of which had four to five hundred kids enrolled.[157] Newton bemoaned the sad state of education among the youth of England, but praised Campbell, saying that "these evils are diminishing partly by the Sunday schools."[158]

When Campbell pursued formal ministerial training, Newton was always nearby, coaching the young man to focus his ministry on the central truths of the gospel.[159] This entrepreneur soon found his way into publishing, starting a tract society in Edinburgh, one of the first in Britain.[160] Newton's hymns, of course, were among the works he published; Newton returned the favor by writing the introduction for one of Campbell's projects.[161]

At the same time, Campbell was busy pioneering another initiative, this time to help prostitutes. He personally invited thirty or forty people to a meeting where he (like Thomas Scott) cast the vision to start a ministry where former prostitutes could get on their feet and be restored to the community. The Edinburgh Magdalen Society was such a success that he replicated the idea in Glasgow.[162] Both outfits were in operation forty years later when Campbell reminisced about the women "who had no way of extricating themselves from being real *outcasts* from society. . . . the erection of such an institution was the opening of one door of hope."[163] In addition to all of this, John Campbell had a fruitful prison ministry.[164]

The only logical reason one can assume that Campbell so desperately wanted to leave all of that behind in order to go to Africa is because of Newton's constant chattering about the place! In 1796, the Edinburgh missionary society was formed; Campbell became the director.[165] With all of Newton's passion for missions, one would think that he was always in favor of sending people out; that was not the case here. Twice Newton discouraged Campbell from taking a request to serve in India; in Newton's mind, Campbell was quite useful right where he was.[166] Newton cared enough about Campbell to give him honest feedback. Campbell was hurt, and discouraged for a time, but his passion for missions was never quenched.

Sierra Leone became the mission society's primary focus, rather than India,[167] and Campbell began to itinerate and preach more.[168] Though Campbell had been wounded by Newton, the relationship continued strong, and Campbell's influence continued to grow. Eventually he was itinerating four to five months a year,[169] even building a Tabernacle in Edinburgh that could hold ten thousand people.[170] Clearly, crowds were coming to listen to those preachers who were invited to fill the pulpit. When Campbell came under attack during construction, Newton reminded him,

> If you are about a good work, Satan will do all he can to discourage and hinder you; but he cannot break his chain, nor go beyond it. He cannot hurt us, unless we give him advantage by indulging unbelief or impatience.[171]

Yet, even with a thriving ministry at home, Africa was never far from Campbell's mind. He adamantly opposed slavery and longed to see the Sierra Leone experiment flourish.[172] After a conversation with Newton, Campbell wrote in his diary, "Speaking of the little success of the Sierra Leone settlement—'Wait,' said [Newton], 'an hundred years first. God is not often so quick with his works as men would have him to be."[173] But Campbell could not wait. His heart broke for the African continent; he had to do something.

If he could not go to Africa, then he would bring Africa home. Late in life, Campbell reflected, "Now, you will be able to see how all my future life, for nearly forty years, depended upon a single thought, whilst stepping out of bed, viz., to bring Africa to England."[174] In 1796, Campbell had conceived an idea, a "Seminary for Africans." Campbell's proposal was simple: to create a boarding school and bring twenty to thirty African children to England for a five-year period. During that time, Campbell would care for them, educate them, help them to know and follow Jesus, and then send them back as missionaries to their native land.[175]

Henry Thornton and William Wilberforce both liked the idea; undoubtedly, Campbell had access to both of them through Newton.[176] When the governor of Sierra Leone, Zachary Macaulay, made a visit to Scotland, he carried a letter of introduction to John Campbell in his hand from Newton "to procure more labourers to go with him into the black vineyard."[177] Campbell acquired the funding, Macaulay found willing participants, and in the end, twenty-four African children landed on the shores of England.[178] Newton had the opportunity to visit the children, even speaking to them in an African language he had learned years ago.[179] In the end, however, Macaulay apparently grew fond of the children himself, and could not bring himself to leave the children under Campbell's care.[180]

It must have been a joyful day for John Campbell when three African children finally became part of his congregation, and even more exciting for him over a decade later when his dream of traveling to Africa now came to pass.[181] He spent nearly two years visiting missionary stations across the continent, seeking out new mission opportunities, and traveling some three thousand miles, much of it on foot.[182] Five years later he did it again for another two-year stint.[183] One of his sad observations was the reality of Africans enslaving other Africans. Campbell's reflections sound very much like those of his mentor: "We have long treated black people in the same way, and ought to be considered savages by the Africans."[184] The echoes of Newton's *Thoughts Upon the African Slave Trade* ring loud and clear.

But perhaps the most striking thing about Campbell's last trip to Africa is his letter to a cousin, written at sea, on the return voyage. The man who was orphaned at six years old shared that he was now returning home with an African orphan named Paul.[185] Campbell stayed in Britain the rest of his life, but Africa was never far from his thoughts. In time, he published three books about Africa, one of which was a work of three volumes detailing his mission work on the continent.[186]

* * *

A dozen seemingly random people: A winsome child. A depressed recluse. An accomplished playwright. A divinity student. A heretic. A guy hoping to keep his job. A neighboring pastor. A proud teenager. A shoe cobbler. A traveling fiddler. A newlywed. A successful businessman. All of them knew John Newton.

With all of them, Newton became a genuine friend:

- sharing tales of the high seas with William Wilberforce from his boyhood;

- keeping vigil for William Cowper through dark seasons of depression;
- filling Hannah More's pockets with sermons after her discovery of new life;
- hosting Thomas Charles as a young ministry student during the summer holiday;
- enduring Thomas Scott's controversial jousting;
- assuring the young pastor, Charles Simeon, that his new congregation would not eat him alive;
- enjoying long theological conversations with William Bull over a good pipe;
- helping John Ryland Jr. navigate relationships with girls and his dad;
- advising William Carey to obey God rather than man;
- welcoming the vagrant, Claudius Buchanan, as he would his own son;
- vouching for Richard Johnson to take a post he probably was not prepared for;
- and even dissuading John Campbell from going overseas because of a belief that he was too valuable at home.

History attests to the authenticity of these friendships, how influential Newton was in each case, and incredibly, the pervasive thread of justice and compassion that weaves its way through the story of each of their lives and even ties them together. The overwhelming trend of Newton's friends, after spending time with him, is to tackle issues of mercy. It is striking. What are the odds?

- The child becomes a politician who leads the abolition campaign.
- The recluse emerges as a voice for the oppressed.
- The playwright turns into the leading female figure of the day for human rights and job training.
- The student becomes the Welsh educator.
- The heretic becomes the defender of prostitutes in London.

- The guy with a tenuous job creates jobs for others who share evangelical convictions and compassionate global concerns.
- The neighboring pastor starts training new pastors to help the poor in their midst.
- The teenager learns to send others out with gracious humility to serve the least of these.
- The shoe cobbler tackles the horror of widow-burning in India.
- The traveling fiddler opposes the Indian Inquisition.
- The newlywed pioneers prison ministry and orphan care in Australia.
- The businessman bleeds for orphans and Africa.

The compassionate trajectory of their lives is remarkably consistent.

Although friendships take work and require intentional effort, Newton's legacy reminds us that it is clearly worth the investment: No one man could effectively spend his life as a politician, poet, educator, chaplain to prostitutes, dean, president of two Bible colleges, and a missionary to three continents at the same time. No one person could tackle issues of slavery, poverty, illiteracy, prostitution, the caste system, widow-burning, the Inquisition, prison ministry, and orphan care with any kind of effectiveness in a single lifetime. It is impossible. Especially for a pastor with sermons to preach, couples to counsel, and meetings to attend.

And yet, John Newton appears to have had his hand in all of the above—to be sure, not always directly. Most of the time Newton was behind the scenes; the work was carried forward through this amazing cast of friends. Nevertheless, John Newton was a common denominator. Many of these folks had no interest in compassionate ministry prior to meeting him; several had not even come to a point of saving faith. Yet after becoming friends with John Newton, each one made unique and considerable contributions to the welfare of humanity. Was it coincidence? A dozen coincidences? Or did old John Newton hope and pray and work toward that end from day one?

I would wager that it was the latter.

What made John Newton such an effective catalyst for compassion, and what can we do to follow in his steps? Those are the questions to which we will turn next.

PART THREE

catalyst for compassion:
LESSONS FROM JOHN NEWTON

CHAPTER SIX

Pray and Preach

When a pastor scans the horizon, the scene is overwhelming: At this very moment, there are 40.3 million people who are victims of the modern day slave trade.[1] According to the U.S. Department of State, there are an estimated 600,000-800,000 men, women, and children trafficked across international borders annually,[2] with over a million children being exploited in the global commercial sex trade.[3] In America, even with abortion rates lower now than at anytime in the past forty years, 860,000 babies are still being aborted annually, or roughly 2,350 every day.[4] Among other travesties in the past decade, Yemen has taken a page from Boko Haram in Nigeria,[5] and The Lord's Resistance Army in Uganda, with no fewer than "842 verified cases" of recruiting child soldiers to do their bidding, sometimes no more than eleven years old.[6] The LRA, of course, for thirty years, forced tens of thousands of boys and girls into combat, often killing family, neighbors, and school teachers in the process. They put these children on the front lines because they are easy to replace by raiding schools or villages.

The Psalmist asks, "Who rises up for me against the wicked? Who stands up for me against evildoers?"[7] Any pastor with a compassionate heart and a desire to make a difference will wonder from time to time if what he is doing is really worthwhile. The problems seem too big, his resources too little, and his influence too meager. People in church argue about carpet colors while little girls are being kidnapped. Maybe he should just quit his job and go do something that matters. Or maybe he should readjust his priorities and spend the bulk of his time volunteering at the shelter for battered women or the local rescue mission.

Yet, if one can learn anything from John Newton, it is this: a pastor can have a far greater impact on issues of justice and compassion by being faithful in his post than by leaving his station to tackle any one particular injustice. One would be hard-pressed to name any person in all of history (aside from Jesus!) who accomplished more for the sake of the oppressed and downtrodden than William Wilberforce. Yet Wilberforce was only one of many men and women that John Newton loved, taught, and empowered in the regular course of his pastoral ministry. It would be wise for all pastors to stew on that; perhaps we should not be so quick to (a) throw up our hands in despair, (b) redefine our role, or (c) quit our jobs to pursue something "worthwhile."

In the stream of the Puritans before him, John Newton viewed the twin callings of Acts 6:4—prayer and preaching—as the two clear priorities of a pastor. When the Greek-speaking widows in the early church were being unintentionally overlooked in the daily distribution of food, a complaint arose. Yet instead of throwing themselves into this ministry of mercy, the apostles were quite clear about being faithful to carry out certain responsibilities with which they had been entrusted:

> And the twelve summoned the full number of the disciples and said, "It is not right that we should give up preaching the word of God to serve tables. Therefore, brothers, pick out from among you seven men of good repute, full of the Spirit and of wisdom, whom we will appoint to this duty. But we will devote ourselves to prayer and to the ministry of the word."[8]

Speaking for many in the Puritan stream from which Newton drank deeply,[9] Charles Bridges once wrote:

> Prayer is one half of our Ministry; and it gives to the other half all its power and success. It is the appointed medium of receiving spiritual

> communications for the instruction of our people. Those who walk most closely with God are most spiritually intelligent in "the secret of his covenant." Many can set their seal to Luther's testimony, that he often obtained more knowledge in a short time by prayer, than by many hours of laborious and accurate study. It will also strengthen our habitual engagedness of our hearts in our work, and our natural exercises and capacities for it. Living near to the fountain-head of influence, we shall be in the constant receipt of fresh supplies of light, support, and consolation—to assist us in our duties, to enable us for our difficulties, and to assure us of our present acceptance, and a suitable measure of ultimate success.[10]

At Olney, Newton had thriving prayer meetings several times a week, and counted those who prayed for him as his dearest friends.[11] The Tuesday evening prayer meeting had to be moved to a room that would hold 130 people,[12] every Sunday morning forty to fifty prayed for Newton before he preached,[13] and Sunday nights he gathered people to sing and pray. Moreover, he spent daily time in the Word and prayer, often recording his prayers in his journal.[14] Preaching was not far behind. It could be argued that while prayer was one half of Newton's ministry, preaching was the other. In addition to Sunday mornings, Newton preached to packed crowds during midweek services throughout his tenure at St. Mary Woolnoth in London.[15] Frankly, his preaching load would make most pastors today blush in embarrassment.

In a letter to a divinity student, Newton's understanding of this twofold calling of a pastor shines through:

> The chief means for attaining wisdom, and suitable gifts for the ministry, are the holy Scriptures, and prayer. The one is the fountain of living water, the other the bucket with which we are to draw. And I believe you will find, by observation, that the man who is most frequent and fervent in prayer, and most devoted to the word of God, will shine and flourish above his fellows.[16]

It would be a mistake to conclude, after reading about Newton's amazing impact in helping the poor, needy, and oppressed, that pastors should therefore rearrange their calendars or leave the pastorate altogether in order to follow in his steps. Quite the opposite would be true. Newton never left his primary calling as a pastor to effect change. "His chief way of working with people was to point them to the Lord Jesus Christ, the Fountain Head, for their direction."[17]

What better way to do that than to consistently pray for, pray with, and model prayer before those whom we hope to influence? Is there a better way to accomplish that goal than to faithfully and powerfully proclaim, week after week, the riches of God's grace in Jesus Christ? For every pastor who hopes and longs to follow in Newton's footsteps, prayer and the proclamation of the Word must remain central. It only makes sense.

E. M. Bounds once argued,

> Prayers must be red hot. It is the fervent prayer that is effectual and that availeth. Coldness of spirit hinders praying; prayer cannot live in a wintery atmosphere. Chilly surroundings freeze out petitioning; and dry up the springs of supplication. It takes fire to make prayers go. Warmth of soul creates an atmosphere favorable to prayer, because it is favorable to fervency. By flame, prayer ascends to heaven. Yet fire is not fuss, nor heat, noise. Heat is intensity—something that glows and burns. Heaven is a mighty poor market for ice.[18]

While E.M. Bounds makes a strong case for warm-hearted praying that would undoubtedly impact those who hear us cry out with such fervency, it should also be noted that the converse is equally true: not only does warmth of soul create an atmosphere that is favorable to prayer, but also prayer creates an atmosphere that warms the soul. It goes both ways. Prayer is the means that God uses to break our hearts for the things that break His. Yes, a warm heart makes prayer more fervent, more intense, even more enjoyable. But prayer also kneads the heart. And though the hearts around us may be like lumps of dough that are cold and stiff and hard at the beginning, the exercise of prayer cannot but create warmth and compassion that was not previously there.

Praying for and with those around you, in your flock, and under your care may actually be the most effective way to pass on your passion for the least of these. In fact, "prayer discipleship" has gained traction as a model for mentoring. "Prayer discipleship uses the Holy Spirit's power in community in conjunction with Scripture to transform and grow followers of Jesus. It is contextual, cross-cultural, reproducible, and cheap."[19] It brings people into the presence of God, to be dependent upon Him, where God can shape one's heart, and one can hear God's call. In prayer, God will melt the hearts of His people, make them soft in His gentle hands, and give them a burden to make right those situations, systems, and structures that are deeply wrong.

Pastor, begin to pray, and behold your people as they announce, "No child in our city should go to bed hungry; I want to do something about it," or "No one is fighting human trafficking in North Africa; that is why we are going there." Imagine the effect on Richard Johnson, visiting the Eclectic Society with John Newton, watching the men discuss various needs, and hearing them pray fervently for God's answer.[20] Only prayer could convince a man who was inclined to turn down the offer to go to Australia, to join with Isaiah before him, and say, "Here I am! Send me."[21]

Yet Newton would not have pastors stop at prayer. He would also encourage us to preach, because the pastor is the prophetic voice for God's people. The great Puritan William Perkins understood the pastorate in the tradition of Israel's prophets; Newton would lend his hearty agreement.[22] Preaching, as "one calling out in the wilderness," is his duty and mantle. While God gently softens and melts our hearts through prayer, preaching works like a fire or a hammer (Jer. 23:29).

A perusal of Newton's published sermons reveals that he clearly viewed himself in that prophetic light:

> But can we read the history of Israel, without remarking how strongly it resembles our own? . . . We have much reason to rejoice in the goodness of the Lord; but we have reason to temper our joy with trembling. . . . May our hearts be suitably affected, while I attempt a brief sketch of the abounding evils and abominations prevalent among us, which might justly provoke the Lord to sweep this land.[23]

Thus Newton spoke out against slavery before it was fashionable to do so, his prophetic voice stirring many to action. We would do well to follow his example.

If the church is to be a city on a hill, a beacon in a dark world, where others may see our good works and glorify our Father in heaven, then the pastor as preacher fulfills a unique and strategic role within the Body of Christ that he should never abdicate. It does not necessarily require any essential change in his preaching, nor does it require special worship services to bring attention to certain injustices. That may be the case; there could be times when a pastor should utilize a special occasion to call for a compassionate response to a particular need. Newton repeatedly did this. Yet in truth, a regular practice of systematic exposition of the Word provides ample opportunity for a pastor to serve as the prophetic voice for God's people. How is it possible to preach through Proverbs, Amos, Luke, or Acts, and not deal with issues of justice and compassion?

Contrary to many popular opinions today, Newton would remind us that preaching is not wasted effort, or an ineffective use of our time. Rather, the call to preach is a gift that should be treasured and has the potential to shake nations. It would take a dull student of history to deny that it shook England in Newton's day.

CHAPTER SEVEN

Love Others

BEFRIEND ALL

How did Newton have such a great impact on issues of justice and compassion? The answer is deceptively simple: John Newton loved people. Everyone, in fact.

One would search in vain to find a particular type of person that John Newton singled out in order to befriend and influence. This is in stark contrast to many leaders of recent years. Bill Bright, for example, the founder of Campus Crusade for Christ International, said of his own ministry, "the vision was gigantic, but the strategy was simple: reach the college campuses for Christ, and you will reach tomorrow's men and women of influence in all society."[1] Bright believed that by reaching college students, he could therefore reach the entire world. But Newton did not seem to think in that way. There was no "Saddleback Sam"[2] or "Unchurched Harry & Mary"[3] that captured Newton's imagination. It would seem that he never felt beholden to go after future movers and shakers. Sure, he befriended many promising young leaders, as anyone in ministry does, but he certainly never limited his contact to people in that category. Unlike other wonderful leaders in the history of the church, John Newton did not have a particular demographic in mind.

He seemed to love and genuinely befriend all who crossed his path. For instance, upon his death, over a hundred letters between Newton and his household servants were extant.[4] He spoke of his servants frequently, treating them like family, and even included details about their health in his correspondence with others.[5]

It would be difficult to come up with a more eclectic bunch of friends. Spending time—lots of time—with a suicidal person like William Cowper would be discouraged by church-growth experts. Let's face it: from a strategic ministry standpoint, William Cowper was a time-consuming emotional drain. Was the best thing for Newton's ministry to welcome Cowper into his home to live with John and Mary? Not likely, at least by today's standards. As one church planting expert puts it,

> New churches attract all kinds of troubled people who want the care of an idealistic, energetic, people-loving, people-seeking church planter. As a result, the planter can get overwhelmed ministering to these troubled people. As hard as it is, the church planter should focus on people who seem likely to become reproducing leaders and on those who are able to minister to others.[6]

Though this is in reference to church planting, it is typical ministry parlance.

Yet this type of counsel did not seem to guide the life and ministry of Newton, who befriended people of all ages, backgrounds, and theology. Newton could say of Cowper, "Besides the submission I owe to the Lord, I think I can hardly do or suffer too much for such a friend."[7] Certainly, there were relationships that he sustained over the years that went nowhere, but it is hard to argue against the end result of his all-are-welcome-to-my-friendship approach. History records the outcome: Newton befriended people. They changed the world.

Age did not matter. The eleven-year-old William Wilberforce is a prime example. This kid did not attend Newton's church, did not live in

Newton's neighborhood, and had a mother who really did not approve of Newton in the first place. Befriending little Wilber was hardly a strategic decision. Even so, the boy delighted Newton; the old sea captain could not pass up an opportunity to tell his stories to a child who so loved to hear them.

Background did not matter. Some of Newton's friends came from among the elite of society, such as Hannah More. Others had money, like the Thornton family. A few were cut out for great things, like Charles Simeon. Newton loved them all. Yet others were not so spectacular, such as Claudius Buchanan, who was little more than a homeless runaway when the two met. The fact that Buchanan had no money and no future did nothing to dissuade Newton from welcoming the wanderer in, and loving him as he would his own son.

Even theological differences did not choke out the possibility of authentic friendship. This is especially poignant in an age where the circles that pastors are willing to run in seem to grow smaller and smaller. The obvious example in Newton's life is the heretic Thomas Scott, with whom Newton entered into a lengthy correspondence. How many evangelical pastors today would do the same with an extremely liberal pastor even of our own denomination?

But perhaps even more instructive is how Newton befriended other evangelical believers of different stripes as friends of the dearest order. If William Bull had been "too independent" for Newton's taste, there would have never been the establishment of a Bible school to train ministers at Newport Pagnell. If John Ryland, Jr. had been "too Baptist" or "too Calvinistic" for Newton, Newton would have had no influence on Bristol Academy. Even more curious is the question of whether the Baptist Missionary Society would have been born if the hyper-Calvinism of the day had prevailed.

Yet Newton bridged those age, background, and theological gaps through true friendship.

This is good news for the typical pastor who does not have the luxury to decide that he will only invest his time in the best and brightest.

Most of us minister among those who are pockmarked with sin, who struggle with deep doubts and deeper wounds, who walk through life with limps and warts. Perhaps it is time for us to love the people God has put before us—all of them—becoming more like the One we follow, the One who was known as a friend of sinners.

DON'T USE THEM

Not only was John Newton remarkable in the way that he seemed to befriend all who crossed his path, he also avoided the all-too-common pastoral tendency to use people. Frankly, he did not gain much from the majority of the friendships recounted in these pages; if he gained anything, it was typically a headache! Of the dozen friendships explored here, none of them stayed in his congregation to beef up his attendance or giving numbers. When the relationships were being formed, few were in a position to advance Newton's personal agenda or social standing. Even when some of these people had risen to a degree of notoriety, John Newton remained a safe friend.

Newton did not abuse these gifts of grace for his own ends; this is clear by the way his friends cherished the relationship. There was no question in the back of anyone's mind: "Is he my friend because he wants to get something from me?" William Bull spoke for many when he wrote to Newton, "It refreshes me to feel how warm a place I have in your heart. Sometimes I think nobody loves me, and it makes me very low. But I know you do, and I am sure Jonathan did not love David more than I do you."[8]

Unfortunately, using people is a plague on the church today that Newton somehow seemed to avoid. We are not even bashful about this when introducing people to one another: "I want you to meet So-and-so. He will be a great resource for you in this project that you are doing." We not only use other people; we expect to be used, and feel as though we have little value if we are not! We do not want to be a friend; we want to be a resource. Somehow, we forget that all people are created in the *Imago Dei*, possessing value not for what they do, but for who they are.[9]

Though your parishioners may want to be useful to you, what they need is friendship with you. It has been stated that "Friendship is a much underestimated aspect of spirituality. It's every bit as significant as prayer and fasting."[10] This is a truth that John Newton knew well. However, a quick look around the church scene today reveals that this is not the norm. Excellence trumps relationship. Progress trumps friendship. Programs trump people, and achieving goals trumps achieving intimacy. And while "Hospital calls, home visits and time spent with parishioners are all acts of friendship,"[11] these pastoral responsibilities often are turned into something else. "Pastoral calling whose motivation is church growth—visiting to 'sell' the church—isn't friendship. It's peddling."[12]

Too often the church has become a place to peddle, and pastors have been some of the worst culprits. While Newton longed to see people come to faith, and join his church, and link arms in bringing about justice and mercy, he could never be labeled a "peddler." People can spot a peddler a mile away. No, his friends knew that what Newton got out of their friendship was, well, them.

I wonder if the same could be said of me?

Or you?

SPOT STRATEGIC MOMENTS

What made John Newton particularly influential went well beyond his willingness to be a genuine friend to any and all. He had a unique and undeniable knack of recognizing significant moments in the lives of others, and an ability to bolster them at just the right time. It is uncanny how Newton seemed to be right at the side of almost every one of our dozen case studies whenever a life-changing decision was on the line. Many times, the persons concerned did not even recognize the significance of the moment. It appears, however, that Newton intuitively did.

Consider the evidence: When William Carey did not know what to do about India, Newton was there. Carey felt called to go, but also faced the daunting reality of prohibitions against it. Newton reminded Carey that if God had a work for him there, the gates of hell would not prevail against it. Carey went, and the rest is history.

When Thomas Scott was spiritually searching, Newton was ready to engage him. Again, when it was time to get into a new parish, Newton helped him land the job at Olney. Not surprisingly, it was Newton who put Scott's name in the hat for the job at Lock Hospital, which would become his life's work.

When John Ryland, Jr. was forming his theological convictions as a teenager, Newton was there. He was there when Ryland had conflict with his father, when he moved to Bristol to take over the seminary, and when Ryland lost his wife. In fact, when Newton heard that she had passed away, he made time to write a letter even though he was about to go preach that morning: "You have received a wound, but faithful is the Friend who has wounded you."[13] That letter could not wait until the worship service was over.

The first time Hannah More visited Newton's church, afterwards, he sat with her an hour to encourage her in the faith. While Claudius Buchanan was sick for the first eighteen months in his new ministry in India, discouraged that he was making no impact, he told Newton, "You are the only person who has written to me regularly since I left England." [14] When Thomas Charles was a divinity student, when William Cowper was depressed, when Charles Simeon was starting out in a hostile parish, when William Bull was starting a Bible school, and when William Wilberforce was about to quit politics, John Newton just happened to be there. He could spot a significant moment a mile away, and he made it his aim to bolster faith and strengthen hands in just those kinds of situations.

It may not be possible that everyone can be as intuitive as Newton was in this regard. Even so, the things that made Newton so sensitive to these kinds of moments in the lives of others can be ours. First of all, he prayed for his friends. He told them so, and in his letters we find prayers to God scattered throughout. It is conceivable that part of the reason Newton was able to spot significant crossroads so readily is because he was in constant communion with One who possesses exhaustive foreknowledge! Time and again, when there was a turning point in a person's life, Newton brought them back to the truth of Scripture. When all seemed lost, or resources were too small, or the task was too big, Newton was there with just the right words.

His example is convicting. Many pastors are guilty of only thinking about the people they minister to when they are sitting down together over a cup of coffee. Once the appointment is over, that person is out of mind. Yet even that may be a stretch. Too often I have seen pastors checking email, answering calls, and texting while some poor person is trying to spill their guts. We might as well hang a sign on our office wall, stating the obvious, "Here's a quarter. Call someone who cares."

Newton was so good at spotting these strategic moments, in part, because, unlike many of us, he spent time thinking about his friends when he was not even with them. Wilberforce had the assurance that he received a "double portion" of Newton's thoughts and prayers. There is no way most of the friendships recorded here could have been sustained if it were not for Newton taking time to reflect on another's situation, and initiating with them through letter writing. When we pastors are so caught up with our own troubles, so focused on ourselves, it is nigh impossible to bolster others at just the right instant.

It takes a selfless soul, a real shepherd, to care about the needs of others more than his own. It takes a degree of self-forgetfulness to be the kind of leader who can see where grace is sprouting in someone else's soul, see the storm clouds rising, and be there to say:

> The Lord has given you a heart to serve him, and he will stand by you. The sailors have a saying, that if it was always fine weather the old women would go to sea; but the skill of the mariner is seen in the storm. Trust in your pilot, and manage your sails, and all will be well.[15]

There are people in your ministry who need just that—a friend to bolster their weak faith and trembling knees. It could be a turning point of epic proportion in their lives. But will you see it? Only if you heed Paul's words: "in humility count others more significant than yourselves. Let each of you look not only to his own interests, but also to the interests of others."[16]

OVER THE LONG HAUL

Though Newton reasserted his commitment to friendship at particular strategic moments in the lives of others, perhaps even more remarkable is the longevity of these relationships. The average length of the twelve friendships studied is over twenty-five years! Even William Carey and John Newton, who barely knew each other when Carey left for India, were still corresponding almost ten years later. To my knowledge, the only one who quit corresponding with Newton was Richard Johnson, and that, after fifteen years. Eventually Newton became so old and blind and frail that he quit writing letters. Yet, even then, old friends like William Bull and John Campbell came to visit to the very end.

It is ironic that we live in a period of history where social media has taken center stage. People we have not seen since high school take pictures of food and post it so that we can know what kind of bagel they ate for breakfast. Yet, despite all of the ways to connect, despite the ease of travel and convenience of communication, the truth remains that sustained friendship is a rare bird indeed. We tend to lose touch with each other, despite how many "friends" we claim to have on Facebook.

Pastors, especially, have a lot of people with whom they need to connect. The relational drain makes it a challenge to keep other friendships up, especially when we have strong friendships with a few whom we see often and minister alongside. Honestly, it is even difficult to maintain close relationships with those who are dearest to us, let alone people who live far away and do not, in any direct way, help to advance our church's ministry. How did Newton do it?

One could contend that Newton's situation was different, allowing extra time that a pastor today simply does not have, but any way that you slice it, that argument does not hold water. The fact of the matter is, Newton was busy just like we are. He had a wife and two adopted daughters. He pastored a growing church. He preached all over. He had numerous people coming to him for counsel. He had masses of correspondence to keep up. He led meetings with other pastors, sponsored new initiatives for outreach and mission, and served the poor in his local community. John Newton was a busy guy.

How did he sustain so many friendships over the long haul? The only satisfying answer is that Newton intentionally and deliberately carved out time for friendship.

> Many people perceive friendship to be a spontaneous, serendipitous, and surprising experience that just happens to us. Nothing could be further from the truth! Deep and lasting friendships require sensitive and thoughtful reflection, creative planning, and intentional actions to thrive.[17]

Newton worked at it. For instance, he resolved to write to Wilberforce at least four times a year (his "quarterly payment") to encourage him, regardless of how often the two were able to see one another:

> I must not forget my promise of waiting upon you quarterly, with a token of my respect and love, as long as I am able. Indeed for some time past I have thought, Perhaps this may be the last letter I shall write to Mr Wilberforce; and my reason for thinking so, should strike me more forcibly every returning quarter. For now at least (though my health continues firm) I may well account myself an Old Man.[18]

Though Newton always thought he was on the verge of death, he carried on for many more years, continually making friendship a priority. He wrote friends when they did not write back. He initiated, because he honestly cared. As a result, people demonstrated unwavering loyalty to John Newton because they had received the same from him.

Imagine being the recipient of a typical note from Newton:

> how probable is it at my time of life, that every letter I write may be my last. If I thought this would prove so, I should almost fill it with expressions of kindness and love, and in trying to tell you how greatly I have prized and do still prize your friendship.[19]

How would you feel about such a man?

Perhaps you would feel as William Bull did, when he wrote to an elderly Newton, after receiving what was likely the last note from his dear friend:

> I think of you daily, with the most sincere affection and love. . . . Many pleasant interviews have we enjoyed in the house of our pilgrimage, but there is one interview yet to come, better than them all together. . . . I must beg, my very dear sir, your acceptance of my best thanks for a thousand kindnesses bestowed on me all your days.[20]

There is a clear connection between Newton's love and his influence. He loved people, regardless of where they came from, how old they were, or what theological bent they had. He could not resist the possibility of making a new friend. He loved them as people, not as resources, not as something to be used, but because of the inherent value of relationship. He thought about them while they were apart, prayed for them when they struggled, and stood by them when times were tough. He was there during the most critical of moments. And even when others were not consistent in making the friendship a priority, John Newton was. Once he was a friend, he was a friend for life.

What many of us fail to realize is, when you love people like that, they are more than willing to hear anything that you may have to say. In fact, as was the case with Newton, they may very well hang on your every word.

CHAPTER EIGHT

Teach Others

AMAZING GRACE

John Newton was a teacher of the best kind: he modeled what he taught. He wrote about justice, preached on it, and highlighted acts of oppression to numerous people on numerous occasions. But even more, "the life of the speaker was congruent with his message."[1] Acts of compassion and justice were routine in his own life, as anyone around him could see.

Yet the most compelling aspect of Newton's teaching centers on the grace of God found in Christ's cross. To spend time with Newton was to hear him recount the story of God's grace in his life again and again; he never wearied of telling that old, old story. When all seemed lost, Jesus saved him from the coast of Africa.

Consider the effect of repeating your testimony of God's amazing grace to a young friend every time you interact. As Timothy Keller notes, "It takes an experience of beauty to knock us out of our self-centeredness and induce us to become just."[2] Newton was a brilliant painter, using his life as a canvas to portray the beauty of God's grace to his friends time and again. Not only does that gospel-cadence increase our affection and adoration towards a kind and loving Savior; it also melts our hearts for those around us. As Wilberforce learned, "this grace can no where be cultivated with more advantage than at the foot of the cross."[3]

Newton put it this way in one of his sermons:

> We are by nature attached to worldly goods, and wholly influenced by selfish principles. But faith in Jesus communicates new motives, views, and aims, to the soul: it teaches us to have our treasure in heaven; to sit loose to the world; to be satisfied with that station and competence which Divine Providence has allotted us; and to love our neighbours as ourselves, because they are our fellow-sinners, and are capable of being called to a participation with us in the honourable relation and privilege of the children of God. Upon these principles the practice of justice is attainable, but upon no other; for though there are many characters honourable and blameless in the outward concerns of life, and in the judgment of men, there is no person upon earth who does or can love or practise justice in its full extent, till he has received the Spirit of Christ, and lives upon him by faith, for wisdom and strength from day to day.[4]

According to Newton, authentic justice-seeking is unattainable apart from faith in Jesus and the new birth. Many evangelicals today minimize the centrality of the gospel as though it is unrelated to doing justice and loving mercy. That was not the case for Newton or his crew. "Evangelical social action was above all—paradoxically—an outworking of the belief that we are saved by faith."[5]

Newton's protégé, William Wilberforce, clearly got the message:

> Our hearts become tender while we contemplate this signal act of loving-kindness. We grow desirous of imitating what we cannot but admire. A vigorous principle of enlarged and active charity springs up within us; and we go forth with alacrity, desirous of treading in the steps of our blessed Master, and of manifesting our gratitude for his unmerited goodness, by bearing each other's burthens [*sic*], and abounding in the disinterested labours of benevolence.[6]

The cross was central in all of Newton's teaching. He did not promulgate morality; he taught the gospel. To be even more specific, John Newton's message was the application of the gospel in his own life.

The importance of this cannot be overstated. In our desire to teach those around us and pass on a vision for a kind of ministry that brings hope and healing, there must be more than intellectual assent that this type of ministry is legitimate. The motivation must go deeper than pity can reach. Until our depravity is truly appreciated and God's gracious condescension to rescue us takes hold deep within us, mercy ministry will never thrive. Without the gospel, motivations remain hollow, allowing excuses to creep in. As Newton argued, "there is no person upon earth who does or can love or practise justice in its full extent" without a love for the gospel.

Robert Murray M'Cheyne, a Scottish pastor from the early part of the nineteenth century, captures the sentiment well:

> Now, dear Christians, some of you pray night and day to be branches of the true Vine; you pray to be made all over in the image of Christ. If so, you must be like him in giving. . . . "Though he was rich, yet for our sakes he became poor." . . . Objection 1. "My money is my own." Answer: Christ might have said, "My blood is my own, my life is my own" . . . then where should we have been? Objection 2. "The poor are undeserving." Answer: Christ might have said, "They are wicked rebels . . . shall I lay down my life for these? I will give to the good angels." But no, he left the ninety-nine, and came after the lost. He gave his blood for the undeserving. Objection 3. "The poor may abuse it." Answer: Christ might have said the same; yea, with far greater truth. Christ knew that thousands would trample his blood under their feet; that most would despise it; that many would make it an excuse for sinning more; yet he gave his own blood. Oh, my dear Christians! If you would be like Christ, give much, give often, give freely, to the vile and poor, the thankless and the undeserving. Christ is glorious and happy and so will you be. It is not your money I want, but your happiness. Remember his own word, "It is more blessed to give than to receive."[7]

Compassionate ministry thrives where grace is most cherished and adored. Newton reminds us that the gospel must be central and God's glory our chief end.

FAITHFUL PRESENCE

After Nebuchadnezzar took some three thousand Hebrews captive in the first of three deportations, God sent the people a clear message through the prophet Jeremiah:

> Build houses and live in them; plant gardens and eat their produce. Take wives and have sons and daughters; take wives for your sons, and give your daughters in marriage, that they may bear sons and daughters; multiply there, and do not decrease. But seek the welfare of the city where I have sent you into exile, and pray to the Lord on its behalf, for in its welfare you will find your welfare.[8]

James Davison Hunter's landmark book, *To Change the World: The Irony, Tragedy, and Possibility of Christianity in the Late Modern World*, has issued a similar call in our day, the call for "Christians to enact the shalom of God in the circumstances in which God has placed them and to actively seek it on behalf of others."[9] This is the essence of what he calls "faithful presence."[10] Hunter understands that

> faithful presence in our spheres of influence does not imply passive conformity to the established structures. Rather, within the dialectic between affirmation and antithesis, faithful presence means a constructive resistance that seeks new patterns of social organization that challenge, undermine, and otherwise diminish oppression, injustice, enmity, and corruption and, in turn, encourage harmony, fruitfulness and abundance, wholeness, beauty, joy, security, and well-being. In the normal course of social life, the challenge and alternative that faithful presence entails is not so much a direct opposition through a contest of power but, as Miraslov Volf puts it, a "bursting out" of an alternative within the proper space of the old.[11]

Though John Newton never had the opportunity to read Hunter's book, he clearly had read Jeremiah's, and this concept of faithful presence "within every sphere of human activity"[12] was certainly on Newton's radar. As has been observed before, the Evangelical Revival under the leadership of Whitefield and the Wesleys initially did not bring reform to England because, by and large, it had not yet taken root among the upper strata of society.[13] It was not until the second generation of leaders such as Newton and Cowper, and especially the third generation, including Wilberforce and Simeon, that evangelical sentiments worked their way, like leaven, through the whole lump. Newton's emphatic persistence in encouraging people to leverage their gifts for the kingdom within their own spheres of influence was a major factor as to why. As has been previously argued, Newton was not necessarily going after the best and the brightest. He befriended all whom God put in his path, enabling him to have influence across various strata of society.

Whatever station in life a person happened to occupy was the sphere where Newton taught them to exercise their influence. For instance, John Campbell was a good businessman with an effective ministry. Newton did not want him to abandon that in order to pursue full-time missions. His faithful presence in the business world was invaluable; in fact, it was those connections that enabled Campbell to get his Magdalen societies off the ground.[14] Without that network, one of Campbell's ministry outlets would have been severely hampered.

In the same way, Newton viewed Cowper's original literary work to be of significant value.

> His teaching had the effect of carrying the spirit of poetry into thousands of middle-class and poor homes which it had not previously entered. On the other hand, his poetry spread the doctrines and . . . the fuller implications of Evangelicalism among the sophisticated who could perhaps have been reached in no other way. . . . All the new spiritual and ethical values implicit in Evangelicalism—the hatred of slavery, oppression, and cruelty, the love of Nature and of simple domestic joys, the deeper regard for women, children, the poor, and animals—found in him their first clear voice.[15]

No wonder Newton kept urging Cowper to write.

Yet perhaps the clearest example of Newton's commitment to faithful presence is found in his interactions with Wilberforce. When Wilberforce was poised to leave politics to become a pastor, Newton would have none of that! Later, Wilberforce wrote, "Mr. Newton, in the interviews I had with him, advised me to avoid at present making many religious acquaintances. . . to keep up my connection with Pitt, and to continue in Parliament."[16]

Newton taught Wilberforce what faithful presence looks like,[17] reminded him regularly that God raised him up "to be a blessing to the public,"[18] told him that many people who were inaccessible to him were within Wilberforce's reach,[19] and encouraged him that "the present therefore is *our* opportunity. . . of employing our influence to the alleviation of misery. In this view life is truly valuable."[20]

In time, Wilberforce came to appreciate the truth in all of this, even seeing God's providential care in taking him from his aunt when he was just a child:

> How eventful a life has mine been, and how visibly I can trace the hand of God leading me by ways which I knew not! I think I have never before remarked, that my mother's taking me from my uncle's when about twelve or thirteen and then completely a methodist, has probably been the means of my being connected with political men and becoming useful in life.[21]

Wilberforce realized that if he had become labeled a Methodist early on, he would have never had the opportunity to be a faithful presence in politics.

Jesus taught us to be in the world, but not of it. Until, as Newton did, we begin teaching our people the call to faithful presence, to bring God's shalom to our cities and neighborhoods, our churches will be filled with folks who are of the world but not in it. Until we begin teaching that God has a greater purpose for our lives than showing up on Sundays, until we demonstrate that our churches exist for more than ourselves, our ministries will have little real influence in the world around us. And until we help people to see that Christ reigns over all and vocation is a primary avenue by which we glorify our Father in heaven, many wonderful people will go through life without seeing God's providential hand and eternal purpose in placing us in our particular post. That would be a monumental tragedy.

MULTIPLY

John Newton jotted a note to himself on Sunday evening, July 29, 1764: "A good deal of company at home, for I have desired those who come from far to dine with me on the Sunday. I trust that the Lord will enable me to keep up this custom."[22] People who had traveled far to come and worship were welcome to join his family after church for lunch. Those words were penned during his first year in the pastorate; this simple gesture began a practice that would come to shape the entire course of Newton's future ministry. He invited people into his home and his life. He surrounded himself with people—faithful people—who would go on to teach others also, not unlike his Master.

Robert Coleman's instant classic, *The Master Plan of Evangelism*, notes how Jesus went about it:

> It all started by Jesus calling a few men to follow him. This revealed immediately the direction his evangelistic strategy would take. His concern was not with programs to reach the multitudes, but with men whom the multitudes would follow. Remarkable as it may seem, Jesus started to gather these men before he ever organized an evangelistic campaign or even preached a sermon in public. Men were to be his method of winning the world to God.[23]
>
> Having called his men, Jesus made a practice of being with them. This was the essence of his training program—just letting his disciples follow him. . . . Amazing as it may seem, all Jesus did to teach these men his way was to draw them close to himself. He was his own school and curriculum.[24]

John Newton taught people in a similar way. His disciples, like those of Jesus, were around him all the time—at church, in the community, and in his home. He multiplied his life into others and at the same time modeled the way of multiplication for them. It was not always convenient, but discipleship never is: "In company from morning till nearly night, and I see not how to avoid it."[25] "I find some inconvenience from such an incessant round of company."[26]

> I have such a levee of land visitors and inquiries every morning, that I meet with many interruptions in writing. It is pleasing to be beloved, and doubly pleasing to me to know that the favour the Lord has given me here is chiefly for the gospel's sake.[27]

"We are now free from company for the first time since Jan 20th. But the Lord has done great things under our roof. Oh, that everyone whom He sends in His providence to us may receive a blessing amongst us."[28]

Newton spent copious amounts of time with those he befriended. This was Newton's primary way of teaching. Even more, as Coleman states, people were "his method of winning the world."

Newton is not remembered for his powerful preaching campaigns.[29] He was no George Whitefield, keeping crowds spellbound by his oratory skill.[30] In fact, some felt that Newton was not a great preacher because he had a poor voice, lacked eloquence, and often found himself in the pulpit ill-prepared. [31] Nor is he remembered for his theological contribution. Newton was no Jonathan Edwards, locking himself into his study for thirteen hours at a time, contemplating the *End For Which God Created the World.*[32] His letters and writings, though thoroughly Christ-exalting, were typically homespun and down-to-earth. Finally, he had none of the organizational skill of John Wesley, herding multitudes of people into class and society meetings to ensure that accountability, discipline, and growth happened amongst large numbers.[33] No, Newton was not the leader of countless throngs; he was the pastor of two thriving, but not massive, churches.

J. I. Packer writes, "Whitefield was flamboyant, Wesley was masterful, Newton was unobtrusive. Yet Newton was indubitably one of the three greatest eighteenth-century evangelical leaders." [34] John Newton's influence appears to be completely disproportionate to his leadership skill. In my estimation, there is only one way to account for it: Newton multiplied himself. He invested deeply in friendships, into people who would, over time, also be amazed by God's grace, also feel the call to be a faithful presence, and who would, in turn, also teach others. As Robert Coleman puts it, "A few people so dedicated in time will shake the world for God. Victory is never won by the multitudes."[35]

CHAPTER NINE

Empower Others

FRIENDSHIP DENSITY

People who have been well loved and well taught become world-changers once they have been empowered. Newton knew this and actively sought different ways to do so, the first being to connect his friends to one another. Part of John Newton's brilliance as a catalyst for compassion was his intuitive appreciation of a concept now known as "friendship density":

> Friendship density refers to how tightly related the friends in an individual's web of relationships are to one another. If you have a dense friendship circle, this denotes that there are many cross relationships; people in your circles are friends with one another as well as with you. . . . Generally speaking, *discipleship thrives in a group that exhibits high friendship density and strong ties.*"[1]

Discipleship did indeed thrive as most of Newton's friends came under his spell, finding themselves more than ready to pour out their lives for the sake of the poor and oppressed.

Newton was a master networker, time and again creating space for his friends to become friends with one another. In the hard work of justice and compassionate ministry, this network empowered each individual to stay the course, even when it proved to be terribly difficult and overwhelmingly discouraging. "Journeying into places of suffering, abuse, and abandonment takes its toll, but together with friends, we find a way forward, stumbling into the open arms of a loving God."[2] Even after Newton had passed away, these friendships remained, pressing each individual forward in their shared concern for the least of these.

The number of connections can be dizzying.

It was through Newton that Thomas Scott and William Wilberforce got to know one another. In fact, Scott became another mentor to Wilberforce; the latter began to attend to Scott's preaching.[3] When Scott himself was still young in the faith, Newton repeatedly brought him along to breakfast with himself and his good friend, William Bull. Before Scott knew it, he was being welcomed into a fraternity of evangelical pastors.[4]

Bull, an independent, was outside of the Anglican fellowship and had no access to their friendship—or finances—until he became friends with John Newton. Newton introduced him to John Thornton, who financed the academy over which Bull presided until Bull's death twenty-seven years later.[5] It was through Newton that Bull knew Wilberforce and came to know of Richard Johnson's work in Botany Bay.[6] It was also through his connection with Newton that Bull came to know William Cowper. The two met twice a month after Newton's introduction.[7]

As would be expected, when Thomas Charles spent the summer with Newton as a student, the holiday would not be complete without a trip to visit William Bull.[8] That same summer Charles was also introduced to Thomas Scott, who became a lifelong friend and supporter of Charles' work. In a letter containing financial support for the charity schools, Scott wrote, "Had I more in my power I should have been glad; but this will testify my sincere love and affection to you, and to the cause you are engaged in."[9] Years later, these two men, now with the help of William Wilberforce, in their pursuit of providing Welsh Bibles to people without one, would help start the British and Foreign Bible Society together.[10]

When revival broke out in Wales, John Campbell wanted to know more details. Newton encouraged him to write Thomas Charles a letter to find out.[11] He did. When Campbell shared the reports from Wales with his Scottish friends, flames of spiritual awakening began to spread in Scotland too.[12]

Hannah More, who had been so dramatically changed after reading Newton's *Cardiphonia,* was already involved in the abolition movement when she was encouraged by Wilberforce to start her schools.

After Claudius Buchanan came to faith, Newton sent him to study at Cambridge under Charles Simeon. The two would later pass through Cowslip Green; unfortunately, Hannah More was out of town, and so the two visited with the other More sisters.[13] Simeon, of course, was also part of the Eclectic Society that had sent Richard Johnson to Australia a decade before.

After Buchanan moved to India, his initial impression of William Carey was not terribly positive.[14] Newton encouraged him not to be quick to dismiss Carey.[15] Buchanan apparently listened; as time progressed, we find the two men working together.[16] Even more, John Ryland Jr., who had helped establish the agency that sent Carey, corresponded with Newton over the work in India on multiple occasions.[17] In fact, when Ryland was afraid that perhaps Carey had died in India, Newton told Ryland that he had two letters from Buchanan that did not mention Carey's death; it was probably only a rumor.[18]

Despite the fact that these dozen people were different ages, from different denominations, were involved in different ministries, and lived in different places, the web of connections amongst this group is nearly impossible to untangle! They all seem to be connected to one another somehow, generally through a point of contact with John Newton. It almost seems that James Davison Hunter has Newton and his circle in mind when he writes,

> Against this great-man view of history and culture, I would argue (along with many others) that *the key actor in history is not individual genius but rather the network* and the new institutions that are created out of those networks. And the more 'dense' the network—that is, the more active and interactive the network—the more influential it could be. This is where the stuff of culture and cultural change is produced.[19]

John Newton empowered his friends with the gift of friendship to one another. To a pastor without the time or energy to tackle the ills of the world all by himself, this is indeed good news. Creating space for those around us to develop friendships only serves to advance our cause. Newton did this regularly by opening up his home as a place where his friends could befriend each other.

Pastors who deem it a good use of their time to connect like-minded individuals may very well advance the kingdom more than they realize. However, it must be noted, the power of networking increases in direct proportion to the depth of the relationship the networker enjoys with the two people he is introducing to one another. (Remember, people are not resources!) If those relationships are shallow, the new connection is generally a shallow one as well. On the other hand, when deep mutual friends of the same person finally have the opportunity to meet and get to know one another, both are truly empowered: iron sharpens iron, creative new ideas and initiatives take place, camaraderie develops, and built-in support structures are established for those seasons when ministry is tough, fruit is meager, and change is slow.

Hunter continues,

> In all of this, the church—local parishes, consortiums of congregations, and denominational bodies, among others—is of central importance here. As the locus of worship and formation it should not only be the catalyst for the active cultivation of these networks but also the connective tissue among overlapping networks. The church discovers in this a vital manifestation of its call to "go into all the world proclaiming the good news."[20]

CHAMPION THE WORK

> Then Ordinary heard a voice call his name. When he turned to see who it was, he recognized a Somebody. It was Champion, an old friend from Familiar who used to be a Nobody. "Champion!" exclaimed Ordinary. "What are you doing here?" Champion sat down on the rock beside him. "When I heard you had become a Dreamer, I just *had* to come," he said. "I knew you'd need help."[21]

Everybody needs a Champion.

It takes faith and courage, not to mention a fair amount of naiveté, to take on the giants of injustice and oppression. Few things are more empowering than a good friend standing in your corner. A champion is not the person out in front, leading the charge. Nor is a champion involved in the daily grind of the work. Finally, a champion gets no credit if something succeeds. Yet, when justice initiatives fail, it is often because there was no one standing in the background, championing the cause.

Pastors do not need to be involved in the daily grind of every compassionate ministry taking place around them. Newton was a champion, not a volunteer. He did not serve at one of Thomas Charles' charity schools, but he did open up his church to host a fundraiser for it. He did not get involved with John Campbell's plan to bring African children to England, but he did write a letter of introduction for Governor Macaulay and sent him to Campbell with it. Newton did not move to the Mendips to work in Hannah More's schools, but he did visit, preach there, and offer his encouragement and support. Finally, Newton did not set sail for Australia, but when Richard Johnson's load was too much, Newton made sure his pamphlet got printed, covered the costs, and looked for a helper that could be sent to assist him.[22]

In your community, there may be ministries where you are not a volunteer, but you do need to champion the work, throw your weight and encouragement behind it, and be there to help when people that you have befriended begin to take bold steps in the right direction. Being a champion is bragging on another's work, going to bat for them when conflict arises, and leveraging your own influence to their advantage. Newton was quite gifted at empowering people in this way.

First of all, Newton unashamedly bragged about the work of his friends. For example, he raved about Wilberforce's first foray into writing: "I can scarcely talk or write without introducing Mr. Wilberforce's book."[23] Not only did he brag to others; he also bragged about the work to the person doing it! He told Richard Johnson that being sent to Australia "is a greater honour than if you had been made a Bishop or Archbishop, or Cardinal or Pope."[24] Time and again we find him telling people how God has raised them up for such a time as this, or how God is using them beyond what they can see, and how crucial it is for them to stay faithful in the valuable post to which God has called them. You can change the entire culture of a ministry, not to mention a friend's whole day, by your words. Consider this: every time you introduce people to one another, you have the opportunity to brag on them both. It matters little if they feel awkward in the moment, so long as they feel heartened when the conversation is over.

Second, Newton praised the value of the work in the face of conflict. This is an important role for a champion, especially with younger friends, because the greener the person, the harder they tend to take the blows of criticism. Newton clearly stood behind Wilberforce numerous times as he battled political opposition to the abolition of slavery. He did the same when Hannah More came under public fire in a magazine: "Cheer up my dear friend. . . . Be strong, and He shall comfort thy heart. . . . He does and will overrule all the designs of men for the furtherance and accomplishment of his holy plan."[25] Champions are the kind of people who have felt the sting of failure, the frown of disapproval, and have come through it, determined to be a buoy to another who might otherwise sink under waves of discouragement. They are the kind of people who redirect and absorb criticism aimed at someone else, sometimes playing the scapegoat, at others the shield. Your reassurances may well be God's instrument to empower others to go the distance.

Third, Newton leveraged his influence on behalf of his friends. For instance, before Cowper was an accomplished poet, Newton wrote a preface for Cowper's first book, and even found him a publisher. Cowper wrote to a family member, "Mr. Newton, who has a large influence in that quarter also, will, I know, serve me like a brother."[26] Newton helped his friends land jobs, raise funds, garner support, make connections, and in general gave their work credibility because of their connection to him. When others see you put your good name on the line to help advance their cause, not only will they serve in greater earnest, their love for you will deepen, with lasting friendship the result.

Champions can be hard to come by, but a real champion is hard to forget.

GET OUT OF THE WAY

> Pastors, as parables of Jesus, bring Christ to people and then as quickly as possible become unimportant, unnecessary, superfluous to the important thing: the parishioner's relationship with Jesus. Jesus did something similar himself. Jesus brought God to people and then just walked away. In the Gospels Jesus appears to have virtually no follow-up program! Even with his disciples we see him making a point with them and walking away, leaving them shaking their heads time and again. The key is getting out of the way.[27]

To empower someone else is to deliberately avoid stepping in and taking over. Quite the opposite, actually. Perhaps the biggest hindrance to leaders reproducing themselves in the lives of others is their inability *not* to lead. A compulsion to always be at the helm, always steering the ship, cuts off at the knees the opportunity for others to make kingdom impact. In short, when pastors are unable to give leadership and give power away, they stunt the spiritual growth of everyone around them.

A striking note in Newton's life, however, was his eagerness to empower others by affirming their leadership. He was clearly a dynamic enough personality to be center stage in almost any arena. Yet, it seems that Newton deliberately restrained himself in order for others to shine.

As stated previously, when the question came up as to whether Christians should boycott West Indian products, Newton sought out Wilberforce. Instead of speaking his mind, he wanted to support Wilberforce's position publicly.

In short, Newton was happy to get out of the way.

Until we learn that ministry is not all about us, we will have a hard time with this. It will be difficult to hold people with an open hand, sending them off to new ventures in other places when we so desperately need help in our own churches. Had Newton clung to people, he never would have been able to encourage Claudius Buchanan to go to India. Buchanan, was, after all, like a "right hand" to Newton. Yet Newton was able to "[give] him up without reluctance."[28]

Until we can rejoice in our disciples becoming our peers, or even our teachers, getting out of the way is virtually impossible. After reading Wilberforce's book, *A Practical View of Christianity*, Newton was amazed by the former's insight and wisdom: "I believe I must in future alter the tone of my quarterly payments. . . . now I shall be glad to look to you . . . for cautions against the evils that beset my own path."[29]

We must vigilantly fight against any type of messiah complex as though people need us. Who they need is Jesus. When we have been good friends to them on their journey, Jesus is who they meet. In Jesus, we are free from competition, free from needing to be needed, free from having to be in control, out in front, and in the spotlight. In Jesus, we empower others by graciously stepping out of the way, joyfully cheering others on from the sidelines, and watching with deep gratitude and an overwhelming sense of humility as our friends go on to conquer kingdoms, enforce justice, and obtain God's promises.

When one thinks highly of Jesus, little of himself, and much of others, he can say, as Newton did when celebrating his seventy-ninth birthday, "Let me retire as a thankful guest from a full table, and rejoice that others are coming forth to serve thee (I hope better) when I can do no more."[30] Newton only wrote one more journal entry before his death. He was content, happy to get out of the way, delighted to see a whole army of friends empowered to lead the charge against the injustices of this world, holding on to the hope that one day in eternity he could shake hands with each dear friend, greeting their final homegoing with joy: "I please myself into thinking I shall be among the first of those, who will be waiting for you, to welcome you home to your Mansion in the Heavenly House."[31]

Conclusion

On December 23, 1807, *The Times* reported Newton's death:

> DIED
> At his house in Coleman Street Buildings, aged 82, the Rev. John Newton, Rector of the United Parishes of St Mary Woolnoth and St Mary Woolchurch Haw of which parishes he had been Rector for 28 years. His unblemished life, his amiable character both as a man and as a Minister and his able writings are too well known to need any comment.[1]

His many years of respectability and kind service had made it easy for people to gloss over those early days when Newton lived anything but a life without blemish.[2] Newton was a self-described "wild creature, whom the Lord in a measure tamed, and brought from Africa, to stand as a memorable proof, that His mercy can pardon the most atrocious wickedness, and His grace can change the most obstinate habits of sin."[3] In the course of one lifetime, this man went from being a degenerate slave, to hardened slaver, to Christian abolitionist.

His early years were, by his own admission, horrid and shameful. He was calloused and proud, foolhardy and selfish, driven by his own lusts, and even cruel. But Jesus changed him. Grace gripped him. So profound was the experience that he penned his own epitaph:

JOHN NEWTON,
CLERK,
ONCE AN INFIDEL AND LIBERTINE,
A SERVANT OF SLAVES IN AFRICA,
WAS,
BY THE RICH MERCY OF OUR LORD AND SAVIOUR
JESUS CHRIST,
PRESERVED, RESTORED, PARDONED,
AND APPOINTED TO PREACH THE FAITH
HE HAD LONG LABOURED TO DESTROY.[4]

Newton's past haunted him in some ways, yet grace abounded where there was once only shame. In October of 1780, Newton went on a preaching tour that would bring him to the coast of England. Knowing Newton's grasp of grace, William Cowper wrote Mary Newton a letter while John was out of town:

> The sight of his old acquaintance [the ocean] will revive in his mind a pleasing recollection of past deliverances, and when he looks at him from the beach, he may say, "You have formerly given me trouble enough, but I have cast anchor now where your billows can never reach me." It is happy for him that he can say so.[5]

Little did Cowper know that the day before, Newton said almost those very words in a poem he composed while standing beside a lighthouse, overlooking that old acquaintance, the ocean:

> Thus on a height in safety I survey
> That wide deceitful storm-vexed sea, the world;
> How often there the thoughtless and the gay,
> Are lost, on rocks, or on each other hurled!
>
> Kindled by Thee, dear Lord, may I thus shine,
> And timely warn them of each dangerous shelf,
> Remembering well their perils once were mine:
> I fear for them though now secure myself.[6]

Newton was secure; he had an Anchor. Though his life had been a windblown one and tossed about violently, Christ became his rock. And though he had formerly walked in darkness, he had seen a great light that at once both kindled his heart with love and also made his life shine out with a certain brilliance. What a friend he found in Jesus!

And in Jesus, what a friend Newton became to others! Before long, numerous people were finding their way into his life and his heart. With deep gratitude for the rich mercy God had condescended to show him, Newton humbly nurtured these friendships with a steady diet of grace. He who had been forgiven much clearly loved much. As one of his friends put it, "In short, Mr. Newton could *live* no longer than he could *love.*"[7] His own profound sense of sinfulness and God's holiness turned a selfish prodigal into a selfless pastor.

His was, as James 1:27 says, a true religion: "Religion that is pure and undefiled before God, the Father, is this: to visit orphans and widows in their affliction, and to keep oneself unstained from the world." He became drawn to those who found themselves in the very position where he had once been—lost and lonely, mistreated and maligned. Both Newton's love for God and his love for others burned brightly for well over forty years. In fact, Newton's last sermon was at a fundraiser for orphans and widows.[8]

It was only natural that those whom he befriended would in turn pick up the baton that he handed them. This was no program. It was his life. Having so fond an affection for his friends, John Newton was well pleased to impart to them not only the gospel of God but also his own life, because they had become very dear to him. Imparting his life meant imparting a concern for justice and compassion, a heart for the least of these, and a cry for some balm in Gilead.

And so, some cried for relief of the afflicted and oppressed while others tended to the wounded. Some changed structures and systems; others changed bandages. Some pulled drowning people out of the river while others went upstream to keep people from falling in.

Some loosened the bonds of wickedness, undoing the straps of the yoke, letting the oppressed go free, and breaking every yoke. Others shared their bread with the hungry, brought the homeless poor into the house, and covered the naked. But all lent their hand to the needy, not hiding themselves from their own flesh. They poured themselves out for the hungry, and satisfied the desire of the afflicted.

Together, as friends, their light rose in darkness. The Lord continually guided them. They were like a watered garden, a spring of water that did not run dry. Ancient ruins were rebuilt. Together, they became repairers of the breach, and restorers of the streets in which to dwell. Finally, as the prophet Isaiah promised, they did indeed raise up the foundations of many generations.

And the world was changed.

* * *

Poor, weak, and worthless, though I am,
I have a rich, almighty Friend;
Jesus, the Saviour, is his name,
He freely loves, and without end.

He ransom'd me from hell with blood,
And by his pow'r my foes controll'd;
He found me wand'ring far from God,
And brought me to his chosen fold.

He cheers my heart, my want supplies,
And says that I shall shortly be
Enthron'd with him above the skies—
Oh! what a friend Christ is to me![9]

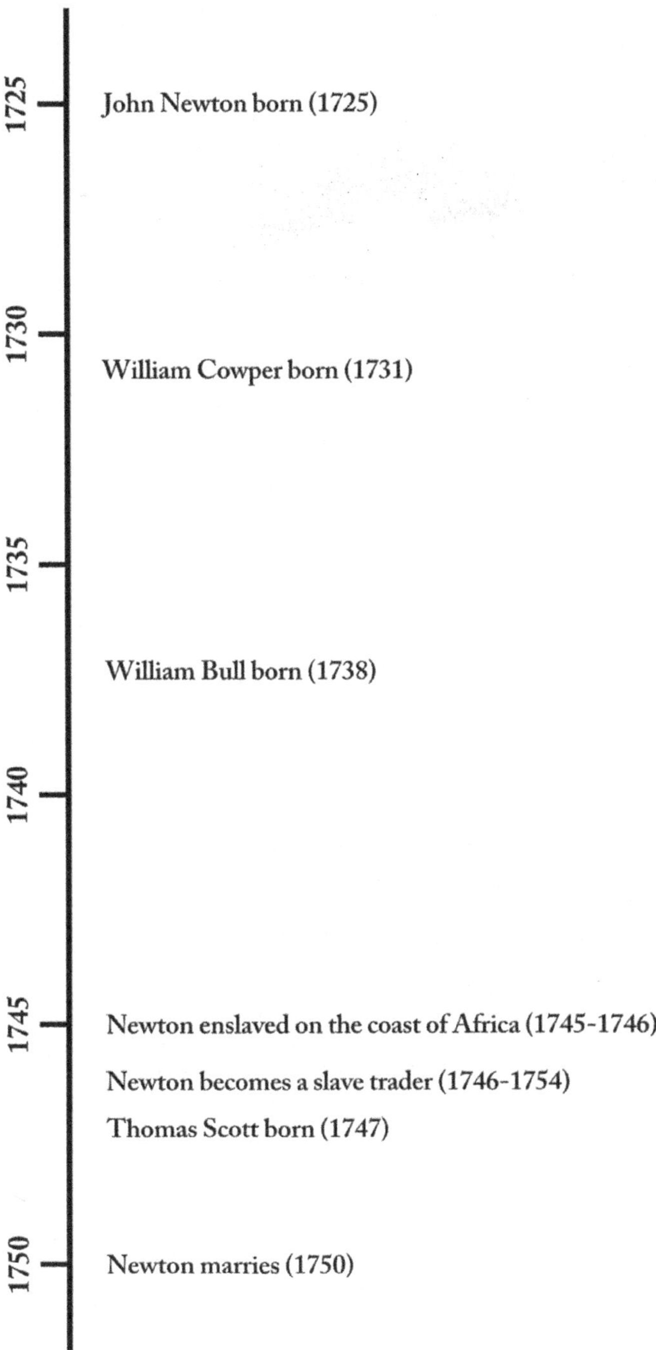

Figure 14. Timeline.

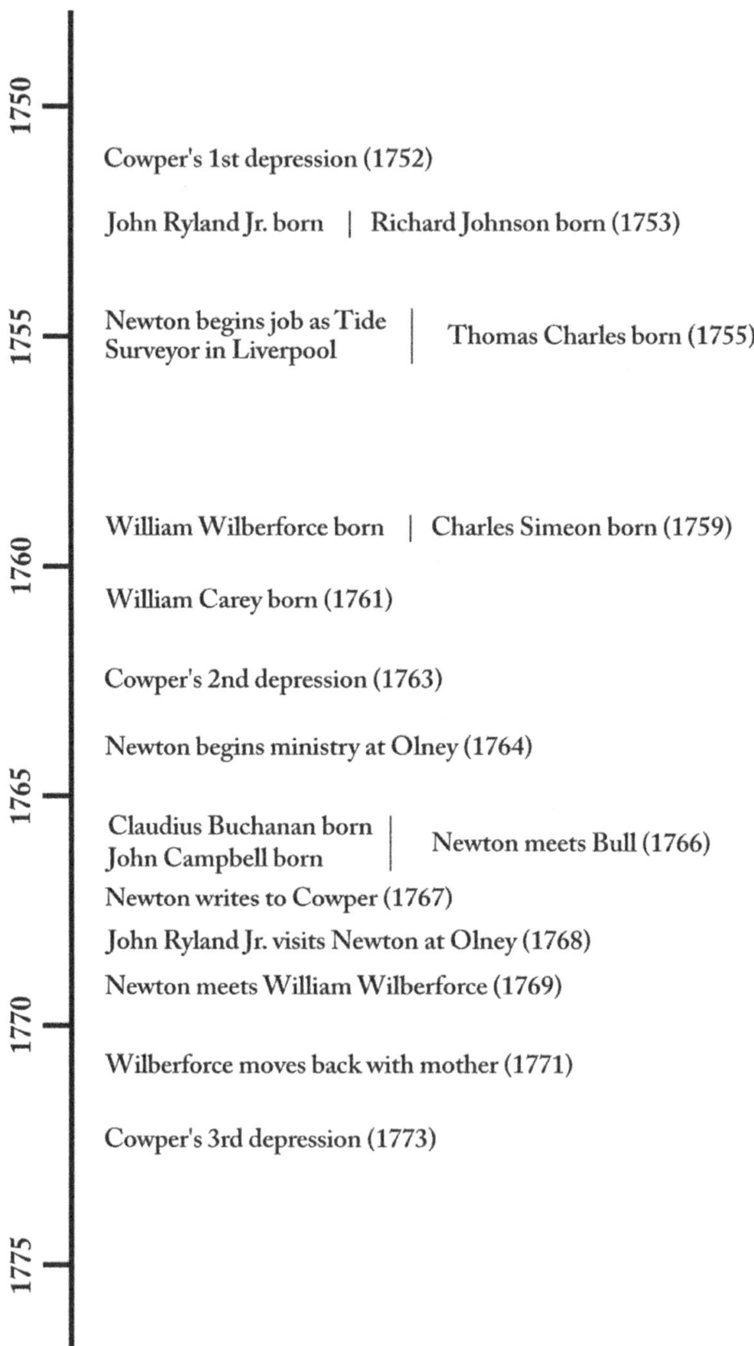

Figure 14. Timeline (cont.).

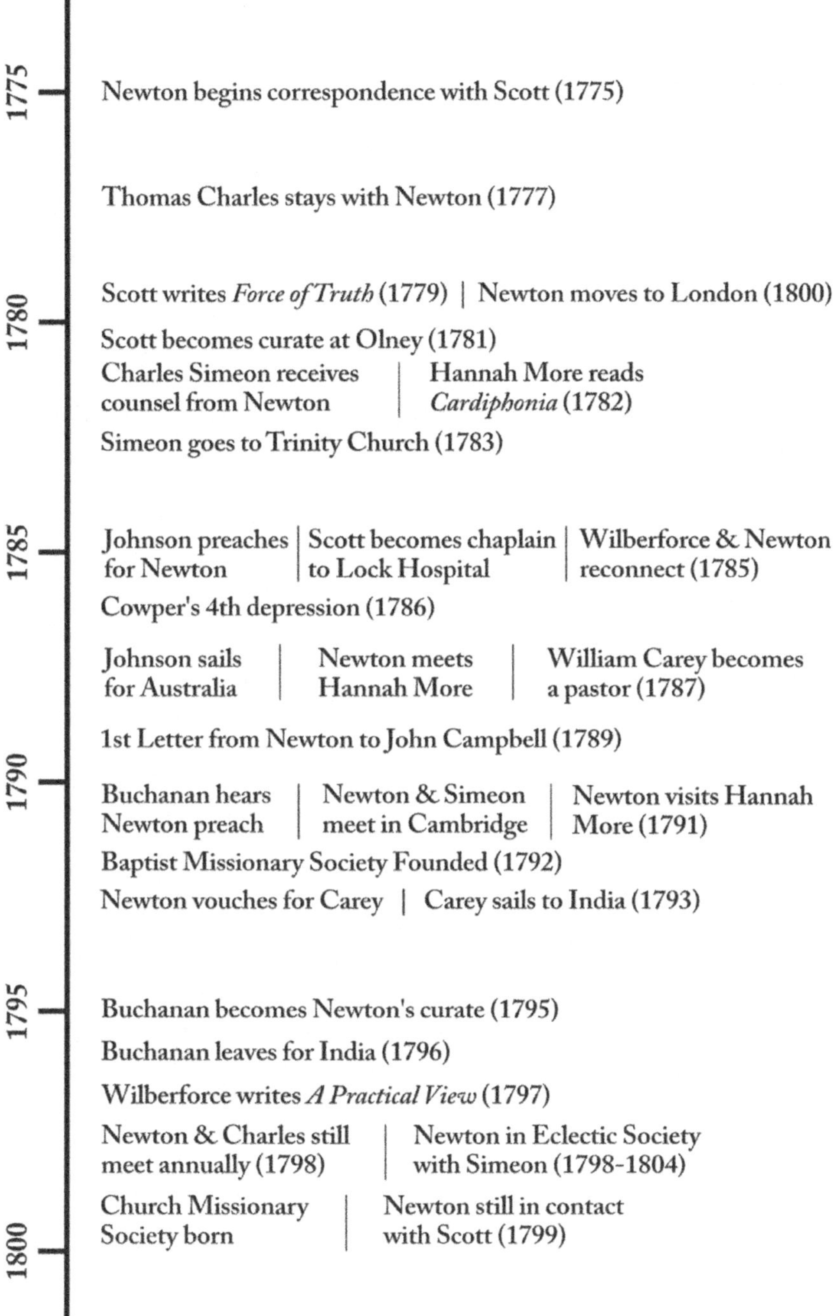

Figure 14. Timeline (cont.).

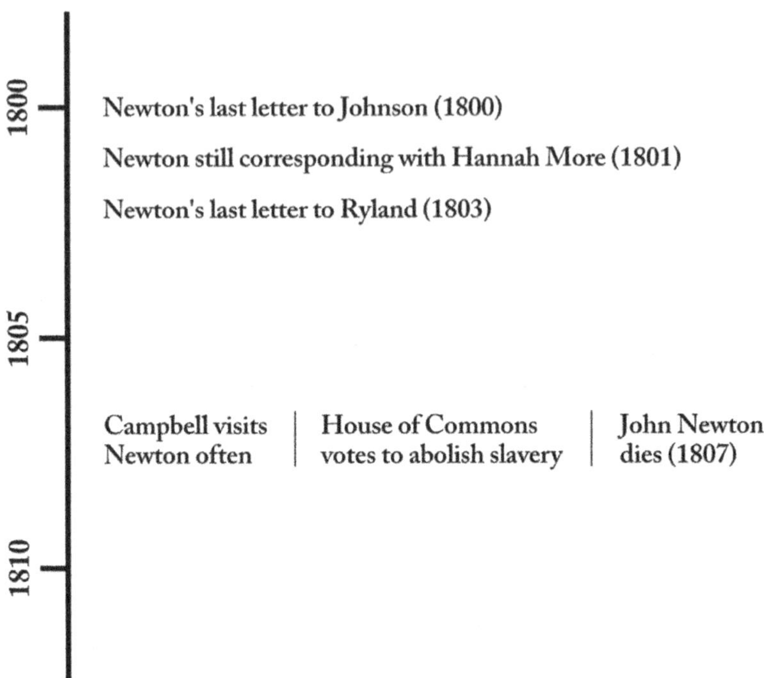

Figure 14. Timeline (cont.).

Image Credits

CHAPTER ONE

Figure 1. John Newton: Joseph Collyer creator QS:P170,Q6282206 After John Russell creator QS:P170,Q4233718,P1877,Q6255995 (https://commons.wikimedia.org/wiki/File:Newton_j.jpg), "Newton J", marked as public domain, more details on Wikimedia Commons: https://commons.wikimedia.org/wiki/Template:PD-old marked as public domain, more details on Wikimedia Commons: https://commons.wikimedia.org/wiki/Template:PD-old

CHAPTER TWO

Figure 2. Young William Wilberforce: John Russell (died 1806) (https://commons.wikimedia.org/wiki/File:William_Wilberforce_by_John_Russell.jpg), "William Wilberforce by John Russell", marked as public domain, more details on Wikimedia Commons: https://commons.wikimedia.org/wiki/Template:PD-old

Figure 3. Thomas Scott: Fergus Pearson (https://commons.wikimedia.org/wiki/File:Thomas_Scott.jpg), "Thomas Scott", marked as public domain, more details on Wikimedia Commons: https://commons.wikimedia.org/wiki/Template:PD-old

Figure 4. Hannah More: William Henry Worthington creator QS:P170,Q21465450 After Henry William Pickersgill creator QS:P170,Q4233718,P1877,Q3133160 published by J. Hudson (https://commons.wikimedia.org/wiki/File:Hannah_More.jpg), "Hannah More", marked as public domain, more details on Wikimedia Commons: https://commons.wikimedia.org/wiki/Template:PD-old

Figure 5. Claudius Buchanan: Unidentified engraver (https://commons.wikimedia.org/wiki/File:Claudius_Buchanan00.jpg), "Claudius Buchanan00", marked as public domain, more details on Wikimedia Commons: https://commons.wikimedia.org/wiki/Template:PD-old

Figure 6. William Cowper: Lemuel Francis Abbott artist QS:P170,Q725410 (https://commons.wikimedia.org/wiki/File:William_Cowper_by_Lemuel_Francis_Abbott.jpg), "William Cowper by Lemuel Francis Abbott", marked as public domain, more details on Wikimedia Commons: https://commons.wikimedia.org/wiki/Template:PD-old

Figure 7. William Bull: Unknown engraver (https://commons.wikimedia.org/wiki/File:William_Bull.jpg), "William Bull", marked as public domain, more details on Wikimedia Commons: https://commons.wikimedia.org/wiki/Template:PD-old

Figure 8. Charles Simeon: Engraving by William Finden after a portrait by Sir William Beechey (https://commons.wikimedia.org/wiki/File:CharlesSimeon.jpg), "CharlesSimeon", marked as public domain, more details on Wikimedia Commons: https://commons.wikimedia.org/wiki/Template:PD-old

Figure 9. John Ryland, Jr.: Unknown engraver After Nathan Cooper Branwhite creator QS:P170,Q4233718,P1877,Q6968987 (https://commons.wikimedia.org/wiki/File:John_Ryland_Branwhite.jpg), "John Ryland Branwhite", marked as public domain, more details on Wikimedia Commons: https://commons.wikimedia.org/wiki/Template:PD-old

Figure 10. William Carey: Unknown (https://commons.wikimedia.org/wiki/File:William_Carey.jpg), "William Carey", marked as public domain, more details on Wikimedia Commons: https://commons.wikimedia.org/wiki/Template:PD-old

Figure 11. Thomas Charles: Anonymous (https://en.wikipedia.org/wiki/File:Thomas_Charles.jpg), "Thomas Charles", marked as public domain, more details on Wikimedia Commons: https://commons.wikimedia.org/wiki/Template:PD-US

Figure 12. Richard Johnson: Garnet Terry (https://commons.wikimedia.org/wiki/File:Richard_Johnson.jpg), "Richard Johnson", marked as public domain, more details on Wikimedia Commons: https://commons.wikimedia.org/wiki/Template:PD-old

Figure 13. John Campbell: Drawn by Rev. W.T. Stoult. Engraving by H. Meyer. John Campbell (1766-1840) (https://commons.wikimedia.org/wiki/File:John_Campbell_(missionar y)02.jpg), "John Campbell (missionary)02", marked as public domain, more details on Wikimedia Commons: https://commons.wikimedia.org/wiki/Template:PD-old

Note: All images from Wikimedia Commons are in the public domain.

Bibliography

Aitken, Jonathan. *John Newton: From Disgrace to Amazing Grace.* Wheaton, IL: Crossway Books, 2007.

Anstey, Roger. *The Atlantic Slave Trade and British Abolition 1760–1810.* Atlantic Highlands, NJ: Humanities Press, 1975.

Beeke, Joel R. and Brian G. Najapfour, eds. *Taking Hold of God: Reformed and Puritan Perspectives on Prayer.* Grand Rapids, MI: Reformation Heritage Books, 2011.

Belmonte, Kevin. *William Wilberforce: A Hero for Humanity.* Grand Rapids, MI: Zondervan, 2007.

Bonwick, James. *Australia's First Preacher; the Rev. Richard Johnson, First Chaplain of New South Wales.* London: Sampson, Low, Marston, and Co., 1898.

Book of Common Prayer. Oxford: Oxford University Press, 1990.

Bounds, E. M. *The Complete Works of E. M. Bounds on Prayer: Experience the Wonders of God through Prayer.* New ed. Grand Rapids, MI: Baker Books, 2004.

Bright, Bill. *Come Help Change the World.* Orlando, FL: NewLife Publications, 1999.

Brooke, Stopford A. *Theology in the English Poets.* 8th ed. London: Kegan Paul, Trench, Trubner & Co., 1896.

Brown, Ford K. *Fathers of the Victorians: The Age of Wilberforce.* Cambridge: Cambridge University Press, 1961.

Buchanan, Claudius. *The Works of the Rev. Claudius Buchanan.* Montpelier, VT: Lucius Q. C. Bowles, 1813.

Bull, Frederick William. *A History of Newport Pagnell.* Kettering: W. E. & J. Goss, 1900.

Bull, Josiah. *John Newton of Olney and St. Mary Woolnoth.* London: The Religious Tract Society, 1868.

———. *Memorials of the Rev. William Bull, of Newport Pagnel.* 2nd ed. London: Elliot Stock, 1865.

Campbell, John. *Travels in South Africa.* London: Black and Parry, 1815.

Carey, Brycchan. "John Wesley's *Thoughts Upon Slavery* and the Language of the Heart." *The Bulletin of the John Rylands University Library of Manchester* 85:2-3 (Summer/Autumn 2003): 269-84.

———. "Slavery, Emancipation, and Abolition." Accessed August 20, 2019. www.brycchancarey.com.

Carey, S. Pearce. *William Carey D.D., Fellow of Linnaean Society.* 3rd ed. London: Hodder and Stoughton, 1924.

Carus, William, ed. *Memoirs of the Life of the Rev. Charles Simeon, M.A.* London: Hatchard and Son, 1847.

Cecil, Richard, ed. *The Life of the Rev. John Newton, Rector of St. Mary Woolnoth, London. Written by himself to A.D. 1763, and Continued to his Death in 1807, by Rev. Richard Cecil.* New York: American Tract Society, 1850.

Coleman, Robert E. *The Master Plan of Evangelism.* 2nd ed. Abridged. Grand Rapids, MI: Fleming H. Revell, 1994.

Collins, Kenneth J. *John Wesley: A Theological Journey.* Nashville: Abingdon Press, 2003.

Colquhoun, John Campbell. *William Wilberforce: His Friends and His Times.* 2nd ed. London: Longmans, Green, Reader, and Dyer, 1867.

Correspondence and Papers of John Newton. Lambeth Palace Library, London. MS 3973.

Cowper, William. *Letters of William Cowper.* London: The Religious Tract Society, 1862.

Culross, James. *The Three Rylands.* London: Elliot Stock, 1897.

Dallimore, Arnold. *George Whitefield: The Life and Times of the Great Evangelist of the Eighteenth-Century Revival.* 2 vols. 1970. Reprint, Edinburgh: Banner of Truth Trust, 2001.

Danker, Ryan Nicholas. *Wesley and the Anglicans: Political Division in Early Evangelicalism*. Downers Grove, IL: InterVarsity Press, 2016.

de Souza, Teotonio R. "Goa Inquisition for Colonial Disciplining." *oHeraldo* (Goa). 13 March 2010.

Demaray, Donald E. *The Innovation of John Newton (1725-1807): Synergism of Word and Music in Eighteenth Century Evangelism*. Lewiston, NY: The Edwin Mellen Press, 1988.

Downer, A. C. *Thomas Scott the Commentator*. London: Chas. J. Thynne, 1909.

Furneaux, Robin. *William Wilberforce*. 1974. Reprint, Vancouver, BC: Regent College Publishing, 2005.

General Correspondence of John Newton. Newton to George Whitefield. William Carey to Newton. Lambeth Palace Library, London. MS 2935.

George, Timothy. *Faithful Witness: The Life and Mission of William Carey*. Birmingham, AL: New Hope Publishers, 1991.

Gordon, Grant. *A Great Blessing to Me: John Newton Encounters George Whitefield*. Fearn, Ross-shire: Christian Focus, 2016.

———, ed. *Wise Counsel*. 2009. Reprint, Edinburgh: Banner of Truth Trust, 2011.

Grimshawe, T. S. *The Life and Works of William Cowper*. 2nd ed. Vol. 1. London: Saunders and Otley, 1836.

Hague, William. *William Wilberforce: The Life of the Great Anti-Slave Trade Campaigner*. New York: Harcourt Publishing Company, 2007.

Hansen, David. *The Art of Pastoring: Ministry Without All The Answers*. Downers Grove, IL: InterVarsity Press, 1994.

Harford, John S. *Recollections of William Wilberforce, Esq., M.P. for the County of York During Nearly Thirty Years; With Brief Notices of Some of His Personal Friends and Contemporaries*. 2nd ed. London: Longman, Green, Longman, Roberts, and Green, 1865.

Hatch, Nathan. *The Democratization of American Christianity*. New Haven, CT: Yale University Press, 1989.

Haykin, Michael, ed. *The British Particular Baptists 1638–1910*. 3 vols. Springfield, MO: Particular Baptist Press, 2000.

Hennell, Michael M. *John Venn and the Clapham Sect*. London: Lutterworth Press, 2003.

Heuertz, Christopher L. and Christine D. Pohl. *Friendship at the Margins: Discovering Mutuality in Service and Mission*. Downers Grove, IL: InterVarsity Press, 2010.

Hindmarsh, D. Bruce. *John Newton and the English Evangelical Tradition*. Grand Rapids, MI: Eerdmans, 1996.

Hole, Charles. *The Early History of the Church Missionary Society*. London: Church Missionary Society, 1896.

Hopkins, Hugh. *Charles Simeon of Cambridge*. London: Hodder and Stoughton, 1977.

Hopkins, Mary Alden. *Hannah More and Her Circle*. New York: Longmans, Green and Co., 1947.

Hunter, James Davison. *To Change the World: The Irony, Tragedy, & Possibility of Christianity in the Late Modern World*. Oxford: Oxford University Press, 2010.

Jenkins, D. E. *The Life of the Rev. Thomas Charles B.A. of Bala*. 3 vols. Denbigh: Llewelyn Jenkins, 1908.

Jones, John Morgan and William Morgan. *The Calvinistic Methodist Fathers of Wales*. 2 vols. Translated by John Aaron. Edinburgh: Banner of Truth Trust, 2008.

Karr, Allan and Linda Bergquist. *The Wholehearted Church Planter: Leadership from the Inside Out*. St. Louis: Chalice Press, 2013.

Keller, Timothy. *Generous Justice: How God's Grace Makes us Just*. New York: Dutton, 2010.

Letters to John Newton. Claudius Buchanan to Newton. Lambeth Palace Library, London. MS 3972.

Letters to Newton. Charles Simeon to Newton. Claudius Buchanan to Newton. Lambeth Palace Library, London. MS 3096.

Lovelace, Richard F. *Dynamics of Spiritual Life: An Evangelical Theology of Renewal.* Downers Grove, IL: InterVarsity Press, 1979.

Mangalwadi, Vishal and Ruth. *The Legacy of William Carey: A Model for the Transformation of a Culture.* Wheaton, IL: Crossway Books, 1999.

Marsden, George M. *Jonathan Edwards: A Life.* New Haven, CT: Yale University Press, 2003.

Martin, Bernard. *John Newton: A Biography.* London: William Heinemann LTD, 1950.

Metaxas, Eric. *Amazing Grace: William Wilberforce and the Heroic Campaign to End Slavery.* New York: HarperOne, 2007.

More, Hannah. *Cheap Repository Tracts: Entertaining, Moral, and Religious.* Revised ed. New York: American Tract Society, 1800.

Moule, Handley. *Charles Simeon.* Reprint, London: InterVarsity Press, 1965.

Murray, Iain H. *Heroes.* Edinburgh: Banner of Truth Trust, 2009.

————. *Puritan Hope.* 1971. Reprint, Edinburgh: Banner of Truth Trust, 1998.

Nash, Ronald H. *Social Justice and the Christian Church.* Milford, MI: Mott Media, Inc., 1983.

Newton, John. *Letters and Conversational Remarks by the Late Rev. John Newton, Rector of St. Mary Woolnoth.* Edited by John Campbell. New York: S. Whiting & Co. Theological and Classical Booksellers, 1811.

————. *Letters of John Newton.* Edited by Josiah Bull. 1869. Reprint, Edinburgh: Banner of Truth Trust, 2007.

————. *The Life and Spirituality of John Newton.* Edited by Bruce Hindmarsh. Vancouver, BC: Regent College Publishing, 2003.

————. *Memoirs of the Life of Rev. William Grimshaw.* London: W. Baynes and Son, 1825.

———. *Ministry on My Mind.* Edited by Marylynn Rouse. 2008. Reprint, Stratford-upon-Avon: The John Newton Project, 2010.

———. *One Hundred and Twenty Nine Letters from the Rev. John Newton, Late Rector of St. Mary Woolnoth, London, to the Rev. William Bull, of Newport Pagnell.* Edited by Thomas Palmer Bull. London: Hamilton, Adams, and Co., 1847.

———. *The Searcher of Hearts: A New Discovery of Writings on Romans 8*. Edited by Marylynn Rouse. Fearn, Ross-shire: Christian Heritage, 1997.

———. *Thoughts Upon the African Slave Trade*. London: J. Buckland, 1788.

———. *The Works of John Newton*. Edited by Richard Cecil. 6 vols. 1820. Reprint, Edinburgh: Banner of Truth Trust, 1988.

Noll, Mark. *The Rise of Evangelicalism: The Age of Edwards, Whitefield and the Wesleys*. Downers Grove, IL: InterVarsity Press, 2003.

Pearson, Hugh. *Memoir of Rev. Claudius Buchanan, D.D.* Abridged ed. New York: American Tract Society, [18--].

Periodical Accounts Relative to the Baptist Missionary Society. Vol. 1. London: Clipstone, 1800.

Perkins, John. *With Justice For All.* Ventura, CA: Regal Books, 1982.

Perkins, William. *The Art of Prophesying*. 1606. Reprint, Edinburgh: Banner of Truth Trust, 1996.

Peterson, Eugene H. *Christ Plays in Ten Thousand Places*. Grand Rapids, MI: Eerdmans, 2005.

———. *The Contemplative Pastor: Returning to the Art of Spiritual Direction.* Grand Rapids, MI: Eerdmans, 1989.

———. *Leap Over a Wall: Earthly Spirituality for Everyday Christians.* San Francisco: HarperSanFrancisco, 1997.

———. *Under the Unpredictable Plant: An Exploration in Vocational Holiness*. Grand Rapids, MI: Eerdmans, 1992.

Philip, Robert. *The Life, Times, and Missionary Enterprises of the Rev. John Campbell.* London: John Snow, 1841.

Piper, John. *The Hidden Smile of God: The Fruit of Affliction in the Lives of John Bunyan, William Cowper, and David Brainerd.* Wheaton, IL: Crossway Books, 2001.

———. *The Roots of Endurance: Invincible Perseverance in the Lives of John Newton, Charles Simeon, and William Wilberforce.* Wheaton, IL: Crossway Books, 2002.

Pollock, John. *Wilberforce.* Tring: Lion Publishing, 1977.

Pratt, John H., ed. *Eclectic Notes.* 2nd ed. London: James Nisbet and Co., 1865.

Prior, Karen Swallow. *Fierce Convictions: The Extraordinary Life of Hannah More.* Nashville, TN: Thomas Nelson, 2014.

Redford, George, and John Angell James, eds. *The Autobiography of the Rev. William Jay.* 3rd ed. London: Hamilton, Adams, and Co., 1855.

Reeves, Dudley. "John Newton Under Amazing Grace." Banner of Truth. Accessed September 5, 2019. http://banneroftruth.org/us/resources/articles/2006/john-newton-under-amazing-grace/.

Reinke, Tony. *Newton on the Christian Life.* Wheaton, IL: Crossway, 2015.

Roberts, William. *The Life and Correspondence of Mrs. Hannah More.* 3rd ed. Vol. 3. London: R. B. Seeley and W. Burnside, 1835.

———. *Memoirs of the Life of Mrs. Hannah More.* Abridged ed. London: R. B. Seeley and W. Burnside, 1839.

Rouse, Marylynn. *365 Days with Newton.* 2006. Reprint, Leominster: Day One Publications, 2010.

———. "A Double Portion of My Thoughts and Prayers: John Newton's Letters to William Wilberforce." *Midwestern Journal of Theology* 17, no. 2 (Fall 2018): 15-41.

———. "John Newton & William Wilberforce Correspondence." Unpublished manuscript.

Scott, John. *Letters and Papers of the Late Rev. Thomas Scott, D.D.* Boston: Samuel T. Armstrong, and Crocker, & Brewster, 1825.

———. *The Life of the Rev. Thomas Scott, D.D.* Abridged ed. New York: American Tract Society, 1835.

Scott, Thomas. *Force of Truth: An Authentic Narrative*. Boston: J. Belcher; S. T. Armstrong, 1814.

Seeley, M. *The Later Evangelical Fathers*. London: Seeley, Jackson, & Halliday, 1879.

Smith, Timothy. *Revivalism & Social Reform: American Protestantism on the Eve of the Civil War*. Eugene, OR: Wipf & Stock, 1957.

Spitzer, Lee B. *Making Friends, Making Disciples*. Valley Forge, PA: Judson Press, 2010.

Spoto, Donald. *Reluctant Saint: The Life of Saint Francis of Assisi*. New York: Penguin Compass, 2002.

Stein, Stephen J., ed. *The Cambridge Companion to Jonathan Edwards*. Cambridge: Cambridge University Press, 2007.

Stetzer, Ed. *Planting New Churches in a Postmodern Age*. Nashville, TN: Broadman & Holman, 2003.

Stott, Anne. *Hannah More: The First Victorian*. Oxford: Oxford University Press, 2003.

———. *Wilberforce: Family and Friends*. Oxford: Oxford University Press, 2012.

Strobel, Lee. *Inside the Mind of Unchurched Harry and Mary*. Grand Rapids, MI: Zondervan, 1993.

Thomas, Gilbert. *William Cowper and the Eighteenth Century*. London: Ivor Nicholson and Watson, 1935.

Tomkins, Stephen. *The Clapham Sect: How Wilberforce's Circle Transformed Britain*. Oxford: Lion Hudson, 2010.

———. *William Wilberforce: A Biography*. Oxford: Lion Hudson, 2007.

Tyson, John R. *Assist Me To Proclaim: The Life and Hymns of Charles Wesley*. Grand Rapids, MI: Eerdmans, 2007.

Van Doren, Mark, ed. *The Selected Letters of William Cowper*. New York: Farrar, Straus and Young, Inc., 1951.

Warren, Rick. *The Purpose Driven Church: Growth Without Compromising Your Message & Mission*. Grand Rapids, MI: Zondervan, 1995.

Whelan, Timothy. "An Evangelical Anglican Interaction with Baptist Missionary Society Strategy: William Wilberforce and John Ryland, 1807-1824." *Interfaces: Baptists and Others*, edited by David Bebbington and Martin Sutherland. Studies in Baptist History and Thought, vol. 44: 56-85. Milton Keynes: Paternoster Press, 2013.

Wilberforce, Robert and Samuel Wilberforce, eds. *The Correspondence of William Wilberforce*. 2 vols. London: John Murray, 1840.

———. *The Life of William Wilberforce*. 5 vols. London: John Murray, 1838.

Wilberforce, William. *A Practical View of the Prevailing Religious System of Professed Christians, in the Higher and Middle Classes in this Country, Contrasted with Real Christianity*. 4th ed. Glasgow: William Collins, 1833.

Wilkinson, Bruce. *The Dream Giver*. Sisters, OR: Multnomah Press, 2003.

Williams, David Innes. *The London Lock: A Charitable Hospital for Venereal Disease 1746-1952*. London: Royal Society of Medicine Press, 1995.

Wolffe, John. *The Expansion of Evangelicalism: The Age of Wilberforce, More, Chalmers and Finney*. Downers Grove, IL: InterVarsity Press, 2007.

Wood, David. "The Eccentric Vicar of Everton: John Berridge, the Cambridgeshire Revival, and the Life of Pastoral Ministry." Doctor of Ministry thesis, Gordon-Conwell Theological Seminary, 2012.

Wyler, Liana Sun and Alison Siskin. "Trafficking in Persons: U.S. Policy and Issues for Congress." Congressional Research Service, 2010.

Notes

INTRODUCTION

[1] Timothy Keller, *Generous Justice: How God's Grace Makes Us Just* (New York: Dutton, 2010), 112.

[2] Lee B. Spitzer, *Making Friends, Making Disciples* (Valley Forge, PA: Judson Press, 2010), 137.

[3] Bruce Hindmarsh notes that Newton has been "largely overlooked by modern historians." D. Bruce Hindmarsh, *John Newton and the English Evangelical Tradition* (Grand Rapids, MI: Eerdmans, 1996), vii.

[4] Ibid, viii. Hindmarsh, for instance, acknowledges that he discusses Newton's involvement in the abolition movement only in passing.

[5] Lovelace speaks of the Clapham Sect, the Eclectic Society, and Charles Simeon's training of future pastors as the "instruments effecting these changes." All of them were directly impacted by Newton. Richard F. Lovelace, *Dynamics of Spiritual Life: An Evangelical Theology of Renewal* (Downers Grove, IL: InterVarsity Press, 1979), 47-48.

[6] "Established" refers to the Anglican church, while "Dissenting" refers to non-Anglican Protestants.

CHAPTER ONE: NEEDING A FRIEND

[1] In 1750, Great Britain's Parliament passed The Calendar Act, implementing a transition from the old Julian calendar to a Gregorian calendar, which took effect in 1752. As such, the calendar was advanced by eleven days, putting Newton's birthday after that point on August 4th.

[2] John Newton, *The Life and Spirituality of John Newton* (Vancouver, BC: Regent College Publishing, 2003), 17-18.

[3] Ibid., 18-19.

[4] Ibid.

[5] Ibid., 19.

[6] Ibid., 20.

[7] Ibid., 20-21.

[8] Ibid., 21-22.

[9] Ibid., 24.

[10] Ibid., 28.

[11] Ibid.

[12] Ibid.

[13] Ibid., 29.

[14] Ibid., 30.

[15] Ibid., 34-35.

[16] Ibid., 36.

[17] Ibid., 35.

[18] John Newton, *One Hundred and Twenty Nine Letters from the Rev. John Newton, Late Rector of St. Mary Woolnoth, London, to the Rev. William Bull, of Newport Pagnell*, ed. Thomas Palmer Bull (London: Hamilton, Adams, and Co., 1847), 34.

[19] Newton, *Life and Spirituality of John Newton*, 37.

[20] John Newton, *The Works of John Newton*, ed. Richard Cecil (Edinburgh: Banner of Truth Trust, 1988), 6:522.

[21] Newton, *Life and Spirituality of John Newton*, 41-42.

[22] John Newton, *Letters and Conversational Remarks by the Late Rev. John Newton, Rector of St. Mary Woolnoth*, John Campbell, ed. (New York: S. Whiting & Co. Theological and Classical Booksellers, 1811), 172.

[23] Josiah Bull, *John Newton of Olney and St. Mary Woolnoth* (London: The Religious Tract Society, 1868), 197.

[24] Newton, *Life and Spirituality of John Newton*, 45.

[25] Ibid., 52.

[26] Bull, *John Newton*, 81.

[27] Newton, *Life and Spirituality of John Newton*, 50.

[28] Ibid., 53.

[29] Ibid., 52.

[30] Ibid., 54.

[31] Ibid., 56-57.

[32] Ibid., 60.

[33] Ibid., 58.

[34] Ibid., 64.

[35] Ibid.

[36] Ibid., 66.

[37] Jonathan Aitken, *John Newton: From Disgrace to Amazing Grace* (Wheaton, IL: Crossway Books, 2007), 91.

[38] Ibid., 93.

[39] The wedding would take place after Newton returned from his next voyage. See Newton, *Life and Spirituality of John Newton*, 75.

[40] D. Bruce Hindmarsh, *John Newton and the English Evangelical Tradition* (Grand Rapids, MI: Eerdmans, 1996), 62.

[41] Iain H. Murray, *Heroes* (Edinburgh: Banner of Truth Trust, 2009), 102.

[42] Newton, *Life and Spirituality of John Newton*, 69-70.

[43] Ibid., 70-71.

[44] Hindmarsh, *English Evangelical Tradition*, 57.

[45] Bull, *John Newton*, 38.

[46] Newton, *Life and Spirituality of John Newton*, 74.

[47] Ibid., 77.

[48] Ibid., 81.

[49] Newton, *Works*, 6:523.

[50] Newton, *One Hundred and Twenty-Nine Letters*, 274.

[51] Bull, *John Newton*, 59.

[52] Newton, *Life and Spirituality of John Newton*, 87.

[53] Ibid., 88.

[54] Ibid., 88-89.

[55] Hindmarsh, *English Evangelical Tradition*, 107-108.

[56] John Newton, February 15, 1755, MS Diary, 1751-1756, Firestone Library, Princeton, NJ, quoted in Marylynn Rouse, email message to author, June 26, 2012.

[57] Hindmarsh, *English Evangelical Tradition*, 70.

[58] Newton, *Life and Spirituality of John Newton*, 90.

[59] Hindmarsh, *English Evangelical Tradition*, 75.

[60] Bull, *John Newton*, 82.

[61] Hindmarsh, *English Evangelical Tradition*, 72.

[62] John Newton to George Whitefield, January 2, 1756, MS 2935, fol. 233, General Correspondence of John Newton, Lambeth Palace Library, London.

[63] Hindmarsh, *English Evangelical Tradition*, 73.

[64] Ibid., 71.

[65] Bull, *John Newton*, 105.

[66] Hindmarsh, *English Evangelical Tradition*, 139.

[67] Bull, *John Newton*, 289.

[68] Hindmarsh, *English Evangelical Tradition*, 77. It had been thought that the work had not survived; however, Marylynn Rouse found a copy of it at Manchester University. John Newton, *Some Thoughts on the Advantages and Expediency of Religious Associations* (Liverpool: John Sadler, 1756).

[69] Bull, *John Newton*, 87.

[70] Hindmarsh, *English Evangelical Tradition*, 78.

[71] Newton, *Life and Spirituality of John Newton*, 93.

[72] Hindmarsh, *English Evangelical Tradition*, 78.

[73] Ibid., 86. Newton's reflection and prayer during this period is well worth reading for anyone contemplating their call to the ministry. See John Newton, *Ministry on My Mind*, ed. Marylynn Rouse (2008; repr., Stratford-upon-Avon: The John Newton Project, 2010).

[74] Hindmarsh, *English Evangelical Tradition*, 86-87.

[75] Bull, *John Newton*, 106.

[76] Hindmarsh, *English Evangelical Tradition*, 89, 92.

[77] Ibid., 90.

[78] Ibid., 98-99.

[79] Ibid., 103.

[80] Ibid., 95.

[81] Newton, *Life and Spirituality of John Newton*, 13.

[82] Stephen Tomkins, *The Clapham Sect: How Wilberforce's Circle Transformed Britain* (Oxford: Lion Hudson, 2010), 25. "You would have liked to have been with me last Wednesday. I preached at Westminster Bridewell. It is a prison and house of correction. . . . I preached from 1 Tim. i. 15; and began with telling them my own story: this gained their attention more than I expected. I spoke to them near an hour and a half. I shed many tears myself, and saw some of them shed tears likewise." Newton, *Works*, 2:150.

[83] Hindmarsh, *English Evangelical Tradition*, 31-32.

CHAPTER TWO: BEING A FRIEND

[1] Josiah Bull, *John Newton of Olney and St. Mary Woolnoth* (London: The Religious Tract Society, 1868), 121.

[2] D. Bruce Hindmarsh, *John Newton and the English Evangelical Tradition* (Grand Rapids, MI: Eerdmans, 1996), 44-45. As Hindmarsh notes, the first half of Newton's life had been rather turbulent, but the second half, beginning the year that he was ordained into the Church of England, was stable.

[3] Lee B. Spitzer, *Making Friends, Making Disciples* (Valley Forge, PA: Judson Press, 2010), 95.

[4] John Newton, *One Hundred and Twenty Nine Letters from the Rev. John Newton, Late Rector of St. Mary Woolnoth, London, to the Rev. William Bull, of Newport Pagnell*, Thomas Palmer Bull, ed. (London: Hamilton, Adams, and Co., 1847), 71.

[5] John Newton, *The Works of John Newton*, Richard Cecil, ed. (Edinburgh: Banner of Truth Trust, 1988), 2:380.

[6] Bull, *John Newton*, 365.

[7] Hindmarsh, *English Evangelical Tradition*, 192.

[8] Ibid., 196-197.

[9] Ibid., 198.

[10] Bull, *John Newton*, 207.

[11] Ibid., 264.

[12] Jonathan Aitken, *John Newton: From Disgrace to Amazing Grace* (Wheaton, IL: Crossway Books, 2007), 342-343.

[13] Bull, *John Newton*, 366.

[14] Kevin Belmonte, *William Wilberforce: A Hero for Humanity* (Grand Rapids, MI: Zondervan, 2007), 23-24.

[15] John Newton to Hannah Wilberforce, June 9, 1770, Cowper and Newton Museum, Olney, quoted in Marylynn Rouse, "John Newton & William Wilberforce Correspondence," unpublished manuscript.

[16] Belmonte, *William Wilberforce*, 26.

[17] John Newton to William Wilberforce [uncle], July 4, 1771, c. 49, fols. 120-121, Wilberforce Papers, Bodleian Library, Oxford, quoted in Rouse, "John Newton."

[18] Ibid.

[19] Marylynn Rouse, "A Double Portion of My Thoughts and Prayers: John Newton's Letters to William Wilberforce," *Midwestern Journal of Theology* 17, no. 2 (Fall 2018): 17.

[20] John S. Harford, *Recollections of William Wilberforce*, 2nd ed. (London: Longman, Green, Longman, Roberts, and Green, 1865), 218.

[21] Aitken, *John Newton*, 239.

[22] Rouse, "A Double Portion," 16.

[23] Stephen Tomkins, *The Clapham Sect: How Wilberforce's Circle Transformed Britain* (Oxford: Lion Hudson, 2010), 44.

[24] John Newton to William Wilberforce [uncle], November 25, 1774, c. 49, fol. 122, Wilberforce Papers, Bodleian Library, Oxford, quoted in Rouse, "John Newton."

[25] Bull, *John Newton*, 282.

[26] Hindmarsh, *English Evangelical Tradition*, 186-188. See also Bull, *John Newton*, 179.

[27] Hindmarsh, *English Evangelical Tradition*, 198-199.

[28] Ibid., 201.

[29] Ibid., 189.

[30] Ibid., 199.

[31] Ibid., 203.

[32] Ibid., 192.

[33] Thomas Scott, *Force of Truth: An Authentic Narrative* (Boston: J. Belcher; S. T. Armstrong, 1814), 26.

[34] Ibid., 31.

[35] Ibid., 32-33.

[36] Bull, *John Newton*, 210-211.

[37] Scott, *Force of Truth*, 12. Socinians deny the divinity of Christ.

[38] Ibid., 17. Pelagians deny original sin in humans.

[39] The *Thirty-Nine Articles of Religion* is the doctrinal statement of the Church of England. *Book of Common Prayer* (Oxford: Oxford University Press, 1990), 867-876.

[40] Scott, *Force of Truth*, 20.

[41] Ibid., 25.

[42] Bull, *John Newton*, 210.

[43] Newton, *Works*, 1:562.

[44] Ibid., 1:570.

[45] Ibid., 1:572.

[46] Ibid., 1:585.

[47] Ibid., 1:588.

[48] Scott, *Force of Truth*, 34.

[49] Newton, *Works*, 1:618.

[50] Bull, *John Newton*, 214.

[51] Scott, *Force of Truth*, 87.

[52] John Piper, *The Roots of Endurance: Invincible Perseverance in the Lives of John Newton, Charles Simeon, and William Wilberforce* (Wheaton, IL: Crossway Books, 2002), 58.

[53] Bull, *John Newton*, 224.

[54] Ibid., 225.

[55] Ibid., 228.

[56] Ibid., 232.

[57] Iain H. Murray, *Puritan Hope* (1971; repr., Edinburgh: Banner of Truth Trust, 1998), 145.

[58] Bull, *John Newton*, 333.

[59] Hindmarsh, *English Evangelical Tradition*, 213.

[60] Bull, *John Newton*, 239.

[61] Aitken, *John Newton*, 270.

[62] "My connections have enlarged—my little name is spread." Hindmarsh, *English Evangelical Tradition*, 289.

[63] Bull, *John Newton*, 323.

[64] Newton, *One Hundred and Twenty-Nine Letters*, 38-39.

[65] John Newton, *Letters of John Newton*, Josiah Bull, ed. (1869; repr., Edinburgh: Banner of Truth Trust, 2007), xi.

[66] Bull, *John Newton*, 101-102.

[67] Tomkins, *Clapham Sect*, 62.

[68] William Roberts, *Memoirs of the Life of Mrs. Hannah More*, abridged ed. (London: R. B. Seeley and W. Burnside, 1839), 101.

[69] Tomkins, *Clapham Sect*, 62.

[70] Newton, *Letters*, 346.

[71] Anne Stott, "Hannah More: Biography," The Victorian Web, accessed August 20, 2019, http://www.victorianweb.org/authors/more/bio.html.

[72] Roberts, *Hannah More*, 153.

[73] Mary Alden Hopkins, *Hannah More and Her Circle* (New York: Longmans, Green and Co., 1947), 147.

[74] Roberts, *Hannah More*, 156.

[75] Ibid., 244-245.

[76] The Mendips is the area where the Mores lived.

[77] John Newton to William Wilberforce, August 3-4, [1792], c. 49, fol. 43, Wilberforce Papers, Bodleian Library, Oxford, quoted in Rouse, "John Newton."

[78] Roberts, *Hannah More*, 172.

[79] William Roberts, *The Life and Correspondence of Mrs. Hannah More*, 3rd ed. (London: R. B. Seeley and W. Burnside, 1835), 3:7.

[80] Roberts, *The Life and Correspondence of Mrs. Hannah More*, 3:99.

[81] Roberts, *Hannah More*, 196.

[82] Ibid., 157.

[83] Bull, *John Newton*, 306-307.

[84] Ibid., 307.

[85] Tomkins, *Clapham Sect*, 213.

[86] Claudius Buchanan to John Newton, October 24, 1792, MS 3096, fol. 117, Letters to Newton, Lambeth Palace Library, London.

[87] Bull, *John Newton*, 307.

[88] Claudius Buchanan to John Newton, October 24, 1792, MS 3096, fol. 118, Letters to Newton, Lambeth Palace Library, London.

[89] Claudius Buchanan to John Newton, MS 3972, fol. 30v, Letters to John Newton, Lambeth Palace Library, London.

[90] Claudius Buchanan to John Newton, August, 1792, MS 3972, fol. 34v, Letters to John Newton, Lambeth Palace Library, London.

[91] Claudius Buchanan to John Newton, August 17, 1793, MS 3972, fol. 36v, Letters to John Newton, Lambeth Palace Library, London.

[92] John Newton, *Letters and Conversational Remarks by the Late Rev. John Newton, Rector of St. Mary Woolnoth*, John Campbell, ed. (New York: S. Whiting & Co. Theological and Classical Booksellers, 1811), 82.

[93] Bull, *John Newton*, 329.

[94] Josiah Bull, *Memorials of the Rev. William Bull, of Newport Pagnel*, 2nd ed. (London: Elliot Stock, 1865), 72.

[95] Newton, *One Hundred and Twenty Nine Letters*, 105.

[96] Ibid., 112.

[97] Cowper was born on November 15, 1731 (Old Style date, New Style Gregorian Calendar is November 26).

[98] John Piper, *The Hidden Smile of God: The Fruit of Affliction in the Lives of John Bunyan, William Cowper, and David Brainerd* (Wheaton, IL: Crossway Books, 2001), 85-86, 106-107.

[99] Ibid., 89.

[100] Ibid., 87.

[101] Ibid., 91.

[102] Ibid., 94.

[103] Ibid., 94-95.

[104] John Newton to William Wilberforce, July 4, 1795, c. 49, fol. 62, Wilberforce Papers, Bodleian Library, Oxford, quoted in Rouse, "John Newton."

[105] Bull, *John Newton*, 158.

[106] Newton, *Letters*, 151.

[107] T. S. Grimshawe, *The Life and Works of William Cowper*, 2nd ed. (London: Saunders and Otley, 1836), 1:93.

[108] Bull, *John Newton*, 185.

[109] Piper, *Hidden Smile of God*, 97.

[110] Bull, *John Newton*, 184.

[111] Piper, *Roots of Endurance*, 56; Bull, *John Newton*, 185. The first stay with Newton was due to the fact that Cowper and Unwin's house was being remodeled; the second because of Cowper's depression.

[112] Newton, *Letters*, 157-158.

[113] Grimshawe, *William Cowper*, 1:118.

[114] Piper, *Hidden Smile of God*, 95.

[115] Bull, *John Newton*, 189.

[116] Grimshawe, *William Cowper*, 1:177.

[117] Newton, *Works,* 3:301.

[118] Grimshawe, *William Cowper*, 1:120-121.

[119] Donald E. Demaray, *The Innovation of John Newton (1725-1807): Synergism of Word and Music in Eighteenth Century Evangelicalism* (Lewiston, NY: The Edwin Mellen Press, 1988), 230. Contra Bull, *John Newton*, 233-234.

[120] Bull, *John Newton*, 238.

[121] Bull, *Memorials*, 98.

[122] Ibid., 99.

[123] Aitken, *John Newton*, 246.

[124] Newton, *Works*, 3:586. Cowper authored this hymn.

[125] Ibid., 3:392. Cowper authored this hymn.

[126] Ibid., 3:353.

[127] Newton, *One Hundred and Twenty-Nine Letters*, 20.

[128] Ibid., iii.

[129] Bull, *Memorials*, 24.

[130] As the title of the work suggests, 129 letters survive from John Newton to William Bull.

[131] Newton, *One Hundred and Twenty-Nine Letters*, 101.

[132] Ibid., 283.

[133] "If you come, you'll find Roast beef and a hearty welcome!" Bull, *John Newton*, 230.

[134] "Theosophic pipes." Bull, *John Newton*, 255.

[135] Newton, *One Hundred and Twenty-Nine Letters*, 7.

[136] Newton wrote to William Bull, "I find few or any with whom I converse with equal advantage, whose manner of thinking is so deep and solid." Bull, *Memorials*, 50.

[137] Newton, *One Hundred and Twenty-Nine Letters*, 142.

[138] Bull, *John Newton*, 257.

[139] Tomkins, *Clapham Sect*, 24.

[140] Bull, *Memorials*, 202.

[141] Ibid., 170.

[142] Newton, *One Hundred and Twenty-Nine Letters*, 47.

[143] Ibid., 124.

[144] Ibid., 262. At first glance, it appears somewhat surprising that Newton would speak of the investigation as though it shed new light on the horror of the trade, when he himself was an active participant and first-hand witness to the atrocities of slave trading. However, I don't think Newton is suggesting that he just now understands how wrong it was (he preached against it long before Parliament began investigating; see Newton, *Works*, 5:152). Newton is saying that the investigation has brought a national awareness to the intricacies of the trade, which, if ignored, now makes the whole nation culpable.

[145] Newton, *One Hundred and Twenty-Nine Letters*, 265.

[146] Bull, *Memorials*, 302.

[147] Bull, *John Newton*, 242.

[148] Bull, *Memorials*, 261.

[149] Bull, *John Newton*, 262.

[150] Hindmarsh, *English Evangelical Tradition*, 313.

[151] Newton, *One Hundred and Twenty-Nine Letters*, 168.

[152] Grant Gordon, ed., *Wise Counsel* (2009; repr., Edinburgh: Banner of Truth Trust, 2011), 202.

[153] Hindmarsh, *English Evangelical Tradition*, 313.

[154] John H. Pratt, ed., *Eclectic Notes*, 2nd ed. (London: James Nisbet and Co., 1865), 536.

[155] Piper, *Roots of Endurance*, 92.

[156] Pratt, *Eclectic Notes*, 536. As a country member, Simeon's attendance was likely sporadic.

[157] FP Porteus 37, fol. 9, Lambeth Palace Library, London; Tomkins, *Clapham Sect*, 176.

[158] Charles Simeon to John Newton, April 1, 1784, MS 3096, fol. 148, Letters to Newton, Lambeth Palace Library, London.

[159] Bull, *John Newton*, 310.

[160] Robert and Samuel Wilberforce, eds., *The Correspondence of William Wilberforce* (London: John Murray, 1840), 1:58.

[161] John Newton to William Wilberforce, 1789, c. 49, fol. 23, Wilberforce Papers, Bodleian Library, Oxford, quoted in Rouse, "John Newton."

[162] Charles Simeon to John Newton, April 1, 1784, MS 3096, fol. 148v, Letters to Newton, Lambeth Palace Library, London.

[163] William Carus, ed., *Memoirs of the Life of the Rev. Charles Simeon, M.A.* (London: Hatchard and Son, 1847), 537-538.

[164] Ibid., xxvii.

[165] Rouse, "A Double Portion," 40.

[166] Gordon, *Wise Counsel*, 7.

[167] Ibid., 9.

[168] James Culross, *The Three Rylands* (London: Elliot Stock, 1897), 69.

[169] Hindmarsh, *English Evangelical Tradition*, 149; Gordon, *Wise Counsel*, 6.

[170] Gordon, *Wise Counsel*, 10.

[171] Ibid., 13.

[172] Ibid., xvii.

[173] Ibid., ix.

[174] Ibid., 30.

[175] Ibid., Newton's political understanding, in short, was that the Lord reigns, and that the problems between Britain and America were largely due to sin.

[176] Ibid., 92.

[177] Ibid., 111. They even talked about vaccines on June 3, 1777.

[178] Ibid., 74.

[179] Ibid., 191.

[180] Ibid., 236.

[181] Ibid., 17.

[182] Ibid., 15.

[183] Hindmarsh, *English Evangelical Tradition*, 147.

[184] Gordon, *Wise Counsel*, 151.

[185] Culross, *Three Rylands*, 74.

[186] Gordon, *Wise Counsel,* 220.

[187] Ibid., 255.

[188] Ibid., 223.

[189] Ibid., 253.

[190] Ibid., 265.

[191] Ibid., 273.

[192] Ibid., 23.

[193] Ibid., 65.

[194] Timothy George, *Faithful Witness: The Life and Mission of William Carey* (Birmingham: New Hope Publishers, 1991), 6.

[195] Ibid., 17.

[196] Murray, *Puritan Hope*, 145.

[197] Gordon, *Wise Counsel*, 190.

[198] George, *Faithful Witness*, 77. George calls them "the faithful four."

[199] Ibid., 33.

[200] Ibid., 77.

[201] Tomkins, *Clapham Sect*, 122-123.

[202] Ibid., 123.

[203] George, *Faithful Witness*, 81.

[204] Ibid., 82.

[205] John Newton to William Wilberforce, May 27, 1793, c. 49, fol. 46, Wilberforce Papers, Bodleian Library, Oxford, quoted in Rouse, "John Newton."

[206] George, *Faithful Witness*, 91.

[207] William Carey to John Newton, November 19, 1802, MS 2935, fol. 275, General Correspondence of John Newton, Lambeth Palace Library, London.

[208] Gordon, *Wise Counsel*, 339.

[209] William Carey to John Newton, December 5, 1798, MS 2935, fol. 273, General Correspondence of John Newton, Lambeth Palace Library, London.

[210] Iain H. Murray, *Heroes* (Edinburgh: Banner of Truth Trust, 2009), 121.

[211] John Mayor, a friend of Thomas Charles, wanted to be tutored by Newton, and made the arrangements for them to stay at Olney. Newton had previously visited Oxford on more than one occasion. Perhaps it was there that Newton first met Mayor and possibly Charles, or Mayor may have introduced them.

[212] D. E. Jenkins, *The Life of the Rev. Thomas Charles B.A. of Bala* (Denbigh: Llewelyn Jenkins, 1908), 1:50.

[213] Ibid., 1:49.

[214] John Morgan Jones and William Morgan, *The Calvinistic Methodist Fathers of Wales*, trans. John Aaron (Edinburgh: Banner of Truth Trust, 2008), 2:246.

[215] Ibid., 2:267, note 11.

[216] Jenkins, *Thomas Charles*, 1:57.

[217] Ibid., 1:57.

[218] Jones, *Calvinistic Methodist Fathers of Wales*, 2:253.

[219] Ibid., 2:255.

[220] Jenkins, *Thomas Charles*, 1:246.

[221] Ibid., 1:492-496.

[222] Ibid., 1:228, 331. Especially in matters concerning courtship and marriage.

[223] Ibid., 2:187.

[224] Gordon, *Wise Counsel*, 203.

[225] Prior to the American Revolution, North America had been the recipient of these criminals. The independence of the United States, however, forced England to find a new destination.

[226] Gordon, *Wise Counsel*, 203.

[227] Bull, *John Newton*, 286.

[228] Newton, *One Hundred and Twenty-Nine Letters*, 205.

[229] James Bonwick, *Australia's First Preacher; the Rev. Richard Johnson, First Chaplain of New South Wales* (London: Sampson, Low, Marston, and Co., 1898), 39.

[230] John Newton to William Wilberforce, November 15, 1786, c. 49, fol. 13, Wilberforce Papers, Bodleian Library, Oxford, quoted in Rouse, "John Newton." See also Tomkins, *Clapham Sect*, 56.

[231] Bull, *John Newton*, 287.

[232] Bonwick, *Australia's First Preacher*, 67.

[233] Gordon, *Wise Counsel*, 218.

[234] Ibid., 307.

[235] Ibid.

[236] Bonwick, *Australia's First Preacher*, 90.

[237] Ibid., 154.

[238] Gordon, *Wise Counsel*, 307.

[239] Bonwick, *Australia's First Preacher*, 90.

[240] Ibid., 112. Newton notes his concern for Johnson to others as well: "Poor Johnson! The Lord mercifully holds him up, but I long for him to have a friend and fellow labourer to assist or comfort him." John Newton to William Wilberforce, August 3-4, [1792], c. 49, fol. 43, Wilberforce Papers, Bodleian Library, Oxford, quoted in Rouse, "John Newton."

[241] Bonwick, *Australia's First Preacher*, 165.

[242] Ibid., 152.

[243] Ibid., 62, 155, 60.

[244] Ibid., 60.

[245] Ibid., 156.

[246] Ibid., 166.

[247] Robert Philip, *The Life, Times, and Missionary Enterprises of the Rev. John Campbell* (London: John Snow, 1841), 81.

[248] "Significant Scots: Rev. John Campbell," Electric Scotland, accessed August 20, 2019, http://www.electricscotland.com/history/other/campbell_john3.htm.

[249] John Newton, *Letters and Conversational Remarks by the Late Rev. John Newton, Rector of St. Mary Woolnoth*, ed. John Campbell (New York: S. Whiting & Co. Theological and Classical Booksellers, 1811).

[250] Philip, *John Campbell*, 81.

[251] Newton, *Conversational Remarks*, 148.

[252] Ibid., 74-75.

[253] Ibid., 36.

[254] Ibid., 135.

[255] Philip, *John Campbell*, 80.

[256] Ibid., 82.

[257] Hindmarsh, *English Evangelical Tradition*, 311.

[258] Bull, *John Newton*, 357.

[259] Philip, *John Campbell*, 97-98.

[260] Newton, *Conversational Remarks*, 187.

CHAPTER THREE: INFLUENCING FRIENDS

[1] See David Wood, "The Eccentric Vicar of Everton: John Berridge, the Cambridgeshire Revival, and the Life of Pastoral Ministry" (DMin thesis, Gordon-Conwell Theological Seminary, 2012), 107.

[2] D. Bruce Hindmarsh, *John Newton and the English Evangelical Tradition* (Grand Rapids, MI: Eerdmans, 1996), 311. Hindmarsh notes that Cecil followed Newton around and recorded what fell from his lips.

[3] Ibid., 234.

[4] MS 3973, fol. 145, Correspondence and Papers of John Newton, Lambeth Palace Library, London. See also John Newton, *The Works of John Newton*, ed. Richard Cecil (Edinburgh: Banner of Truth Trust, 1988), 1:90.

[5] Timothy Keller, *Generous Justice: How God's Grace Makes us Just* (New York: Dutton, 2010), xix-xx.

[6] Just as Newton describes Christian growth from Mark 4:28: "first the blade, then the ear, then the full grain in the ear." See John Newton, *The Life and Spirituality of John Newton* (Vancouver, BC: Regent College Publishing, 2003), 6, 96-112.

[7] Josiah Bull, *John Newton of Olney and St. Mary Woolnoth* (London: The Religious Tract Society, 1868), 54.

[8] Jonathan Aitken, *John Newton: From Disgrace to Amazing Grace* (Wheaton, IL: Crossway Books, 2007), 325.

[9] Hindmarsh, *English Evangelical Tradition*, 171-172.

[10] Bull, *John Newton*, 136.

[11] Hindmarsh, *English Evangelical Tradition*, 171.

[12] Bull, *John Newton*, 150.

[13] Ibid., 155.

[14] Ibid., 144.

[15] Hindmarsh, *English Evangelical Tradition*, 205.

[16] Bull, *John Newton*, 219.

[17] Ibid., 88.

[18] Hindmarsh, *English Evangelical Tradition*, 197.

[19] Ibid., 309.

[20] Bull, *John Newton*, 353.

[21] Ibid., 136.

[22] Grant Gordon, ed. *Wise Counsel* (2009; repr., Edinburgh: Banner of Truth Trust, 2011), 369.

[23] For instance, see John Newton, *One Hundred and Twenty-Nine Letters from the Rev. John Newton, Late Rector of St. Mary Woolnoth, London, to the Rev. William Bull, of Newport Pagnell*, ed. Thomas Palmer Bull (London: Hamilton, Adams, and Co., 1847), 240-303; Gordon, *Wise Counsel*, 371-396.

[24] Newton, *One Hundred and Twenty-Nine Letters*, 225.

[25] Ibid., 239-240.

[26] Gordon, *Wise Counsel*, 232. In this case, it was a needy pastor.

[27] Newton, *One Hundred and Twenty-Nine Letters*, 47.

[28] John Newton to William Wilberforce, July 5, 1788, c. 49, fols. 17-18, Wilberforce Papers, Bodleian Library, Oxford, quoted in Marylynn Rouse, "John Newton & William Wilberforce Correspondence," unpublished manuscript.

[29] Newton, *Works*, 2:86.

[30] John Newton, *Letters and Conversational Remarks by the Late Rev. John Newton, Rector of St. Mary Woolnoth*, ed. John Campbell (New York: S. Whiting & Co. Theological and Classical Booksellers, 1811), 18.

[31] Gordon, *Wise Counsel*, 198.

[32] Newton, *One Hundred and Twenty-Nine Letters*, 263.

[33] Fast Days were times for national repentance and prayer.

[34] Newton, *Works*, 5:141, 152.

[35] It must be stated that numerous factors contributed to the cessation of slavery, not simply the actions of a few devout people such as Wilberforce. "Historians are divided on the reasons for the success of these campaigns, variously arguing that it was the reward for diligence of a body of virtuous 'saints' such as William Wilberforce and Thomas Clarkson, that it was realized that the institution of slavery was no longer profitable, that there was a fundamental shift in popular sensibility, that the campaign was the expression of a new middle-class capitalist ideology that insisted on the importance of free labour in a free market, or that slave resistance made the plantations untenable. Few historians now doubt that a combination of several of the above led to abolition of the slave trade, with social, economic and cultural factors in the metropolis probably providing the impetus." Brycchan Carey, "John Wesley's *Thoughts Upon Slavery* and the Language of the Heart," *The Bulletin of the John Rylands University Library of Manchester* 85:2-3 (Summer/Autumn 2003): 270-71.

[36] Tomkins makes the statement that "even Newton, for all his experience and participation, only seems to have had his conscience pricked by the public campaign." Contrary to Tomkins, by 1781 Newton's conscience had been thoroughly pricked; in fact, he was pricking the conscience of others. See Stephen Tomkins, *The Clapham Sect: How Wilberforce's Circle Transformed Britain* (Oxford: Lion Hudson, 2010), 70.

[37] Later in life, Wilberforce wrote, "As long ago as in 1781, the very first year of my being in parliament, and when I was not twenty-two years of age, I wrote a letter to James Gordon expressing my hopes that some time or other I might become the instrument of breaking, or at least easing, the yoke of [West Indian slaves]." Robert and Samuel Wilberforce, *The Life of William Wilberforce* (London: John Murray, 1838), 4:306. Of course, the Quakers had been actively working against the trade since the 1770s. See Tomkins, *Clapham Sect*, 66.

[38] Wesley published his *Thoughts upon Slavery* in 1774. See Carey, "John Wesley's *Thoughts*": 275.

[39] John Wesley, *Letters of the Rev. John Wesley, A.M.,* 8 vols, ed. John Telford (London: The Epworth Press, 1931), 7:359-60, quoted in Carey, "John Wesley's *Thoughts*": 277.

[40] To be fair, once the decision had been made to move forward, Pitt supported Wilberforce wholeheartedly, employing his remarkable oratorical skill to the fullest degree. See Robin Furneaux, *William Wilberforce* (1974; repr., Vancouver, BC: Regent College Publishing, 2005), 111.

[41] Newton, *One Hundred and Twenty-Nine Letters*, 262.

[42] Newton, *Works*, 5:262-263.

[43] Ibid., 5:290-291.

[44] Such as his sermon on November 21, 1787 at the annual meeting for the Society for Promoting Religious Knowledge Amongst the Poor. He had been a member of the society for almost twenty years. After commending the support of societies to spread the gospel, Newton said, "Among these there are few, in any, which I can more warrantably commend to your attention, than the laudable and benevolent object of the Society for Promoting Religious Knowledge among the Poor; an institution which it has pleased God signally to prosper." Ibid., 5:221.

Newton also preached at charity benefits on other occasions, including one for the Langbourn-Ward Charity School on March 30, 1800. See Ibid., 6:491-517.

[45] Bull, *John Newton*, 357.

[46] Aitken, *John Newton*, 241.

[47] Ibid., 243.

[48] Newton goes on to say that Jesus' teaching in Luke 14:12-14 indicates that "in some respects our duty is to give a preference to the poor." Newton, *Works*, 1:133-136.

[49] Newton began work on the project in 1795, and it was published early in 1799. See Newton, *Conversational Remarks*, 86; Bull, *John Newton*, 340.

[50] John Newton, *Memoirs of the Life of Rev. William Grimshaw* (London: W. Baynes and Son, 1825), 90.

[51] Ibid., 111.

[52] Ibid., 115.

[53] Newton, *Conversational Remarks*, 86. John Newton to John Campbell.

[54] Gordon, *Wise Counsel*, 350.

[55] Ibid., 295.

[56] Newton, *Works,* 5:308.

[57] Ibid., 5:406-407 footnote.

[58] Ibid., 6:521.

[59] Aitken, *John Newton*, 322.

[60] Gordon, *Wise Counsel*, 304.

[61] Aitken, *John Newton*, 320.

[62] Newton, *Works*, 6:529.

[63] Ibid., 6:530.

[64] Ibid., 6:533.

[65] Ibid., 6:534.

[66] Ibid., 6:543.

[67] Ibid., 6:544.

[68] Ibid., 6:544.

[69] Ibid., 6:537.

[70] Ibid., 6:548.

[71] Aitken, *John Newton*, 323.

[72] Ibid.

[73] Newton once told John Ryland Jr., "My whole concern with politics is to tell people that the Lord reigns, that all hearts are in his hand, that creatures are all instruments of his will, and can do neither more nor less than he, for wise reasons, appoints or permits; that sin is the procuring cause of all misery; that they who sigh and mourn for our abominations and stand in the breach pleading for mercy, are better patriots than they who talk loudly about men and measures, of either side." Gordon, *Wise Counsel*, 324.

[74] Gordon, *Wise Counsel*, 204.

[75] Aitken, *John Newton*, 325.

[76] Ibid., 325-326.

[77] Gordon, *Wise Counsel*, 225.

[78] George Redford and John Angell James, eds., *The Autobiography of the Rev. William Jay*, 3rd ed. (London: Hamilton, Adams, and Co., 1855), 278-279. A "D.D." is a Doctor of Divinity degree.

[79] Bernard Martin, *John Newton: A Biography* (London: William Heinemann LTD, 1950), 324.

[80] John Pollock, *Wilberforce* (Tring: Lion Publishing, 1977), 211; Kevin Belmonte, *William Wilberforce: A Hero for Humanity* (Grand Rapids, MI: Zondervan, 2007), 151.

[81] John Newton to Hannah More, June 4, 1793, c. 49, fols. 127-128, Wilberforce Papers, Bodleian Library, Oxford, quoted in Rouse, "John Newton."

[82] Keller, *Generous Justice*, 102.

CHAPTER FOUR: TO CHANGE SOCIETY

[1] Robert and Samuel Wilberforce, *The Life of William Wilberforce* (London: John Murray, 1838), 1:93.

[2] Ibid.

[3] Ibid., 1:96.

[4] Ibid., 1:96-97. See also, Kevin Belmonte, *William Wilberforce: A Hero for Humanity* (Grand Rapids, MI: Zondervan, 2007), 80-82.

[5] Wilberforce, *Life of William Wilberforce*, 1:96-97.

[6] Belmonte, *William Wilberforce*, 67.

[7] Ibid., 84.

[8] Wilberforce, *Life of William Wilberforce*, 1:96-97.

[9] Ibid., 1:99.

[10] Ibid.

[11] Ibid., 1:100-101.

[12] John Newton to William Wilberforce, March 21, 1786, c. 49, fol. 4, Wilberforce Papers, Bodleian Library, Oxford, quoted in Marylynn Rouse, "John Newton & William Wilberforce Correspondence," unpublished manuscript.

[13] Belmonte, *William Wilberforce*, 100.

[14] Stephen Tomkins, *The Clapham Sect: How Wilberforce's Circle Transformed Britain* (Oxford: Lion Hudson, 2010), 48.

[15] John Newton to William Wilberforce, May 18, [1786], c. 49, fol. 9, Wilberforce Papers, Bodleian Library, Oxford, quoted in Rouse, "John Newton."

[16] John Newton to William Wilberforce, November 15, 1786, c. 49, fols. 12-13, Wilberforce Papers, Bodleian Library, Oxford, quoted in Rouse, "John Newton."

[17] John Newton to William Wilberforce, July 31, 1799, c. 49, fol. 94, Wilberforce Papers, Bodleian Library, Oxford, quoted in Rouse, "John Newton."

[18] Robert and Samuel Wilberforce, eds. *The Correspondence of William Wilberforce* (London: John Murray, 1840), 1:x.

[19] Donald E. Demaray, *The Innovation of John Newton (1725-1807): Synergism of Word and Music in Eighteenth Century Evangelicalism* (Lewiston, NY: The Edwin Mellen Press, 1988), 89.

[20] Wilberforce, *Life of William Wilberforce*, 1:9.

[21] John Newton to William Wilberforce, November 1, 1787, c. 49, fols. 14-15, Wilberforce Papers, Bodleian Library, Oxford, quoted in Rouse, "John Newton."

[22] Jonathan Aitken, *John Newton: From Disgrace to Amazing Grace* (Wheaton, IL: Crossway Books, 2007), 310.

[23] Belmonte, *William Wilberforce*, 152.

[24] Eric Metaxas, *Amazing Grace: William Wilberforce and the Heroic Campaign to End Slavery* (New York: HarperOne, 2007), 83.

[25] John Pollock, *Wilberforce* (Tring: Lion Publishing, 1977), 60.

[26] Metaxas, *Amazing Grace*, 83. See also Belmonte, *William Wilberforce*, 157-159.

[27] Belmonte, *William Wilberforce*, 102.

[28] Ibid., 104-106. That said, a bill was passed at this time, reducing how many slaves a ship could legally transport, based on its size.

[29] Ibid., 105.

[30] Tomkins, *Clapham Sect*, 86.

[31] William Wilberforce to John Newton, September 6, 1788, c. 49, fol. 19-20, Wilberforce Papers, Bodleian Library, Oxford, quoted in Rouse, "John Newton."

[32] Ibid.

[33] Robin Furneaux, *William Wilberforce* (1974; repr., Vancouver, BC: Regent College Publishing, 2005), 100.

[34] Ibid., 102.

[35] Pollock, *Wilberforce*, 115-116.

[36] Belmonte, *William Wilberforce*, 114.

[37] Ibid., 125.

[38] Ibid., 134.

[39] John Newton to William Wilberforce, May 29, 1789, c. 49, fol. 28, Wilberforce Papers, Bodleian Library, Oxford, quoted in Rouse, "John Newton."

[40] John Newton to William Wilberforce, June 10, 1791, c. 49, fol. 34, Wilberforce Papers, Bodleian Library, Oxford, quoted in Rouse, "John Newton."

[41] John Newton to William Wilberforce, August 3-4, [1792], c. 49, fol. 43, Wilberforce Papers, Bodleian Library, Oxford, quoted in Rouse, "John Newton."

[42] Ibid.

[43] John Newton to William Wilberforce, March 19, 1795, c. 49, fol. 60, Wilberforce Papers, Bodleian Library, Oxford, quoted in Rouse, "John Newton."

[44] John Newton to William Wilberforce, July 4, 1795, c. 49, fol. 63, Wilberforce Papers, Bodleian Library, Oxford, quoted in Rouse, "John Newton."

[45] Belmonte, *William Wilberforce*, 134, 136.

[46] John Newton to William Wilberforce, March 30, 1796, c. 49, fol. 69-70, Wilberforce Papers, Bodleian Library, Oxford, quoted in Rouse, "John Newton."

[47] John Newton to William Wilberforce, July 21, 1796, c. 49, fols. 71-72, Wilberforce Papers, Bodleian Library, Oxford, quoted in Rouse, "John Newton."

[48] Belmonte, *William Wilberforce*, 244, 247.

[49] "I doubt if I shall ever change my situation." Furneaux, *William Wilberforce*, 161.

[50] Belmonte, *William Wilberforce*, 255-256.

[51] Ibid., 253.

[52] Wilberforce, *Life of William Wilberforce*, 5:218.

[53] Belmonte, *William Wilberforce*, 140-141.

[54] Furneaux, *William Wilberforce*, 253; Pollock, *Wilberforce*, 211; Belmonte, *William Wilberforce*, 150.

[55] Belmonte, *William Wilberforce*, 151.

[56] Robert and Samuel Wilberforce, eds., *The Correspondence of William Wilberforce* (London: John Murray, 1840), 1:302.

[57] Ibid., 1:303.

[58] Wilberforce, *Life of Wilberforce*, 3:170.

[59] Metaxas, *Amazing Grace*, xvii; Ford K. Brown, *Fathers of the Victorians: The Age of Wilberforce* (Cambridge: Cambridge University Press, 1961), 357.

[60] M. Seeley, *The Later Evangelical Fathers* (London: Seeley, Jackson, & Halliday, 1879), 150.

[61] Gilbert Thomas, *William Cowper and the Eighteenth Century* (London: Ivor Nicholson and Watson, 1935), 258.

[62] Demaray, *Innovation of John Newton*, 278.

[63] Seeley, *Later Evangelical Fathers*, 112-113.

[64] John Piper, *The Hidden Smile of God: The Fruit of Affliction in the Lives of John Bunyan, William Cowper, and David Brainerd* (Wheaton, IL: Crossway Books, 2001), 97.

[65] Thomas, *Cowper and the Eighteenth Century*, 262. See also Josiah Bull, *John Newton of Olney and St. Mary Woolnoth* (London: The Religious Tract Society, 1868), 254.

[66] Thomas, *Cowper and the Eighteenth Century*, 266. Some editions, however, kept the introduction.

[67] William Cowper, *Letters of William Cowper* (London: The Religious Tract Society, 1862), 200-201.

[68] Thomas, *Cowper and the Eighteenth Century*, 267.

[69] Brycchan Carey, "Anti-Slavery Poems by William Cowper," Slavery, Emancipation, and Abolition, accessed August 20, 2019, http://www.brycchancarey.com/slavery/cowperpoems.htm.

[70] Demaray, *Innovation of John Newton*, 138.

[71] Cowper, *Letters of William Cowper*, 179.

[72] Bull, *John Newton*, 278.

[73] Thomas, *Cowper and the Eighteenth Century*, 265.

[74] Bernard Martin, *John Newton: A Biography* (London: William Heinemann LTD, 1950), 340. Letter to Hannah More.

[75] Mark Van Doren, ed. *The Selected Letters of William Cowper* (New York: Farrar, Straus, and Young, Inc., 1951), 132-133.

[76] Aitken, *John Newton*, 325.

[77] Thomas, *Cowper and the Eighteenth Century*, 358-359.

[78] Tomkins, *Clapham Sect*, 71.

[79] Van Doren, *Selected Letters of William Cowper*, 239-241.

[80] John Newton, *The Works of John Newton*, ed. Richard Cecil (Edinburgh: Banner of Truth Trust, 1988), 6:532.

[81] Carey, "Anti-Slavery Poems by William Cowper."

[82] Ibid.

[83] Stopford A. Brooke, *Theology in the English Poets*, 8th ed. (London: Kegan Paul, Trench, Trubner & CO., 1896), 56-57.

[84] Thomas, *Cowper and the Eighteenth Century*, 333.

[85] John Newton, *Letters of John Newton*, ed. Josiah Bull (1869; repr., Edinburgh: Banner of Truth Trust, 2007), 355.

[86] Martin, *John Newton*, 316, 318.

[87] John Wolffe, *The Expansion of Evangelicalism: The Age of Wilberforce, More, Chalmers and Finney* (Downers Grove, IL: InterVarsity Press, 2007), 134-137.

[88] "That More gave up writing dramatic tragedies because she came to doubt the heroic ideals of the classical world shows how much she was influenced by evangelical religion." Mark Noll, *The Rise of Evangelicalism: The Age of Edwards, Whitefield and the Wesleys* (Downers Grove, IL: InterVarsity Press, 2003), 238-239.

[89] Martin, *John Newton*, 316-317, 319.

[90] Grant Gordon, ed. *Wise Counsel* (2009; repr., Edinburgh: Banner of Truth Trust, 2011), 204.

[91] Brycchan Carey, "Hannah More: *Slavery, A Poem*," Slavery, Emancipation, and Abolition, accessed August 20, 2019, www.brycchancarey.com/slavery/morepoems.htm.

[92] Carey, "Hannah More: *Slavery, A Poem*." More's words, from a footnote in "Slavery, A Poem."

[93] Despite some of More's conservative and traditional views concerning women's roles and paternalistic posture toward the poor, she deserves a fair hearing and appreciation for the context from which she created a significant role for herself.

[94] Brycchan Carey, "Hannah More (1745-1833)," Slavery, Emancipation, and Abolition, accessed August 20, 2019, www.brycchancarey.com/abolition/more.htm.

[95] Martin, *John Newton*, 343.

[96] Wolffe, *Expansion of Evangelicalism*, 134.

[97] Tomkins, *Clapham Sect*, 140, 142, 144.

[98] Nathan Hatch, *The Democratization of American Christianity* (New Haven, CT: Yale University Press, 1989), 143. Stephen Tompkins notes, "But their writings, whether about the poor, such as the *Mendip Annals*, or for them, such as the later Cheap Repository tracts, reveal them to be manipulative and arrogantly controlling as well as concerned and generous." Tomkins, *Clapham Sect*, 79.

[99] Martin, *John Newton*, 343.

[100] See, for instance, "The Cottage Cook" or "The History of Hester Wilmot." Hannah More, *Cheap Repository Tracts: Entertaining, Moral, and Religious*, rev. ed. (New York: American Tract Society, 1800), 4:8-35, 47-86.

[101] Martin, *John Newton*, 321.

[102] Timothy Smith, *Revivalism and Social Reform: American Protestantism on the Eve of the Civil War* (Eugene, OR: Wipf & Stock, 1957), 146. See also Tomkins, *Clapham Sect*, 136.

[103] Carey, "Hannah More (1745-1833)." Perhaps 2.8-3 million British Pounds. See "Five Ways to Compute the Relative Value of a UK Pound Amount, 1270 to Present," Measuring Worth, accessed August 20, 2019, https://www.measuringworth.com/calculators/ukcompare/.

[104] Tomkins, *Clapham Sect*, 75.

[105] Ibid., 75-77.

[106] William Roberts, *Memoirs of the Life of Mrs. Hannah More*, abridged ed. (London: R. B. Seeley and W. Burnside, 1839), 246.

[107] Tomkins, *Clapham Sect*, 75-77. Some feel that More's work was anything but educational; Ford Brown makes this argument. Though Brown admits that "The Mores went into them Sunday after Sunday for many years, on horseback when they had to, for ten miles or sometimes twenty miles, over 'dreadful roads,' in spite of weather and illness and always in the face of steady discouragements" (230), he also asserts, "Thus no pains are required to discover that to educate her children, youths and adults was far from Hannah More's aim" (189), and, "Mrs More took pains to teach her scholars to read as little as it is humanly possible to do and did not teach anybody to write" (190). Brown argues that More's only purpose was to spread evangelical principles (191). Ford K. Brown, *Fathers of the Victorians: The Age of Wilberforce* (Cambridge: Cambridge University Press, 1961). While that may have be the impulse which led to such commitment, Brown overstates his case, neglecting to account for the real learning and training that did, in fact, undeniably take place at Hannah More's schools.

[108] Tomkins, *Clapham Sect*, 75-77.

[109] Roberts, *Hannah More*, 245.

[110] Ibid., 246. See also William Roberts, *The Life and Correspondence of Mrs. Hannah More, 3rd ed.* (London: R. B. Seeley and W. Burnside, 1835), 3:7.

[111] Roberts, *The Life and Correspondence of Mrs. Hannah More*, 3:7.

[112] More, *Cheap Repository Tracts*, 3:74-95.

[113] Ibid., 4:12-15.

[114] Martin, *John Newton*, 341.

[115] Newton, *Letters*, 346.

[116] Wilberforce, *Correspondence of William Wilberforce*, 1:113. Letter penned December 13, 1791; it is mistakenly dated 1794 in this work.

[117] Newton, *Letters*, 358-359.

[118] Roberts, *The Life and Correspondence of Mrs. Hannah More*, 3:6-7, 10.

[119] Ibid., 3:23-24.

[120] Anne Stott, "Hannah More: Biography," The Victorian Web, accessed August 20, 2019, http://www.victorianweb.org/authors/more/bio.html. In fact, two of her women's benefit clubs existed until 1949 and 1950.

[121] John Morgan Jones and William Morgan, *The Calvinistic Methodist Fathers of Wales*, trans. John Aaron (Edinburgh: Banner of Truth Trust, 2008), 2:269, 272.

[122] D. E. Jenkins, *The Life of the Rev. Thomas Charles B.A. of Bala* (Denbigh: Llewelyn Jenkins, 1908), 1:552.

[123] Ibid., 1:563.

[124] Jones, *Calvinistic Methodist Fathers of Wales*, 1:47.

[125] Ibid., 2:288.

[126] Iain H. Murray, *Heroes* (Edinburgh: Banner of Truth Trust, 2009), 129.

[127] Jones, *Calvinistic Methodist Fathers of Wales*, 2:287.

[128] Jenkins, *Thomas Charles*, 1:566-567.

[129] Jones, *Calvinistic Methodist Fathers of Wales*, 2:282, 285.

[130] Jenkins, *Thomas Charles*, 2:88.

[131] Ibid., 2:95-96, 103-104.

[132] Jones, *Calvinistic Methodist Fathers of Wales*, 2:289.

[133] Jenkins, *Thomas Charles*, 2:30.

[134] Ibid., 2:286.

[135] Ibid., 2:184.

[136] Ibid., 2:215, 462.

[137] Jones, *Calvinistic Methodist Fathers of Wales*, 2:317.

[138] Ibid., 2:300.

[139] Jenkins, *Thomas Charles*, 2:183. Two sermons were preached; Newton was one of the speakers.

[140] Ibid., 1:598-599.

[141] Jones, *Calvinistic Methodist Fathers of Wales*, 2:303.

[142] Jenkins, *Thomas Charles*, 2:115.

[143] Murray, *Heroes*, 136.

[144] "The people surrounded the carrier that bore the Bibles like starving people pressing around a delivery of bread." Jones, *Calvinistic Methodist Fathers of Wales*, 2:303.

[145] Ibid., 2:301; Murray, *Heroes*, 136.

[146] Tomkins, *Clapham Sect*, 220.

[147] Jenkins, *Thomas Charles*, 1:228.

[148] Jones, *Calvinistic Methodist Fathers of Wales*, 2:341.

[149] George Redford and John Angell James, eds., *The Autobiography of the Rev. William Jay*, 3rd ed. (London: Hamilton, Adams, and Co., 1855), 279.

[150] A conservative estimate, based on Jenkins, *Thomas Charles*, 3:575.

[151] Jones, *Calvinistic Methodist Fathers of Wales*, 2:337.

CHAPTER FIVE: TO CHANGE THE CHURCH

[1] D. E. Jenkins, *The Life of the Rev. Thomas Charles B.A. of Bala* (Denbigh: Llewelyn Jenkins, 1908), 1:571-572.

[2] John Newton, *One Hundred and Twenty Nine Letters from the Rev. John Newton, Late Rector of St. Mary Woolnoth, London, to the Rev. William Bull, of Newport Pagnell*, ed. Thomas Palmer Bull (London: Hamilton, Adams, and Co., 1847), 129 note.

[3] John Scott, *The Life of the Rev. Thomas Scott, D.D.*, abridged ed. (New York: American Tract Society, 1835), 132-133.

[4] A. C. Downer, *Thomas Scott the Commentator* (London: Chas. J. Thynne, 1909), 27, 29.

[5] Ibid., 47.

[6] Donald E. Demaray, *The Innovation of John Newton (1725-1807): Synergism of Word and Music in Eighteenth Century Evangelicalism* (Lewiston, NY: The Edwin Mellen Press, 1988), 218.

[7] Downer, *Thomas Scott the Commentator*, 49.

[8] Ibid., 50.

[9] Eric Metaxas, *Amazing Grace: William Wilberforce and the Heroic Campaign to End Slavery* (New York: HarperOne, 2007), 76.

[10] Scott, *The Life of the Rev. Thomas Scott,* 186.

[11] Jenkins, *Thomas Charles*, 1:571.

[12] "The aristocratic congregation, connected with the Hospital, did not take kindly to Scott's blunt preaching." Thomas Scott, *The Force of Truth* (1779; repr., Edinburgh: Banner of Truth Trust, 1984), 17.

[13] Scott, *The Life of the Rev. Thomas Scott*, 183.

[14] Downer, *Thomas Scott the Commentator*, 59.

[15] Donald Spoto, *Reluctant Saint: The Life of Saint Francis of Assisi* (New York: Penguin Compass, 2002), 58.

[16] Jenkins, *Thomas Charles*, 1:571.

[17] John Scott, *Letters and Papers of the Late Rev. Thomas Scott, D.D* (Boston: Samuel T. Armstrong, and Crocker, & Brewster, 1825), 78.

[18] Downer, *Thomas Scott the Commentator*, 69.

[19] Scott, *Letters and Papers*, 79.

[20] Scott, *The Life of the Rev. Thomas Scott,* 185.

[21] Downer, *Thomas Scott the Commentator*, 68.

[22] Scott, *The Life of the Rev. Thomas Scott,* 188-189.

[23] Ibid., 326-327.

[24] Downer, *Thomas Scott the Commentator*, 53.

[25] Ibid., 59.

[26] Ibid., 69. It was still in operation at the date of publication of *Scott the Commentator* in 1909 under the name "Lock Rescue House." The institution finally closed in 1952. See David Innes Williams, *The London Lock: A Charitable Hospital for Venereal Disease 1746-1952* (London: Royal Society of Medicine Press, 1995).

[27] John H. Pratt, ed. *Eclectic Notes*, 2nd ed. (London: James Nisbet and Co., 1865), 536. Scott continued in the Eclectic Society until 1807, the year of Newton's death.

[28] Downer, *Thomas Scott the Commentator*, 75.

[29] "Simeon came to be a leading apostle of the Mission cause, as Wilberforce had already begun to be of the Abolition cause." Charles Hole, *The Early History of the Church Missionary Society* (London: Church Missionary Society, 1896), 12. See all of chapter one for Simeon's influential role leading up to the formation of the CMS.

[30] M. Seeley, *The Later Evangelical Fathers* (London: Seeley, Jackson, & Halliday, 1879), 245-248.

[31] Handley Moule, *Charles Simeon* (repr., London: InterVarsity Press, 1965), 42.

[32] Ibid., 179.

[33] John Piper, *The Roots of Endurance: Invincible Perseverance in the Lives of John Newton, Charles Simeon, and William Wilberforce* (Wheaton, IL: Crossway Books, 2002), 103.

[34] An advowson is the right of a patron to name the next pastor to take over a particular congregation when the position becomes open.

[35] Seeley, *Later Evangelical Fathers*, 275-276.

[36] Ibid., 260.

[37] Ibid., 277.

[38] D. Bruce Hindmarsh, *John Newton and the English Evangelical Tradition* (Grand Rapids, MI: Eerdmans, 1996), 326.

[39] Hole, *The Early History of the Church Missionary Society*, 32.

[40] Bernard Martin, *John Newton: A Biography* (London: William Heinemann LTD, 1950), 325.

[41] Hole, *The Early History of the Church Missionary Society*, 10-11.

[42] Seeley, *Later Evangelical Fathers*, 271.

[43] The caste system in India particularly bothered Simeon, which he referred to as a "horrid structure" that he hoped to "undermine." Caste distinctions were theologically offensive: "Now Christ regards the very least and meanest of His people as members of His body: and consequently, the separations occasioned by caste are contrary to the very spirit of His religion, which makes all His people to be one. Therefore the *distinctions of caste are inadmissible in a Christian community*." William Carus, ed. *Memoirs of the Life of the Rev. Charles Simeon, M.A.* (London: Hatchard and Son, 1847), 759, 761.

[44] Hugh Hopkins, *Charles Simeon of Cambridge* (London: Hodder and Stoughton, 1977), 202, 176.

[45] Carus, *Memoirs of the Life of the Rev. Charles Simeon*, 537-538.

[46] Seeley, *Later Evangelical Fathers*, 279.

[47] Josiah Bull, *Memorials of the Rev. William Bull, of Newport Pagnel*, 2nd ed. (London: Elliot Stock, 1865), 55.

[48] Hindmarsh, *English Evangelical Tradition*, 238. See also Frederick William Bull, *A History of Newport Pagnell* (Kettering: W. E. & J. Goss, 1900), 281.

[49] Newton, *One Hundred Twenty-Nine Letters*, 91-92.

[50] Ibid., 115, 124.

[51] Ibid., 133.

[52] Ibid., 138.

[53] Ibid., 101.

[54] Bull, *Memorials*, 302.

[55] Ibid., 252.

[56] Ibid., 268-269.

[57] The Bull family—William (father), Thomas (son), and Josiah (grandson)—pastored the independent congregation at Newport Pagnell for over one hundred years. See Bull, *A History of Newport Pagnell*, 250.

[58] Josiah Bull, *John Newton of Olney and St. Mary Woolnoth* (London: The Religious Tract Society, 1868), 257.

[59] Ibid., 258.

[60] Ibid.

[61] Bull, *A History of Newport Pagnell*, 149.

[62] Bull, *Memorials*, 157.

[63] Ibid., 169.

[64] Ibid., 345.

[65] Bull, *John Newton*, 259.

[66] George Redford and John Angell James, eds., *The Autobiography of the Rev. William Jay*, 3rd ed. (London: Hamilton, Adams, and Co., 1855), 272.

[67] Grant Gordon, ed. *Wise Counsel* (2009; repr., Edinburgh: Banner of Truth Trust, 2011), 257.

[68] Hindmarsh, *English Evangelical Tradition*, 142-159.

[69] Grant Gordon, "John Ryland Jr.," in *The British Particular Baptists 1638-1910,* ed. Michael Haykin (Springfield, MO: Particular Baptist Press, 2000), 2:83.

[70] Ibid., 2:84-85.

[71] Ibid., 2:85. See also Stephen J. Stein, ed. *The Cambridge Companion to Jonathan Edwards* (Cambridge: Cambridge University Press, 2007), 247.

[72] Gordon, "John Ryland Jr.," 2:90.

[73] John Newton, *The Works of John Newton*, ed. Richard Cecil (Edinburgh: Banner of Truth Trust, 1988), 2:113.

[74] Gordon, "John Ryland Jr.," 2:93.

[75] Gordon, *Wise Counsel*, 402.

[76] Ibid., 326-328.

[77] Henry Thornton was the son of John Thornton, Newton's benefactor. Henry was a banker, a Member of Parliament, and the chairman of the Sierra Leone Company.

[78] Gordon, *Wise Counsel*, 318, 341-344.

[79] Ibid., 315-316.

[80] Stephen Tomkins, *The Clapham Sect: How Wilberforce's Circle Transformed Britain* (Oxford: Lion Hudson, 2010), 229. Clearly, the Quakers would be an exception here. Also, Timothy Whelan demonstrates that there were some key Baptist leaders involved in abolition much earlier. See Timothy Whelan, "An Evangelical Anglican Interaction with Baptist Missionary Society Strategy: William Wilberforce and John Ryland, 1807-1824," in *Interfaces: Baptists and Others*, eds. David Bebbington and Martin Sutherland, Studies in Baptist History and Thought (Milton Keynes: Paternoster, 2013), 57-58.

[81] Gordon, *Wise Counsel*, 201.

[82] *Periodical Accounts Relative to the Baptist Missionary Society* (London: Clipstone, 1800), 1:111-112.

[83] Gordon, *Wise Counsel*, 287.

[84] Gordon, "John Ryland Jr.," 2:90.

[85] Gary W. Long, "William Knibb," in *The British Particular Baptists 1638-1910*, ed. Michael Haykin (Springfield, MO: Particular Baptist Press, 2000), 3:220-221.

[86] Ibid., 3:213.

[87] Gordon, *Wise Counsel*, 398 n. 1.

[88] Ibid., 395.

[89] Ibid., 396-397.

[90] Ibid., 395.

[91] Pearce S. Carey, *William Carey D.D., Fellow of Linnaean Society*, 3rd ed. (London: Hodder and Stoughton, 1924), 46.

[92] *Periodical Accounts*, 1:342.

[93] William Carey to John Newton, November 19, 1802, MS 2935, fol. 276, General Correspondence of John Newton, Lambeth Palace Library, London.

[94] William Carey to John Newton, MS 2935, fol. 275, General Correspondence of John Newton, Lambeth Palace Library, London.

[95] Gordon, *Wise Counsel*, 339.

[96] Ibid., 354.

[97] Timothy George, *Faithful Witness: The Life and Mission of William Carey* (Birmingham: New Hope Publishers, 1991), 23.

[98] William Carey to John Newton, December 5, 1798, MS 2935, fol. 273v, General Correspondence of John Newton, Lambeth Palace Library, London.

[99] Vishal and Ruth Mangalwadi, *The Legacy of William Carey: A Model for the Transformation of a Culture* (Wheaton, IL: Crossway Books, 1999), 19.

[100] Ibid., 22.

[101] Ibid., 23.

[102] Ibid., 19-23.

[103] Ibid., 18-25.

[104] Hugh Pearson, *Memoir of Rev. Claudius Buchanan, D.D.*, abridged ed. (New York: American Tract Society, [18--]), 98, 102. After Buchanan's ordination on September 20, 1795, he immediately went to work under Newton at St. Mary Woolnoth. His last Sunday was July 3, 1796.

[105] Claudius Buchanan to John Newton, October 24, 1792, MS 3096, fol. 118, Letters to Newton, Lambeth Palace Library, London.

[106] Martin, *John Newton*, 322. Although the East India Company had traditionally frowned on missionaries (as with William Carey), thinking that they might disrupt the Company's ability to trade and profit, they did appoint chaplains who were supposed to minister to the English workers in India. Charles Grant, Charles Simeon and others sought to put evangelical men in these posts, who would not only serve the English colonists but also the indigenous peoples.

[107] Pearson, *Memoir of Rev. Claudius Buchanan*, 100. Buchanan was appointed March 30, 1796. It should be noted that Charles Simeon was also influential in the appointment, having known Buchanan through the latter's time at Cambridge. See Hole, *The Early History of the Church Missionary Society*, 19.

[108] John Newton, *Letters and Conversational Remarks by the Late Rev. John Newton, Rector of St. Mary Woolnoth*, ed. John Campbell (New York: S. Whiting & Co. Theological and Classical Booksellers, 1811), 82.

[109] Ibid., 93.

[110] Pearson, *Memoir of Rev. Claudius Buchanan*, 39.

[111] Claudius Buchanan to John Newton, August 11, 1796 and October 1, 1798, MS 3972, fols. 37, 41, Letters to John Newton, Lambeth Palace Library, London.

[112] Pearson, *Memoir of Rev. Claudius Buchanan*, 147.

[113] Claudius Buchanan to John Newton, October 1, 1798, MS 3972, fol. 44, Letters to John Newton, Lambeth Palace Library, London.

[114] Claudius Buchanan to John Newton, MS 3972, fol. 41, Letters to John Newton, Lambeth Palace Library, London.

[115] Pearson, *Memoir of Rev. Claudius Buchanan*, 149.

[116] Tomkins, *Clapham Sect*, 213. See also Pearson, *Memoir of Rev. Claudius Buchanan*, 156.

[117] Claudius Buchanan to John Newton, October 24, 1792, MS 3096, fol. 118, Letters to Newton, Lambeth Palace Library, London.

[118] Claudius Buchanan to John Newton, March 26, 1793, MS 3096, fol. 120, Letters to Newton, Lambeth Palace Library, London.

[119] Claudius Buchanan, *The Works of the Rev. Claudius Buchanan* (Montpelier, VT: Lucius Q. C. Bowles, 1813), 14.

[120] Ibid., ii. (Recommendation from page prior to Table of Contents.)

[121] Pearson, *Memoir of Rev. Claudius Buchanan*, 276.

[122] Buchanan, *The Works of the Rev. Claudius Buchanan*, 38-39.

[123] Ibid., 41.

[124] Ibid., 28-29.

[125] Ibid., 30-31.

[126] Ibid., 120, 128, 130.

[127] Ibid., 133.

[128] The Portuguese brought the Catholic Inquisition to Goa, India in the year 1560. It was reportedly both intense and heartless. See "The Portuguese Inquisition in Goa: A brief history," Indiafacts, accessed September 25, 2019, http://indiafacts.org/the-portuguese-inquisition-in-goa-a-brief-history/; Teotonio R. de Souza, "Goa Inquisition for Colonial Disciplining," *oHeraldo* (Goa) (13 March 2010): 8.

[129] Pearson, *Memoir of Rev. Claudius Buchanan*, 384.

[130] Ibid., 412.

[131] Ibid., 424.

[132] Buchanan, *The Works of the Rev. Claudius Buchanan*, 284-286.

[133] Pearson, *Memoir of Rev. Claudius Buchanan*, 438-439.

[134] "Like a moon among lesser fires," from Horace's *Odes* 1.12.

[135] Carus, *Memoirs of the Life of the Rev. Charles Simeon*, 459-460.

[136] Pearson, *Memoir of Rev. Claudius Buchanan*, 149.

[137] James Bonwick, *Australia's First Preacher; the Rev. Richard Johnson, First Chaplain of New South Wales* (London: Sampson, Low, Marston, and Co., 1898), 145.

[138] Ibid., 147-153. Bonwick refers to eleven of Newton's letters to Johnson in this small selection.

[139] Ibid., 167.

[140] Perhaps 27,000-28,000 British Pounds in today's currency. See "Five Ways to Compute the Relative Value of a UK Pound Amount, 1270 to Present," Measuring Worth, accessed August 20, 2019, https://www.measuringworth.com/calculators/ukcompare/.

[141] John Newton to Sir Charles Middleton, December 7, 1786, c. 49 fol. 126, Wilberforce Papers, Bodleian Library, Oxford, quoted in Marylynn Rouse, "John Newton & William Wilberforce Correspondence," unpublished manuscript.

[142] Bonwick, *Australia's First Preacher*, 90.

[143] Ibid., 232.

[144] Ibid., 241.

[145] Ibid., 233-234.

[146] Ibid., 234-237.

[147] Ibid., 250.

[148] Ibid., 198.

[149] Ibid., 221-223.

[150] Ibid., 193-197.

[151] Ibid., 243.

[152] Robert Philip, *The Life, Times, and Missionary Enterprises of the Rev. John Campbell* (London: John Snow, 1841), 56, 73.

[153] Ibid., 67. Campbell began ministering to orphans in 1787, two years before meeting Newton.

[154] Demaray, *Innovation of John Newton*, 165.

[155] Philip, *John Campbell*, 138.

[156] Ibid., 307-308, 363.

[157] Ibid., 128, 130.

[158] Newton, *Conversational Remarks*, 126.

[159] Ibid., 150.

[160] John Newton, *Letters of John Newton*, ed. Josiah Bull (1869; repr., Edinburgh: Banner of Truth Trust, 2007), 362.

[161] Philip, *John Campbell*, 192, 209.

[162] Ibid., 153, 157, 159.

[163] Ibid., 157.

[164] Newton, *Letters*, 363.

[165] Demaray, *Innovation of John Newton*, 171.

[166] Newton, *Conversational Remarks*, 97-98; Philip, *John Campbell*, 261.

[167] Philip, *John Campbell*, 160.

[168] Ibid., 269.

[169] Ibid., 302.

[170] Ibid., 165.

[171] Newton, *Conversational Remarks*, 133.

[172] In 1791, the Clapham Sect established the Sierra Leone Company. "They would create trading links with Africa to replace the soon to be abolished slave trade, establish British legal, political, and social systems, and infuse Christianity, all financed by investors motivated by the winning combination of philanthropy, proselytism, and profit. It was, though, a long way outside their competence and the most colossal failure of their history." Tomkins, *The Clapham Sect*, 91.

[173] Newton, *Conversational Remarks*, 174.

[174] Philip, *John Campbell*, 362.

[175] Ibid., 161-162, 166. One wonders how exactly the children themselves felt about such a plan, or what their experience would be in a foreign land. We do know that those selected were children of African chiefs, who perhaps felt that it was an honor and/or an opportunity. Nevertheless, though Campbell surely had good intentions, the wisdom of the project seems doubtful in retrospect.

[176] Ibid., 161-162.

[177] Ibid., 166; Newton, *Conversational Remarks*, 81.

[178] Philip, *John Campbell*, 167.

[179] Newton, *Conversational Remarks*, 139.

[180] Bull, *John Newton*, 343-344; Philip, *John Campbell*, 177.

[181] Philip, *John Campbell*, 367-368.

[182] Ibid., 400, 509-510.

[183] Ibid., 512.

[184] Ibid., 420.

[185] Ibid., 552-553.

[186] Ibid., 584, 589.

CHAPTER SIX: PRAY AND PREACH

[1] International Labour Organization and Walk Free Foundation, *Global Estimates of Modern Slavery: Forced Labor and Forced Marriage* (Geneva: International Labour Office, 2017), 9.

[2] Liana Sun Wyler and Alison Siskin, "Trafficking in Persons: U.S. Policy and Issues for Congress" (Congressional Research Service, 2010), 3.

[3] International Labour Organization, *Global Estimates*, 40.

[4] Ariana Eunjung Cha, "The U.S. abortion rate falls to lowest level since Roe v. Wade," *Washington Post*, September 18, 2019, accessed September 18, 2019, https://www.washingtonpost.com/health/2019/09/18/us-abortion-rate-falls-lowest-level-since-roe-v-wade/.

[5] Drew Hinshaw and Joe Parkinson, "The 10,000 Kidnapped Boys of Boko Haram," *Wall Street Journal*, August 12, 2016, accessed September 18, 2019, https://www.wsj.com/articles/the-kidnapped-boys-of-boko-haram-1471013062.

[6] US Department of State, *Trafficking in Persons Report June 2019* (Office of the Under Secretary for Civilian Security, 2019), 4.

[7] Ps. 94:16.

[8] Acts 6:2-4.

[9] D. Bruce Hindmarsh, *John Newton and the English Evangelical Tradition* (Grand Rapids, MI: Eerdmans, 1996), 36-40.

[10] Charles Bridges, *The Christian Ministry with an Inquiry into the Causes of Its Inefficiency*, 3rd ed. (London: Seeley and Burnside, 1830), 193, quoted in Joel R. Beeke and Brian G. Najapfour, eds. *Taking Hold of God: Reformed and Puritan Perspectives on Prayer* (Grand Rapids, MI: Reformation Heritage Books, 2011), 228.

[11] Beeke and Najapfour, *Taking Hold of God*, 234.

[12] Hindmarsh, *English Evangelical Tradition*, 198-199.

[13] Ibid., 201.

[14] Ibid., 222-223.

[15] Ibid., 307.

[16] John Newton, *The Works of John Newton*, ed. Richard Cecil (Edinburgh: Banner of Truth Trust, 1988), 1:141.

[17] Marylynn Rouse, e-mail message to author, June 1, 2012.

[18] E. M. Bounds, *The Complete Works of E. M. Bounds on Prayer: Experience the Wonders of God through Prayer*, new ed. (Grand Rapids, MI: Baker Books, 2004), 35.

[19] Allan Karr and Linda Bergquist, *The Wholehearted Church Planter: Leadership from the Inside Out* (St. Louis: Chalice Press, 2013), 132.

[20] Interestingly enough, Johnson was absent at the meeting discussing the best way to reach Botany Bay. James Bonwick, *Australia's First Preacher; the Rev. Richard Johnson, First Chaplain of New South Wales* (London: Sampson, Low, Marston, and Co., 1898), 36.

[21] Isa. 6:8.

[22] William Perkins, so influential to later Puritan pastors, set the course for many after him, stating, "There are two parts to prophecy: preaching the Word and public prayer. For the prophet (that is, the minister of the Word) has only two duties. One is preaching the Word, and the other is praying to God in the name of the people." William Perkins, *The Art of Prophesying* (1606; repr., Edinburgh: Banner of Truth Trust, 1996), 7.

[23] Newton, *Works,* 5:279.

CHAPTER SEVEN: LOVE OTHERS

[1] Bill Bright, *Come Help Change the World* (Orlando, FL: NewLife Publications, 1999), 15.

[2] Rick Warren, *The Purpose-Driven Church* (Grand Rapids, MI: Zondervan, 1995), 170.

[3] Lee Strobel, *Inside the Mind of Unchurched Harry and Mary* (Grand Rapids, MI: Zondervan, 1993).

[4] Bernard Martin, *John Newton: A Biography* (London: William Heinemann LTD, 1950), 336.

[5] Grant Gordon, ed. *Wise Counsel* (2009; repr., Edinburgh: Banner of Truth Trust, 2011), 336-337.

[6] Ed Stetzer, *Planting New Churches in a Postmodern Age* (Nashville, TN: Broadman & Holman, 2003), 91-92. Stetzer's point is well taken. However, Newton's example makes me wonder if we are too eager to dismiss needy people, when they may in fact be God's chosen instrument for a particular task.

[7] Josiah Bull, *John Newton of Olney and St. Mary Woolnoth* (London: The Religious Tract Society, 1868), 201.

[8] Josiah Bull, *Memorials of the Rev. William Bull, of Newport Pagnel*, 2nd ed. (London: Elliot Stock, 1865), 63.

[9] I am indebted to Eugene Peterson's insight here. See Eugene H. Peterson, *Christ Plays in Ten Thousand Places* (Grand Rapids, MI: Eerdmans, 2005), 38-39.

[10] Eugene H. Peterson, *Leap Over a Wall: Earthly Spirituality for Everyday Christians* (San Francisco: HarperSanFrancisco, 1997), 53.

[11] David Hansen, *The Art of Pastoring: Ministry Without All the Answers* (Downers Grove, IL: InterVarsity Press, 1994), 121.

[12] Ibid., 122.

[13] Gordon, *Wise Counsel*, 187, 189.

[14] Claudius Buchanan to John Newton, July 3, 1798, MS 3972, fol. 39, Letters to John Newton, Lambeth Palace Library, London.

[15] Gordon, *Wise Counsel*, 223.

[16] Phil. 2:3-4.

[17] Lee B. Spitzer, *Making Friends, Making Disciples* (Valley Forge, PA: Judson Press, 2010), 108.

[18] John Newton to William Wilberforce, March 30, 1796, c. 49, fol. 69, Wilberforce Papers, Bodleian Library, Oxford, quoted in Marylynn Rouse, "John Newton & William Wilberforce Correspondence," unpublished manuscript.

[19] Gordon, *Wise Counsel*, 349.

[20] Bull, *Memorials*, 317.

CHAPTER EIGHT: TEACH OTHERS

[1] Marc V. Rutter, "Going the Distance: Red Flags and the At-risk Leader" (message at men's lunch, New Staff Training, Campus Crusade for Christ, Daytona Beach, FL, February 1, 2000).

[2] Timothy Keller, *Generous Justice: How God's Grace Makes us Just* (New York: Dutton, 2010), 183.

[3] William Wilberforce, *A Practical View of the Prevailing Religious System of Professed Christians, in the Higher and Middle Classes in this Country, Contrasted with Real Christianity*, 4th ed. (Glasgow: William Collins, 1833), 338.

[4] John Newton, *The Works of John Newton*, ed. Richard Cecil (Edinburgh: Banner of Truth Trust, 1988), 2:548.

[5] Stephen Tomkins, *The Clapham Sect: How Wilberforce's Circle Transformed Britain* (Oxford: Lion Hudson, 2010), 19-20.

[6] Wilberforce, *A Practical View*, 339.

[7] Quoted in Keller, *Generous Justice*, 108.

[8] Jer. 29:5-7.

[9] James Davison Hunter, *To Change the World: The Irony, Tragedy, & Possibility of Christianity in the Late Modern World*, 278.

[10] Ibid., 238.

[11] Ibid., 247-248.

[12] Ibid., 269.

[13] Ford K. Brown, *Fathers of the Victorians: The Age of Wilberforce* (Cambridge: Cambridge University Press, 1961), 46.

[14] Robert Philip, *The Life, Times, and Missionary Enterprises of the Rev. John Campbell* (London: John Snow, 1841), 152-153.

[15] Gilbert Thomas, *William Cowper and the Eighteenth Century* (London: Ivor Nicholson and Watson, 1935), 333.

[16] Kevin Belmonte, *William Wilberforce: A Hero for Humanity* (Grand Rapids, MI: Zondervan, 2007), 80.

[17] See chapter four, above, for his specific instructions. John Newton to William Wilberforce, November 1, 1787, c. 49, fols. 14-15, Wilberforce Papers, Bodleian Library, Oxford, quoted in Rouse, "John Newton."

[18] John Newton to William Wilberforce, c. 49, fol. 16, Wilberforce Papers, Bodleian Library, Oxford, quoted in Marylynn Rouse,"John Newton & William Wilberforce Correspondence," unpublished manuscript.

[19] Brown, *Fathers of the Victorians*, 122. Newton was speaking specifically in reference to Wilberforce's new book.

[20] John Newton to William Wilberforce, July 4, 1795, c. 49, fol. 63, Wilberforce Papers, Bodleian Library, Oxford, quoted in Rouse, "John Newton."

[21] Robert and Samuel Wilberforce, *The Life of William Wilberforce* (London: John Murray, 1838), 1:6-7.

[22] Josiah Bull, *John Newton of Olney and St. Mary Woolnoth* (London: The Religious Tract Society, 1868), 134.

[23] Robert E. Coleman, *The Master Plan of Evangelism*, 2nd ed., abridged. (Grand Rapids, MI: Fleming H. Revell, 1994), 27.

[24] Ibid., 41.

[25] Bull, *John Newton*, 256. Dated August 4, 1781, Newton's birthday.

[26] Ibid., 149.

[27] Ibid., 168.

[28] Ibid., 180-181. Dated May 14, 1772. Newton had a string of constant visitors for almost four months!

[29] Newton certainly made such evangelistic campaigns. For example, in the spring of 1777, Newton took a preaching tour, delivering nineteen sermons in a period of three weeks. However, these campaigns were never the primary thrust of his ministry. See Bull, *John Newton*, 223.

[30] Among others, Benjamin Franklin was impressed with Whitefield's preaching, stating that "every accent, every emphasis, every modulation of voice, was so perfectly well turned and well placed, that, without being interested in the subject, one could not help being pleased with the discourse; a pleasure of much the same kind with that received from an excellent piece of musick." Quoted in Arnold Dallimore, *George Whitefield: The Life and Times of the Great Evangelist of the Eighteenth-century Revival* (1970; repr., Edinburgh: Banner of Truth Trust, 2001), 1:116.

[31] Bull, *John Newton*, 206, 368.

[32] George M. Marsden, *Jonathan Edwards: A Life* (New Haven, CT: Yale University Press, 2003), 133, 460-464.

[33] Kenneth J. Collins, *John Wesley: A Theological Journey* (Nashville, TN: Abingdon Press, 2003), 120-123.

[34] J. I. Packer, "Board of Reference and Endorsements," The John Newton Project, accessed August 20, 2019, www.johnnewton.org/Groups/231004/The_John_Newton/new_menus/About_the_Project/Board_of_Reference/Board_of_Reference.aspx. Presumably, Dr. Packer left Jonathan Edwards out of his statement as he was referring only to the English leaders of the Evangelical Revival.

[35] Coleman, *The Master Plan of Evangelism*, 36.

CHAPTER NINE: EMPOWER OTHERS

[1] Lee B. Spitzer, *Making Friends, Making Disciples* (Valley Forge, PA: Judson Press, 2010), 79-80.

[2] Christopher L. Heuertz and Christine D. Pohl, *Friendship at the Margins: Discovering Mutuality in Service and Mission* (Downers Grove, IL: InterVarsity Press, 2010), 139.

[3] Stephen Tomkins, *The Clapham Sect: How Wilberforce's Circle Transformed Britain* (Oxford: Lion Hudson, 2010), 48-49.

[4] John Newton, *One Hundred and Twenty Nine Letters from the Rev. John Newton, Late Rector of St. Mary Woolnoth, London, to the Rev. William Bull, of Newport Pagnell*, ed. Thomas Palmer Bull (London: Hamilton, Adams, and Co., 1847), 26, 53.

[5] Josiah Bull, *Memorials of the Rev. William Bull, of Newport Pagnel*, 2nd ed. (London: Elliot Stock, 1865), 169.

[6] Ibid., 158.

[7] T. S. Grimshawe, *The Life and Works of William Cowper*, 2nd ed. (London: Saunders and Otley, 1836), 1:123.

[8] D. E. Jenkins, *The Life of the Rev. Thomas Charles B.A. of Bala* (Denbigh: Llewelyn Jenkins, 1908), 1:52.

[9] Ibid., 1:564.

[10] Ibid., 2:108. See also, Tomkins, *Clapham Sect,* 191.

[11] Jenkins, *Thomas Charles*, 2:96.

[12] Ibid., 2:103-104.

[13] M. Seeley, *The Later Evangelical Fathers* (London: Seeley, Jackson, & Halliday, 1879), 262-263.

[14] Claudius Buchanan to John Newton, October 1, 1798, MS 3972, fol. 46, Letters to John Newton, Lambeth Palace Library, London.

[15] Claudius Buchanan to John Newton, June 6, 1799, MS 3972, fol. 57, Letters to John Newton, Lambeth Palace Library, London.

[16] Carey, however, seems to have been favorable toward Buchanan: "Mr. Buchanan I hope to see in a few weeks, as I intend a journey to Calcutta." William Carey to John Newton, December 5, 1798, MS 2935, fol. 273v, General Correspondence of John Newton, Lambeth Palace Library, London.

[17] Grant Gordon, ed. *Wise Counsel* (2009; repr., Edinburgh: Banner of Truth Trust, 2011), 215.

[18] Ibid., 375.

[19] James Davison Hunter, *To Change the World: The Irony, Tragedy, & Possibility of Christianity in the Late Modern World*, 38.

[20] Ibid., 270.

[21] Bruce Wilkinson, *The Dream Giver* (Sisters, OR: Multnomah Press, 2003), 29.

[22] James Bonwick, *Australia's First Preacher; the Rev. Richard Johnson, First Chaplain of New South Wales* (London: Sampson, Low, Marston, and Co., 1898), 152.

[23] Josiah Bull, *John Newton of Olney and St. Mary Woolnoth* (London: The Religious Tract Society, 1868), 335.

[24] Bonwick, *Australia's First Preacher*, 153.

[25] John Newton, *Letters of John Newton*, ed. Josiah Bull (1869; repr., Edinburgh: Banner of Truth Trust, 2007), 359-360.

[26] Seeley, *Later Evangelical Fathers*, 110.

[27] David Hansen, *The Art of Pastoring: Ministry Without All The Answers* (Downers Grove, IL: InterVarsity Press, 1994), 132.

[28] Bull, *John Newton*, 329.

[29] John Newton to William Wilberforce, June 7, 1797, c. 49, fol. 79, Wilberforce Papers, Bodleian Library, Oxford, quoted in Marylynn Rouse, "John Newton & William Wilberforce Correspondence," unpublished manuscript.

[30] Marylynn Rouse, "A Double Portion of My Thoughts and Prayers: John Newton's Letters to William Wilberforce," *Midwestern Journal of Theology* 17, no. 2 (Fall 2018): 40.

[31] John Newton to William Wilberforce, August 3, 1799, c. 49, fol. 95, Wilberforce Papers, Bodleian Library, Oxford, quoted in Rouse, "John Newton."

CONCLUSION

[1] Jonathan Aitken, *John Newton: From Disgrace to Amazing Grace* (Wheaton, IL: Crossway Books, 2007), 348.

[2] Jonathan Aitken notes that Newton "would surely have been unimpressed by the eulogistic reference." Aitken, *John Newton*, 349.

[3] John Newton to William Wilberforce, November 1, 1799, c. 49, fol. 99, Wilberforce Papers, Bodleian Library, Oxford, quoted in Marylynn Rouse, "John Newton & William Wilberforce Correspondence," unpublished manuscript.

[4] Josiah Bull, *John Newton of Olney and St. Mary Woolnoth* (London: The Religious Tract Society, 1868), 360.

[5] T. S. Grimshawe, *The Life and Works of William Cowper*, 2nd ed. (London: Saunders and Otley, 1836), 1:210.

[6] Bull, *John Newton*, 251.

[7] Richard Cecil, ed. *The Life of the Rev. John Newton, Rector of St. Mary Woolnoth, London. Written by himself to A.D. 1763, and Continued to his Death in 1807, by Rev. Richard Cecil* (New York: American Tract Society, 1850), 225. See also John Newton, *The Works of John Newton*, ed. Richard Cecil (Edinburgh: Banner of Truth Trust, 1988), 1:95.

[8] Aitken, *John Newton*, 344. This sermon was preached in October of 1806.

[9] Newton, *Works*, 3:340.

SOLA

five 16th-century truths that
recaptured the heart of the gospel
and why they matter today

Mark Hallock & Ben Haley

Acoma Press exists to make Jesus non-ignorable by equipping and encouraging churches through gospel-centered resources.

Toward this end, each purchase of an Acoma Press resource serves to catalyze disciple-making and to equip leaders in God's Church. In fact, a portion of your purchase goes directly to funding planting and replanting efforts in North America and beyond. To see more of our current resources, visit us at *acomapress.org*.

Thank you.

Made in the
USA
Columbia, SC

80728547R00134